Robokicker

Dave Ridgway

with
David A. Poulsen

Johnson Gorman Publishers

Copyright © 1995 Dave Ridgway and David A. Poulsen

All rights reserved. No part of this book may be reproduced by any means, electronic or mechanical, including photography, recording, or any information and retrieval system, without permission in writing from the publisher.

Johnson Gorman Publishers
Red Deer, Alberta

Cover design: The Design Kitchen/Susan Lee
Text design: Full Court Press/Dennis Johnson
Printed and bound in Canada by Webcom for Johnson Gorman Publishers

Financial support provided by the Alberta Foundation for the Arts, a beneficiary of the Lottery Fund of the Government of Alberta.

COMMITTED TO THE DEVELOPMENT OF CULTURE AND THE ARTS

CANADIAN CATALOGUING IN PUBLICATIONS DATA
Ridgway, Dave, 1959–
Robokicker
ISBN 0921835-44-2 (bound). — ISBN 0-921835-34-5 (pbk.)
1. Ridgway, Dave, 1959– 2. Football players–Saskatchewan–Biography. 1. Poulsen, David A., 1946– 11. Title.
GV939.R52A3 1995 796.335'092 C95-910609-X

For my two sons, Christopher Dallas and Drew Bradley. I miss you both more than you will ever know and love you more than anything in the world. You are truly the sunshine of my life.
–DAVE RIDGWAY

For Mom, Barb, Murray and Kim, Amy, Dave, Brennan, Kyle and Brad ... A Hall of Fame family.
–DAVID A. POULSEN

Acknowledgments

There are so many people to be thanked when a book like this is finally finished. First, I want to express my appreciation to three people who don't hear the words *thank you* nearly as often as they should: my father, Len; my mother, Mary; and my Grandma, Alice. I extend as well my thanks to my past and present teammates and coaches. My special gratitude goes to Roy Antal, Stacey Cattell, John Chaput, Chinook Chapel, Troy Christian, Darrell Davis, Gregg Drinnan, Bill Dubecky, Mitch Englot, Dave Elston, Norm Fong, Alan Ford, Ivan Gutfriend, Bob Hughes, the community of Langenburg, Saskatchewan, Patti Jackson, Doug McConarchie, Jill McDougall, Cheryl McLean, Liz Measner, Nick Miliokas, Lorne Mitchell, Michael Murray, Tony Playter (you were a tremendous help, Tony), Vickie Poitras, Randy Pollock, Carol Rafuse, Dan Rambo, Herb and Arni Scholz, Tom Shepherd, Larry Smith, Barry Taman, Beave Taman, Wayne and Ann Tribe, Nancy Valentino (Ridgway) and Blair Watson.

Thanks as well to the Canadian Football League for providing what I believe is the most exciting football played anywhere, to the Saskatchewan Roughriders football club for allowing me to live my dream and finally to the fans of the Saskatchewan Roughriders—it is a privilege and a joy to play for and write about your team.

–DAVE RIDGWAY

Though many people assisted with and offered encouragement for this project, one deserves special mention. It was the Reverend Guy Scholz who first conceived the idea, who brought us together to write it, and whose encyclopedic knowledge of the CFL was invaluable during the twelve months it has taken to complete it. His fascination with statistics, love of the Riders and belief in this book have earned our undying appreciation.

–D.R. & D.A.P.

Contents

Foreword / 7

1 The Kick – Part One / 10
2 England to North America / 16
3 There Ain't No *E* in Ridgway / 38
4 The Green and White / 59
5 1 – 800 – Phantom / 80
6 The Long, Lean Years / 99
7 A Few Good Men – The Early Years / 134
8 A Few More Good Men – The Recent Years / 162
9 I Got By With a Little Help From My Friend / 186
10 Thrown for a Loss / 202
11 The Twilight Zone / 216
12 We're Taking on Water but the Ship Isn't Sinking / 222
13 That Championship Season / 241
14 The Kick – Part Two / 268

Appendix – The Dave Ridgway Record / 277

FOREWORD

There is a day that sticks in the memory. It was years ago, in the 1980s, and I was standing in the parking lot at Taylor Field, not far from the players' entrance to the Saskatchewan Roughriders' dressing room. I was standing with a Saskatchewan Roughrider coach and it was the month of May, a few weeks removed from the start to training camp.

We were just chatting when a big car rolled into the parking lot, stopped, and out got a kicker named Dave Ridgway, who had been born in England and played college football in Toledo and somehow ended up in Regina.

The coach's eyes squinted and the lines on his face tightened and the sense of his anger could be felt. He glared at Dave Ridgway and then told me, in words that still sizzle to this day, "That guy . . . he'll never make it! He can't do the job. If I don't do another thing while I'm here, I'll get rid of the . . ."

The years have passed, and so has the coach, and Dave Ridgway is still here.

When you talk of the history of the Saskatchewan Roughriders, a team that is as close to the heart of any fan of any team in the world, there are players whose names and accomplishments have been such that they have bridged the decades and touched immortality.

There is number 23, which belonged to Ron Lancaster, the greatest quarterback to ever wear the Green and White.

There is number 34, which belonged to George Reed, the greatest fullback to ever play in the Canadian Football League.

And there is number 36, perhaps the greatest placement kicker to ever put on a football uniform.

When he retires from football, if ever, Ridgway's number 36 will be raised atop the flag poles that stand above the north end zone of Taylor Field, reminding the fans of those days when a guy who came to be known as Robokicker dominated football in Saskatchewan as few before him had.

His records and accomplishments are well known—his career in Saskatchewan underlined forever by the exclamation mark that was The Kick that won the 1989 Grey Cup for the Roughriders.

But this also is a guy who lives to the ultimate the role all Roughriders are expected to live up to when they play in this football-crazy province. And that is, Dave Ridgway is a part of the community.

He involves himself in fund-raisers for various charities, and there are few banquets that light the long Saskatchewan winter nights that Dave Ridgway doesn't appear at.

When he told me he was going to write a book on his career and his life in football, I wondered if it was a little premature, if perhaps he should wait until his playing days are over. But, even though he is into the twilight years of his career, Dave has already seen and experienced and accomplished more than most could ever expect to see.

Foreword

Because he decided not to write one of those tell-all books that too often pockmark great careers, the appeal for Dave's book heightens. And the timing seems right.

The Dave Ridgway who emerges from this book is the same Dave Ridgway I have known for years—a guy who has felt the highs and lows of sports and life and has emerged from them with grace and success.

–BOB HUGHES
Regina, May 1995

CHAPTER I

The Kick – Part One

This is it, folks, this is what it's all about.... One game, there is no tomorrow.... This is for the whole magilla... for the whole ball of wax... for the whole kit 'n' caboodle... for the whole enchilada... the whole shootin' match.... This is for all the marbles. —ROOKIE OF THE YEAR, 1993

WITH 44 SECONDS REMAINING in the 1989 Grey Cup game, Hamilton Tiger-Cat quarterback Mike Kerrigan threw a third-down, nine-yard touchdown pass to Tony Champion. The Hamilton receiver, coming off an outstanding season, made what I believe was one of the greatest catches ever, not just in the history of the Canadian Football League, but in the game of football. I would put that reception—with Champion's body twisting, turning and stretching out backward—alongside any of the great catches: the Super Bowl grabs of Lynn Swann for the Pittsburgh Steelers, the remarkable game-after-game acrobatics of the Saskatchewan Roughriders' Joey Walters, and for sheer drama the Immaculate Reception of the Steelers' Franco Harris.

Champion's catch was all the more memorable because he made it at the most critical time—the dying seconds of a championship game. The touchdown and the convert that followed pulled the Tiger-Cats into a 40–40 tie in a game that had been a shoot-out almost from the outset. And a game the Saskatchewan Roughriders had been on the verge of winning was now suddenly in jeopardy.

What surprises me now, as I look back on the seconds immediately after the Hamilton touchdown, was the absolute certainty I felt that we would get close enough in the remaining time to attempt a field goal. In all my years in football I believe I have seen nobody better at getting his team into position for that last-second shot at victory than the man who was then our quarterback, Kent Austin. I can recall so many instances during Kent's tenure in Saskatchewan when he directed our offense on late-game drives either for a touchdown or field goal attempt and a shot at victory. There was no doubt in my mind that in this, the most critical minute of all of our careers, he would do it again.

On many of those previous occasions, as he was about to head onto the field with the offense, Kent would turn to me and nod, and I would nod back to him. Without any words being spoken, what was being exchanged between us was an agreement, a pact: his nod was saying, *We'll get you a shot* and mine was replying, *Let's do it*.

This time though, there was no nod. As soon as I saw the official's arms go into the air to signal the Tony Champion touchdown, I turned away from the field, put on my helmet and walked down to our kicking net. I didn't see the first few plays of the final drive. In fact, I didn't look up from where I was kicking into the net until our offense had moved the ball over midfield. It was only later on video that I saw the opening moments of the drive.

It began inauspiciously with Austin throwing incomplete on a pass intended for Don Narcisse. On second down Kent threw a pinpoint sideline pass that snaked between Hamilton defenders Pete Giftopolous and Lance Shields and was caught by our ever-reliable slotback, Ray Elgaard. That catch took us to the Hamilton 54. Kent then hit wide receiver Mark Guy for 18 yards. Mark was, in my mind, an unsung hero of that Grey Cup game and this was a huge catch. Mark hung on to the ball despite being simultaneously hit by three Tiger-Cats. At this point I stopped warming up and was ready to go onto the field. As I turned to watch our offense I was convinced, as I think everyone was, that our next play would be a running play to get the ball into position for the field goal attempt.

The sideline was pandemonium. Head Coach John Gregory was running in one direction; Offensive Line Coach Gary Hoffman was running in the other and a lot of other people were running in all directions. Gregory grabbed running back Brian Walling and tried to send him in with a play, but by the time Brian started onto the field, Kent Austin had already called the play and the offense was coming out over the ball. Ray Elgaard yelled to Brian to get off the field, and whatever the coach's play was, it was never called.

Incredibly, the play Kent called (and this is indicative of the confidence he has in his ability) was a passing play, a comeback route to Mark Guy. While we on the sidelines looked on with our hearts in our mouths, Mark caught the perfect throw another 10 yards up field and stepped out-of-bounds at the Hamilton 26. On the next play Kent took the snap from center and went to one knee, stopping the clock with seven seconds showing.

We called a time-out and I started onto the field. There was no conversation and no exchange of signals. We had kicked hundreds of field goals before, and I wanted to treat this kick no differently than any other. I walked to the left hash mark and set my tee down where I wanted the ball placed.

The Kick – Part One

I can't say I was feeling a lot of extra butterflies as I waited to attempt the most important kick of my career. Seeing my teammates so focused as they made the final march downfield reminded me that my role was just one part in the completion of the job. As well, although there was a time-out on the field, I was busy making the preparations for the kick and wasn't thinking of much else.

When Head Referee Dave Yule blew the whistle to signal time back in, Hamilton immediately called their own time-out. This is a common strategy in football, the idea being, of course, to give the kicker as much time as possible to think about the moment and allow the pressure to build that much more. The strategy is very sound because that's exactly what happens.

During the second time-out Coach John Gregory called Glen Suitor, my holder for place-kicks, to the sidelines and gave him instructions to do something we hadn't tried during the course of the game. When Glen came back on the field, I asked him what John had wanted and Glen said, "He wants a shift, but I'm not calling it. Screw it; let's just kick it and get the hell out of here." A shift involves having the offensive line set up in a two-point stance, and on a verbal signal from Glen, usually the word *set*, drop down into their normal stance a fraction of a second before the ball is snapped. This is done in the hope of drawing the defending team offside or at least slowing down their charge off the line and reducing the chance of the kick being blocked.

I nodded agreement with Glen and turned away. But with some time remaining in the time-out, I began to feel my nervousness building. Some of the Tiger-Cat players were putting the time to good use by talking a little trash across the line of scrimmage, most of it directed at me. They were discussing my wife, my kids and anything else they could think of, and I'd have to say that some of their remarks were . . . colorful. By the way, if the situation had been reversed and the Tiger-Cats were lining up to try a game-deciding field goal, our guys would have been doing the same thing. That's part of the game.

I went back to where Glen was standing. I leaned into him until our face masks were almost touching and said, "Talk to me about something other than football."

Glen and I are close friends on and off the field and had been planning a camping trip to the Rockies for the following spring. Never having camped in the mountains before, I had several times expressed concern about bears we might encounter. I had seen enough *National Geographic* specials to know that spring is the time when bears end their hibernation. And when they do they're usually hungry and more than a little grumpy.

Now, as we awaited the calling of time back in, Glen, without a second's hesitation, said, "I've figured out what we're going to do about that camping trip. We'll have a footrace, and then we won't have to think about the bear anymore because the slow guy'll be the bear food."

I laughed, thinking about a footrace between a defensive back and a kicker, knowing what my chances were of winning. But then Glen added, "And, by the way, have you seen the hooters on the blond sitting about four rows behind our bench?"

Crazy though the comment was, Glen wasn't being frivolous or flip about what was about to happen. In fact, just the opposite. He realized I was tensing up, and he knew me well enough to be able to say exactly the right (albeit goofy) thing to lighten me up and get my mind off the game for a few seconds. Still, I'll bet some of the Tiger-Cats were surprised to look over and see an opposition player shaking his head and

The Kick – Part One

laughing as he got ready to attempt a field goal that, if successful, would bring his team its second Grey Cup in history.

I soon stopped laughing and lined up for what I hoped would be the last play of the 1989 Grey Cup game. Though I was trying not to, I was thinking. I guess this wasn't surprising. There was a lot to think about . . .

CHAPTER 2

England to North America

You've got a gift, Roy. But it's not enough. You've got to develop yourself. Rely too much on your own gift and you'll fail. —THE NATURAL, 1988

SPORTS WAS AN IMPORTANT PART of my life as far back as I can remember. As a small boy I spent many crisp fall English afternoons watching my father play soccer for my grandfather's team. One of the first teams I ever cheered for was the Ward Street Old Boys, an amateur team from Stockport that my Grandfather Tom owned and managed. One of the few regrets I have in my life is that neither Grandfather Tom on my father's side nor Grandfather Jim on my mother's were able to see me play either collegiate or professional football. I think both men would have been as proud of their grandson as I was of them.

I was born April 24, 1959, in Stockport, England, a working-class town situated fifteen minutes from Manchester and about an hour's drive inland from Liverpool. My parents, Leonard and Mary (Harrop), had four children of whom I am the oldest. My brother John is next, followed by Neil and then Lyn, the youngest and my only sister. My only living grandparent is my father's mother, Grandma Alice, and she and I stay in regular contact with each other.

In addition to being weaned on soccer I received an early introduction to North American sports that, prior to the 1980s, many British kids had never heard of. The first was baseball. Many of my father's friends were either American servicemen or Canadian businessmen, and they had formed a league to keep their baseball tradition alive while they were overseas.

Not long afterward I was introduced, mostly through magazines like *Sports Illustrated* and *The Sporting News*, to football, or as I came to know it, *Gridiron*, which is, I understand, the correct technical name for what we refer to as football. As a teenager I wrote countless letters to major league baseball teams and American and Canadian football teams in the hope they would send me photos, player cards or other souvenirs. Many did and I still have most of that early collection. It was my introduction to a pastime I still enthusiastically pursue today—I am an avid collector of just about everything associated with sport.

My father regularly sent away to Sears, Roebuck and Co. in the United States for clothing associated with teams—T-shirts, caps and sweat shirts as well as sports toys. My brothers, my sister and I spent many hours poring over the Sears' *Christmas Wish Book*, casting especially longing looks at anything associated with North American sports.

My father's profession was that of an airframe fitter. He served an apprenticeship with Fairey Aviation in Britain, and after two years in the armed forces went to work for the A.V. Roe Corporation. During the late sixties and early seventies, employment in the aviation industry was scarce, and my father began contracting out his services. The result was that he traveled all over the globe working for whoever required his particular skills. He spent the better part of 1971, including the winter, on the air base at Gimli, Manitoba.

When he returned to England, my father spent some time in the South working with a helicopter manufacturer. It was about this time my parents split up. For a while my two brothers and I were raised by my father while my sister stayed with my mother. After a brief attempt at reconciliation in 1972 failed, my sister came to join us as my father took on the task of being a single parent with four children. My parents divorced in 1974, at which time my father was granted formal custody of all four kids.

It wasn't the best way to grow up though it was better than having no parents, as is the case with lots of kids. As the oldest child in the household, I was often made privy to family problems that a twelve-year-old really shouldn't have to know about. I swore to myself that if I ever had children I would never put them through the trauma of being separated from one of their parents. Unfortunately that is exactly what happened, and it is the biggest regret of my life.

We grew up in a rough part of Stockport, an area called Hillgate. The neighborhood's chief claim to fame was that it produced some of the tougher and seedier members of local society. But though my father was a factory worker and we certainly weren't wealthy, I don't remember us wanting for anything as kids. There was always food on the table and decent clothes. Of course, being kids, we were pretty much unaware of anything different in the world, and we didn't spend a lot of time wishing for something better.

Though my mother wasn't with us, there was love in our family. My father provided us with genuine affection, and my brothers, sister and I were quite close, in part, no doubt, because of what we had gone through together. I have talked with my mother about her leaving, and I know she regrets what happened to the relationship between her and my father and subsequently to us as a family. But she felt at the time, and still does, that she had to leave and I can accept it. In the time immediately after their breakup I took the side of my father, but as time has gone on, I hope I've arrived at a point where I don't take either side. My parents' relationship deteriorated, and there isn't much to be gained by my blaming one or the other. I love them both, and I appreciate more than I can say the sacrifices my father made to raise us.

A few months after my parents' divorce, my father made the decision to emigrate to Canada. It was something he had often talked about since his stay in 1971. Unfortunately it was virtually impossible to emigrate with four small children in tow, and it was decided that Neil and I would accompany my dad and that John and Lyn would remain behind in England. Though my father has never discussed this part of our life with me, I know from having been apart from my own kids the kind of anguish he must have experienced.

I have been back to England three times since we emigrated: in 1975, in 1979 and most recently in 1991. My mother, my brother John and my sister, Lyn, still live in Great Britain. When both Neil and I went to England in 1991, it was the first time in eighteen years all four of us had been together. Though there was a little tension in the air at times and still a few hard feelings toward my father on the part of John and Lyn, who still feel they were left behind, it was one of the great experiences of my life to be reunited with all of my siblings and my mother. My brother Neil, who has played professional soccer in the United States, and now lives in Kalamazoo, Michigan, gets back to England at least once a year. He has done a very good job of maintaining his ties with the family and his British heritage. When he gets back to England, he hits a lot of the old haunts, eats fish-and-chips at the local "chippy" and, of course, spends time in the various neighborhood pubs. I hope in the future to be able to follow Neil's lead and reestablish a similar closeness with the rest of my family.

On August 6, 1974, my father, Neil and I arrived in Canada, the stereotypical immigrants. We had left a difficult situation, both economically and emotionally, and when we got to Canada we had nothing. We brought with us a few personal belongings, and my father carried in his pocket one hundred dollars in Canadian money. We were met at the airport by his acquaintance, Paddy Koch, who escorted us to his car, a beautiful, brand new, lime green Capri. It wasn't a very big car, however, and the job of getting the four of us plus suitcases and a steamer trunk into the vehicle is the stuff from which cartoons are made.

I'm not sure what we would have done without Paddy's hospitality. He took us to his apartment in Kitchener, Ontario, and he and his family put us up until we were able to strike out on our own. Paddy's mother, a tiny German woman, made my brother and me feel like family while Paddy undertook to introduce us to hamburgers and other niceties of Canadian culture. He was a character. While walking through a supermarket Paddy liked to make himself a sandwich with ingredients he picked up along the way. Of course, by the time he got to the cash register, the sandwich was totally consumed. In a department store he would often pick up a couple of baseball mitts and a ball and stage an impromptu game of catch in the aisle with my younger brother. Come to think of it, Paddy had the kind of attitude that would fit in pretty well on a football team.

England to North America

My father got work in Kitchener, and I was enrolled in grade ten at Grand River Collegiate Institute. It was there I received my introduction to the game of football. I was tall for my age, about 6' 1", but I weighed only 145 pounds. The coach thought I should try out at tight end. My career as a receiver was short-lived. After the first few times I got schmucked from behind when going for a pass, the world of place-kicking suddenly looked enticing.

My father secured a job in Burlington, Ontario, shortly before Christmas and once again the Ridgways were on the move. It was there, at M. M. Robinson High School, that my football career eventually took shape. I had always been an athletic kid, playing soccer as well as squash, tennis and badminton. Unfortunately I wasn't nearly as dedicated to the academic side of school life and, in fact, came close to being expelled because of poor grades and sporadic attendance. Had this happened, there isn't the slightest doubt in my mind that my life would have gone down a very different path. I was fortunate to have a peer group of level-headed kids and a vice-principal, Bob Langlois, who were more interested in my education than I was. If it hadn't been for them I'm not sure how things might have turned out for me.

It was about that time I discovered a distinct class system operating in the school. Some of the kids were from upper middle-class families and enjoyed many of the advantages important to kids: nice clothes, money and, most important, cars or at least access to them. My father, on the other hand, did not purchase a car until we had been in Canada for three years. Until then we went everywhere on buses, which, because I was used to traveling that way in England, did not seem particularly strange to me.

I played soccer at M. M. Robinson in 1975 but didn't go out

for the football team until the following year. One of our physical education teachers, Scott Smiley, was the football coach, and he encouraged me to try out for the kicking job on the football team. My father had been pushing me constantly to go out and practice on my own. For the previous Christmas he had given me a football and kicking tee. I spent that spring and summer on the football fields of Burlington, kicking that one ball, then running to get it, kicking it again from that spot and repeating the process over and over again.

The thought of playing professional football began to plant itself in my mind. There was one huge obstacle to overcome. My father's income wasn't the sort that could support a college education, and with the marks I had been pulling down, the prospect of my winning an academic scholarship was dim. The only way I would be able to pursue football was by obtaining an athletic scholarship.

I think I showed some natural raw ability to kick a football a long way during my last year of high school, but I've seen dozens of young players who can kick for distance but who never go on to play professional football. It is the ability to kick with accuracy that determines whether the kid who can boom them from way out there is ever going to get beyond high school or college. Bolstered by the encouragement from my father and Scott Smiley and armed with a letter of recommendation from Garney Henley of the Hamilton Tiger-Cats (and after some serious effort to improve my academics) I secured an athletic scholarship to the University of Toledo.

The letter from the Tiger-Cats was a huge help. Scott had called them to arrange an evaluation of my kicking. Garney Henley had completed an outstanding sixteen-year playing career and had just taken a position as an assistant coach to then Tiger-Cat Head Coach Bob Shaw.

England to North America

I went to Ivor Wynne Stadium, and Garney came onto the field and held the ball for me. He watched me kick about thirty balls from varying distances and angles on the field. I later received a letter from him recommending me on behalf of the Tiger-Cats, and not long after I was off to the United States to pursue my goal of one day being a professional football player.

I received a number of replies to the queries I had sent out, and in the spring of 1977 my father and I set out to investigate a few of the schools that had expressed interest in me. The first school was Marietta College, a small school of fifteen hundred students located in southern Ohio. The campus, situated in the valley of the Ohio River, was very pretty. The coach of the football team, which played Division III ball, indicated it was against NCAA recruiting rules for him to watch me kick, but he might leave the gates of the stadium open in the event I wanted to go in and kick a few—just to warm up my leg, of course. The implication was that he just might happen to stroll by the open gate as I was kicking.

My father and I went onto the field and I kicked for a while, after which we went up to the coach's office to meet with him. He indicated that though money was tight in the athletic budget, he could probably wrangle me some financial assistance from the academic scholarship and student loan funds. Though both my father and I were impressed with Marietta, we both felt my chances of playing professionally would be enhanced if I attended a Division I school.

From there we went to Miami of Ohio, then Ohio University and finally the University of Toledo. Chuck Stobart was head coach of Toledo, and when we got there they were just winding up spring football. During one of their last practices, I went onto the field (again unofficially in shorts, T-shirt and kicking shoes) and kicked during the practice in order for the coaches to evaluate me. After the practice, Jim Cameron, a graduate assistant with the football team, toured us around campus and, in effect, recruited me.

One of the interesting sidelights to that trip was the fact that Elvis Presley was to perform in Toledo a few days later. We were offered a pair of tickets to the show. Though I'd been a huge Elvis fan all through high school, I didn't feel right about asking my dad to take more time off work. I remember thinking there would be other opportunities to see the King, especially if I were living in the United States. Four months later, on the eve of my departure for the University of Toledo training camp, a couple of friends called to say Elvis had died. Damn, I wish we'd gone to that concert.

I was offered a two-thirds full-ride scholarship at the University of Toledo, and while this was very exciting for both my father and me, it still left us with the problem of how to raise the other one-third of the money I would need. Nevertheless, we accepted the offer, and I took up residence in the third country of my young life.

I was plain and simply awful in my freshman training camp. Looking back on the experience I can see now that I was much too young and too immature to be there. Though our family had gone through a lot, I was ill-prepared for the loneliness of my first time away from home.

One of the things I liked least about that first year was being assigned as the roommate to the kicker who had been there for three years. He was not particularly interested in forming any sort of friendship with the kid who was trying to take his job. Just as important he was a junior and I was a freshman. Our age and maturity difference made us about as unsuited as it's possible to be in terms of being roommates. A couple of weeks into camp I went to Jim Cameron to tell him I'd had enough. He directed me to Dave Elliot, the defensive backfield coach. I explained my roommate problem, expecting to hear a sympathetic response to what was for me a very real problem. Elliot responded, "Ridgway, there's a good chance things are going to get a lot worse before they get better, so get used to it." This wasn't what a scared, lonely kid going to school in a foreign country wanted to hear.

Elliot was wrong. Gradually things got better. A few days before our first game of the season, another of the assistant coaches, Bob Simmons, asked me to accompany him to a meeting with Head Coach Chuck Stobart. Chuck met us in the hall outside his office and said to Bob, "Did you tell him?"

Bob replied that he hadn't and then announced they were putting me on a full-ride scholarship including the paying of my out-of-state tuition fees. This was the best news I could have received right about then, but I was completely surprised, maybe even shocked, when they told me. Through most of training camp I had kicked like I had a broken leg, and to this day I'm not sure why the coaches decided not only to bump up my scholarship but to name me as the starting kicker for our season-opener.

I wish I could say I responded to their show of confidence by kicking the lights out during my freshman year, but the truth is I was terrible. We attempted 13 field goals over the course of 11 games and I made a paltry four. As a team we were 2 and 9 and there weren't a whole lot of positives to be taken out of the year.

Our troubles started early. The night before our first game of the 1977 season against Ball State, the coaches took the team to see the movie *Rocky*, no doubt to provide inspiration for our debut contest. The movie's message, with its story of

Rocky Balboa's great comeback and never-say-die attitude, was reinforced the next day. Minutes before the kickoff to the game, the school band played the *Rocky* theme. I was pumped. The whole team was pumped.

Unfortunately our competition must have seen a better movie. Ball State pounded us 43–3. The good news was that I made my first field goal attempt as a University of Toledo Rocket, a 40-yarder into the closed end of the Glass Bowl stadium.

This was, however, one of the last pieces of good news in a season that is best forgotten. Well, maybe there was one more. Our Homecoming game that year was against Ohio University. We won it 31–29 on the first kick of my career that was to decide a game. I remember going onto the field with a minute left on the clock in a state of virtual terror. I couldn't make my knees stop shaking, and my mouth guard was stuck to the roof of my mouth. The kick to be a 32-yard attempt, but it looked to me like at least half a mile. I'm pretty sure my mind went blank, but my body fortunately went on automatic pilot. The snap came back and I suppose I must have kicked it because it went through the uprights and we won the game.

My sophomore year was similarly unremarkable. We were not much better than the year before, and the pressure had begun to mount on Coach Stobart to get things turned around or risk being fired.

And sure enough, in my junior year, the fortunes of the Rockets changed for the better, in spite of our second game not being one of the bright lights of the season. We were going up against Arizona State in Tempe. Frank Kush was the coach of the Sun Devils, and they were one of the perennial powers of NCAA football. Kush, you may recall, once punched out his punter after a particularly bad kick.

England to North America

After being touted as one of the two or three best teams in the nation, the Sun Devils had lost their first two games of the season and were a little snarly going into the game against us. The game was a mismatch and they crushed us 49–0. A week earlier our punter had broken his leg, and I wound up handling the punting chores in Tempe. It wasn't the most desirable game in which to start a new phase of my career. The Arizona State defense forced us to punt the ball 15 times, a Pac-10 and Mid-American Conference single-game record and a hell of a lot of punts for four-down football. Although I had a decent average for the day (41.5 yards per kick) there were a couple that, had I been playing for the Sun Devils, might have had Frank Kush dialing up another knuckle sandwich.

We had a decent 1979 and it came down to our second-last game of the year against Central Michigan University. A win would give us the Mid-American title. I missed three field goals that day and we wound up tying the game 7–7. We had another chance to gain a share of the conference championship by beating Northern Illinois in our last game of the season in De Kalb, Illinois. They had won only a couple of games that year, but they increased their total by one by whipping our butts soundly. Of course, in the post-season recaps a lot of fingers were rightly pointed at me for having missed those three field goals against Central.

The following year I went 7 of 8, my most accurate year of college ball by far. I missed the last three games of the season when I was declared ineligible for having signed with a Canadian agent. This was my first big tactical error since I'd been playing the game of football. I had been assured by the agent that signing with him would not affect my eligibility. He was wrong (I suspect deliberately) and this cost me three important games in my senior year.

My college career came to an end and with it the Chuck Stobart experience. Chuck was one hard-ass coach. He had been an assistant to Bo Schembechler at the University of Michigan for eleven years and also had been at Miami of Ohio for a while, a school known as the Cradle of Coaches because of all the great coaches who began their careers there. I liked Chuck despite his toughness. He wasn't a big man, maybe 5' 8" and 185 pounds, but I saw him manhandle players a lot bigger than he was and actually kick a few in the backside during practice. And I don't mean playful kicks.

But the man I enjoyed most while I was at Toledo was Assistant Coach Dan Simrell. We were to become good friends during my time at the University of Toledo, and Dan was one of the main driving forces behind my football career going beyond the college level.

Another mentor was Dr. Herb Sandberg, who taught me a class in children's literature in my senior year. I went into it thinking it would be a class I could take to kill a little time and pick up a few credit hours. It ended up being one of the classes I most enjoyed and found most informative during my time at the University of Toledo. Herb was to have a profound impact on my life both academically and socially. At the end of each quarter he hosted a get-together at his home for his students, and part of their mark depended on their attending. Because Herb is a gourmet, it wasn't much of an imposition and everybody always attended. His house was also big enough that he rented rooms to some of his students. I became one of the tenants. It was at this point that the loneliness and awkwardness of life in a foreign country began to melt away. After several years as a student, athlete and visitor to the United States, I finally started to feel at home.

Herb became a friend to me and Nancy, the girl I was dating. When I was drafted in 1981 by the Montreal Alouettes, Herb held a draft party for me. When Nancy and I were married in 1982, Herb attended the wedding. He has even been up to Saskatchewan to see me play. The stories of Herb's kindness and the great times we had with mutual friends Bob Flynn and Mary Jablon could fill a book. The truth is people like Herb Sandberg don't come along nearly often enough in a lifetime.

Though my college football career had been unspectacular I came out of school believing more than ever there was a future for me in professional football. I didn't have the greatest stats in the world, but I did have a tremendous desire to play the game and a willingness to do whatever was required to make a career for myself in the pro ranks.

In 1981, as if to confound my plans, I made my second major football mistake. I was drafted by the Montreal Alouettes and also received a number of letters from NFL clubs, and a couple, the Seattle Seahawks and the Dallas Cowboys, expressed more than passing interest. A week before the NFL draft I received a call from Gil Brandt, the director of player personnel for the Cowboys. Gil indicated they were thinking of drafting me and wondered what my reaction would be. During the course of our conversation I mentioned I had been drafted by the Alouettes. This was the mistake. At this point there was silence on the other end of the line, and the conversation wound down quickly. Needless to say I was not drafted by the Cowboys. I can only surmise they felt a Canadian kid would automatically take the offer from a Canadian team, and they decided not to waste a draft pick on me.

So I was off to the Montreal Alouettes for my first professional training camp. The team was owned at the time by Nelson Skalbania, a free-spender who was signing big-name NFL superstars, people like Vince Ferragamo, Billy (White Shoes) Johnson, David Overstreet and others. Tom Cousineau, an all-everything linebacker from Ohio State and a first-round NFL draft pick, had also been signed but reported late to camp apparently because he was miffed over what Ferragamo had received for a contract. When he finally showed up, Cousineau refused to wear Alouettes' gear to practice, choosing instead his Ohio State sweater and pants. I don't think Tom exactly endeared himself to the other players or fans, but maybe when you're making the kind of money he was, it doesn't matter what people think of you.

My first coach in the Canadian Football League was Joe Scanella. He had been an assistant with the Oakland Raiders when they won the Super Bowl a year prior to his coming to Canada. I wasn't in camp long enough to get to know him very well, but it seemed to me he would have been good to play for.

One of my recollections about Joe came out of an early training camp practice. I was working on playing the fairly substantial crosswind blowing that day. Joe came over to talk to me. He put his arm around me and pointed at the goalposts with his left hand. He went on to explain the principal of aiming slightly into the crosswind in order to allow the wind to push the ball back on line and through the uprights. What stood out most about the conversation was the Super Bowl ring Joe was wearing. It was an impressive piece of jewelry and, as a matter of fact, was the model for our 1989 Roughrider Grey Cup rings. That morning, with the sun glistening off the ring's many diamonds, it was a stunning sight. I remember thinking that someday I'd like to win a ring like that.

If I thought my first college training camp was an eye-opening experience, it was nothing compared to my first taste of professional football. I remember thinking after I got through my freshman training camp that there is nothing lower than a kid fresh out of high school going off to college to try out for the football team. And that I would never have to experience anything like that again. Boy, was I wrong.

In Montreal, not only was I a rookie with no professional experience, but also I was a rookie kicker. Believe me, there is no one lower on the planet. I decided early on that my strategy would be to shut up, blend in and draw attention to myself only on the field.

Our training camp was held in the community of Victoriaville, of hockey stick fame, and one of the first things I noticed was that very few people there spoke any English. Most of the American players, many of whom were from the Southern and Western United States, had never been closer to a French person than Marcel Marceau, the mime they had maybe seen on TV. I had heard of culture shock and had experienced it to some extent when we had emigrated, but the time I spent in Victoriaville in La Belle Province—now *that* was culture shock.

We were housed at a *College d'ensiegnement General et Professionnel* (the Quebec equivalent of a junior college) and the place was first class in every way. The dormitories were beautiful, the classrooms where we held our meetings were first-rate and the dining room was altogether different from most training camp facilities. Rather than one mass, generic meal for the whole team, we were able to order virtually whatever we wanted. Chris Walby, who would later become a perennial Winnipeg Blue Bomber all-star lineman, was also a rookie in camp, and every time we walked into the dining room, Chris thought he had died and gone to heaven. I sat with him a few times during meals and was amazed at how much he could put away. I can vouch for the fact that Chris didn't get to be 6' 7" and 270 pounds with smoke and mirrors. Every pound of that body has been bought and paid for.

It was intimidating being at a camp that had as many superstars in attendance as Skalbania had assembled. It was during that brief period in CFL history when salaries, at least for some players, rivaled those being paid in the NFL. Nevertheless, I found most superstars to be normal, down-to-earth people. Vince Ferragamo, who had quarterbacked the Los Angeles Rams to the Super Bowl game in 1980 and would eventually leave football to pursue a career in medicine, was a super person. He looked like a cross between Warren Beatty and Ed Marinaro and not surprisingly was a huge hit with women. Whenever we got back to the dorm, no matter what the time was, there would be a throng of female fans standing outside chanting, "Vince . . . Vince." As the rest of us were walking by, they'd stop us, talk for a while and finally say, "Could you go get Vince?"

One of the things I liked best about Vince, a married man, was that despite all the adoration heaped upon him, which would have messed up a lot of guys' heads, he went about his business at training camp seemingly oblivious to the stir he was creating.

I played catch a few times with Vince while he was warming up. I've tossed the ball back and forth with a number of quarterbacks who threw hard—John Hufnagel when I first came into the league comes to mind—but Vince was the only guy I've ever seen who, when you were 15 yards apart, threw the ball so hard and with so much rotation that it made a whistling noise as it rocketed toward you.

Billy (White Shoes) Johnson was another interesting player at the Victoriaville camp. Billy had been a receiver and premiere kick-returner with the Houston Oilers and Atlanta Falcons and had been the first to wear white shoes in the NFL, thus the nickname. In Montreal it became francophonized as Souliers Blancs.

One night after practice I wandered into the dorm's TV room and Billy happened to be the only other person there. I hadn't to that point met him and didn't realize the famed Billy "White Shoes" Johnson was sitting there. I sat down and the two of us watched a program for a while. Eventually I turned to him and said, "Man, am I homesick." Which was true. I was missing Nancy in Ohio and my family in Ontario and it seemed like a year since I'd seen either of them. Billy said he felt the same way and asked if I was married. I replied that I wasn't but I had a girlfriend down in the States. Billy told me he was married, had a couple of kids and was having a tough time being away from them. At this point he stuck out his hand and said, "Billy Johnson." I shook his hand and told him my name, and we went back to watching TV. Except I wasn't seeing much of what was on. Instead, I was thinking, *Man I'm sitting here watching TV with Billy (White Shoes) Johnson. I'm making $21 a week and he's making $200,000 a year and we're just a couple of guys who are homesick together.*

However, there was a difference. The next day Billy flew his wife and kids in from Houston so they could be with him, and I went back to writing letters to Nancy and my dad.

We broke camp in Victoriaville and went to Montreal where the team put us up at the Holiday Inn right next to the Olympic Village that had housed the athletes for the 1976 Olympic Games. We all went to work learning to navigate the subway system in Montreal, which is probably unique among subway systems and is, without a doubt, the best I have ever traveled on. It was because of the subway that I got my first close look at one of the scourges of professional sport. For our first preseason game a number of us had decided to take the subway over to the ballpark. A few hours before the game I wandered down to one of the guy's rooms to check on what time we were going to leave. When I got there several of the players, including a number who were to play that day, were sitting around toking up and getting high.

I was faced with a dilemma. There was no way I wanted to smoke drugs, but there was that old immigrant kid peer pressure thing hanging over me. How could I find a way of refusing without looking like a geek? I couldn't think of any way to turn the stuff down and still be seen as cool by the guys, so I just left. Besides, I figured with my luck I'd be in there and the place would be busted or a coach would wander in, and whether I was smoking up or not wouldn't matter. My career would take a definite downturn. Some of the same thing had gone on in the jock dorm at college, and my reaction to it then was the same as it was in the hotel in Montreal and has been ever since. I really don't have a big problem with what other players do, it's just not for me.

As training camp and the preseason were winding down it was becoming clear I wasn't going to be a member of the 1981 Montreal Alouettes. I had not dressed for a single preseason game so I suppose it should have come as no surprise when the inevitable call came to my room in the hotel. I was told to get my playbook and go down to the Big "O" to see Coach Scanella. I knew there could be only two reasons for the coach to call for me: one, he wanted my opinion of the offense; or two, I was about to get what football players to as an apple and a road map. I admit I tend to be overly optimistic, which is why I believed there was at least a tiny chance the coach and I would be discussing offensive strategy.

My optimism, of course, was misplaced. When I got to

England to North America

Joe's office he told me I was being released. He was decent and considerate as he explained the reason I was being let go: I didn't punt and they had decided to go with a kicker who could perform both punting and place-kicking duties. (This scenario would haunt me a number of times later in my career.) Joe ended the conversation by saying that if he heard of anyone in the league who was looking strictly for a place-kicker, he would mention my name. At this point we shook hands, I thanked Joe and walked out of his office thinking this was the last I would have to do with the Montreal Alouettes. Later, my assumption would be proved wrong.

I was disappointed but also angry. I had been told when I arrived that I was being looked at solely as a place-kicker and now I was being released because I didn't punt.

I arrived home the next morning and that night I was contacted by Paul Robson of the Winnipeg Blue Bombers and asked to report at once to the Bombers' training camp because my services might be required. In a matter of hours I went from the depths of despair to a new high of optimism. I repacked my bags (not a big job since I had barely begun to unpack) and headed for Winnipeg. I arrived at the Bomber camp exhausted as I hadn't slept the night I had been cut or the night of the call from Winnipeg. Nobody was at the airport to meet me, and when I called the Bombers' office, no one seemed to know anything about me or my arrival at training camp. This was a bad sign. Finally I was told to take a cab to the stadium. I got my new equipment, my new number (7) and waited for the afternoon meetings and practice to get underway. The meeting was long as we watched what seemed like endless game film (on an 8 mm projector with that non-stop, mesmerizing *chigida–chigida* noise) and I was all but asleep.

When the lights suddenly came on, Bomber Head Coach Ray Jauch was looking directly at me. I tried to shake myself awake and look alert. I don't think it worked. What I didn't know was the coach was staring intently at me because he was trying to figure out who the hell I was. I would later learn that the idea to bring me in for a tryout had been Paul Robson's alone and Jauch didn't know anything about it.

Near the end of the practice I kicked a few with the incumbents, place-kicker Trevor Kennerd and punter Bob Cameron. Dieter Brock was holding for me (this was before he became a major force in the CFL) and after some major running under Ray Jauch's watchful eye, the practice was over. So, as it turned out, was my short and uneventful career with the Blue Bombers. Ray came over to me and, as politely as he could, asked who I was. When I told him, he said, "Well, Dave, we're just not looking for a place-kicker. I'm happy with the guy we've got so I'm afraid we can't use you." I couldn't blame Ray. Trevor Kennerd was a fine kicker who would go on to have a great career in the league. But I had been cut twice in three days and was feeling about as low as low can be.

When I arrived home again, tail between my legs, I watched TV and wallowed in self-pity for about three weeks after which my father got fed up. He told me it was time to get on with life and face my options: either I could enroll in school for the upcoming year and complete my degree or go out and get a job. I wasn't enthused about the idea of joining the real world so going back to the University of Toledo looked pretty good.

This, by the way, was typical of the way my father raised his kids. He was very British and very proper—he didn't swear and didn't tolerate us doing it either—but he had grown up in a tough neighborhood and believed in strict discipline and a firm hand to enforce it when necessary.

England to North America

A significant problem stood in the way of my returning to school. This time there would be no football scholarship to rely on, and our financial situation had not improved to the extent that my father could afford to put me through that last year of school. It was my future in-laws, Nick and Marlene Valentino, who came to the rescue and enabled me to complete my degree. It was something I appreciated very much.

Though my dream of playing professional football wasn't dead, it was certainly on life support. I had no way of knowing then that Montreal Coach Joe Scanella and Saskatchewan Coach Joe Faragalli were both Italian and happened to be good friends. And that good Italian friends talk. And sometimes they talk about place-kickers. And once in a while during the conversation the talk rolls around to how one Joe needs a place-kicker out in Saskatchewan and the other Joe knows this kid who might be available.

CHAPTER 3

There Ain't No *E* in Ridgway

Whadaya think training camp is, some kind of country club? Is that what you think? Because no man is assured of a job around here. And if you think you are, you've got another think coming.
—BRIAN'S SONG, 1970

On May 17, 1982, a hot, muggy day, I left Toledo, Ohio, for Regina, Saskatchewan. I had just finished the spring quarter of my final year at the University of Toledo and was heading off, full of hope, for the training camp of the Saskatchewan Roughriders.

My journey would take me first by car to Cleveland, then by plane to Toronto, Winnipeg and finally to *Rajeena*, which is how many Americans, ever concerned about the possibility of sounding a touch personal, pronounce the name of the Queen City. I'm not being smug when I say this because, despite receiving my high school education in Eastern Canada, my knowledge of the West, and particularly of the prairies, was embarrassingly limited. As a matter of fact I had only recently learned out of which city the Roughriders football club was based.

I was wearing a pair of dress slacks and a short-sleeved, cotton dress shirt with a button-down collar. I had chosen my clothes on that day partly for the weather, which was great in Ohio, and partly because I saw going to training camp as a kind of job interview, which in a sense it is. After what had happened in Montreal the year before, it would be overstating things to suggest I was confident, but the truth is I had a good feeling about going to Saskatchewan and what the future might hold.

The trip was uneventful until Winnipeg where I had an hour layover. While I was sitting in the airport I noticed a young, athletic-looking guy hustling by. (I would later learn he was almost always in a hurry to get somewhere.) Over his shoulder he had a suit-bag emblazoned with a Saskatchewan Roughriders' emblem. Although I was reluctant to approach him I finally wandered over to where he wound up sitting and asked if he happened to be en route to *Rajeena* and the Roughriders' training camp.

This is how I met Stew Fraser, who was to become one of my first close friends on the team and who would hold the ball for many of the kicks I would subsequently attempt. We talked for a while in the airport holding lounge and then arranged to sit together on the flight to Regina. I had, of course, introduced myself to Stew, but I hadn't mentioned I was also on my way to training camp. As a result, for the first hour or so of our acquaintance, Stew thought I was one of those avid fans of the Green and White who just wanted to talk football. And because of my short haircut, he guessed I just might be an RCMP recruit on my way to the Mounties' training headquarters in Regina. (That was another of the things I didn't know about the city as I made my way to my first Riders' camp.)

As we talked Stew found out the real reason I was Regina-bound. I learned he was close friends with Paul (Doc) Watson, the place-kicker of the previous year. What neither Stew nor I knew at the time was that Paul had torn his Achilles tendon playing volleyball prior to camp. In fact, it was this break—a good one for me, a bad one for Paul—that put me in the running for the job in Saskatchewan. Despite being close to the incumbent kicker, Stew was friendly and went out of his way to make me feel comfortable about the upcoming camp. His generosity was something I have never forgotten.

When we arrived at the airport, Stew, as to be expected, headed off with a couple of veteran players there to meet him while I wandered off in search of anybody who could offer me some direction about what I was to do and where I was to go. At the time, the Roughriders employed a retired RCMP officer, Al Tingle, to shuttle incoming rookies to the stadium for check-in and physicals. (Like Stew he would become a great family friend.)

Al gathered up a half dozen rookies who had arrived on various flights; we collected most of our bags and headed for the van parked outside. I say *most* of our bags because one of mine had not made it to Regina. Once we were in the van, Al had each rookie tell where he was from and what position he was trying out for. When it came my turn I announced I was Dave Ridgway, I was from the University of Toledo and I was trying out for the place-kicking job.

Al turned in his seat, looked at me and said, "Well, if I were you, I wouldn't bother unpacking because we've drafted a hell of a kicker out of the University of Western Ontario." This wasn't the news I most wanted to hear. But Al was right. The Riders had drafted Kevin Rydeard from Western, and Al, a knowledgeable football fan, knew coaches tend to pay more attention to players they have drafted than free agents like I was. Al's pronouncement didn't help my confidence.

Nor did the weather. The light, short-sleeved shirt I'd worn didn't turn out to be such a good choice for my first visit to Saskatchewan. As we made our way from the airport to the stadium, I couldn't help but notice it was sleeting. Sleet is that mixture of rain and snow prairie people are only too familiar with, even in May. The interesting feature about this particular sleet, however, was that it was moving sideways. I had never seen this phenomenon, not in Great Britain where I was born, not in Burlington where I went to high school and certainly not in Ohio where I had spent the last five years of my life. In all those places precipitation traveled as it was supposed to—vertically, not horizontally. The reason this sleet was moving sideways was the near gale-force wind accompanying it.

To a kicker wind is like dust to a house painter, fog to a sailor or ice to a skier: it is the condition he dreads most. Had I known at the time just how often and how hard the wind blows on the prairies, I might have taken Al Tingle's advice and got back on the plane and got the hell out of there.

As we made our way toward Taylor Field and the van rocked from side to side in the wind, I took comfort in the knowledge that any place with both a football team and weather conditions like these must also have a domed stadium. So as we traveled the streets of Regina I busied myself by scanning the horizon for a first glimpse of the dome I was sure would be Taylor Field. As we pulled off Elphinstone Street and up behind what was clearly an *outdoor* stadium, I recall thinking it had to be one of the nicest practice facilities I'd ever seen.

I said to Al, "Where's the stadium?"

He turned to me, laughed and said, "This is it, kid. Welcome to Taylor Field."

Inside the stadium I met another individual who was to

have a large impact on my career. He was equipment manager Norm Fong. One of the things I learned very quickly is that in the world of professional football, two people run the team; they are not the head coach and the general manager, though they undoubtedly think they are. No, the ones who really run the show are the equipment manager and the trainer. They also are the two people one should never upset. In the case of Norm Fong this presents something of a challenge, especially for rookies, because Norm feels life would be a whole lot better if they didn't exist.

As I met Norm that first time, I found myself looking at a person of Chinese descent whose body could best be described as having a great deal in common with the round bales that dot prairie fields. Norm's dimensions are such that Joe Faragalli, when he coached the Riders, insisted on having Norm stand next to him during the singing of the national anthem in televised games. Joe reasoned that when the camera panned the bench, as it often does during anthems, his less-than-svelte physique would look almost anorexic next to Norm's.

After being issued our equipment and before being whisked away for physicals and dental appointments, I managed to steal a moment to go onto the playing field and stand on what was at the time foreign soil for me—the 55-yard line. This geographical region does not exist in the United States where I had played virtually all of my football to that point.

Taylor Field runs from northwest to southeast. I stood facing southeast with the wind buffeting my back. *Kicking this way will be no problem at all,* I thought. Then I turned and faced into the wind, and I remember laughing and thinking that anything longer than 20 yards in such gale wouldn't have a prayer of getting anywhere near the goalposts. I had no idea how prophetic the thought was.

Then it was off to the doctor and dentist and finally to our dorm for rookie camp—Luther College on the University of Regina campus. The rooms were tiny, which wasn't a problem for me, but some of the bigger rookies were bothered by beds only five-and-a-half-feet long. Apparently this school only catered to short scholars.

What *was* troubling me was the fact that my bag had still not shown up. It was the bag in which I had packed my passport, all of my personal items and a number of positive thinking books I was studying at the time. Given the advice I'd received about not bothering to unpack and my certainty that field goals could only be kicked in one direction at Taylor Field, I wouldn't have minded giving a couple of those books a quick browse right about then.

Rookie camp is not particularly demanding for kickers. The coaches are far more interested in evaluating the players who can run, jump and catch than watching punters and place-kickers. In fact, I believe, and I think most coaches would agree, that the only way kickers can truly be evaluated is under fire in game conditions. The major event for me took place about two days into rookie camp when my missing piece of luggage finally arrived with everything still intact.

Rookie camp concluded and we headed for Saskatoon and the University of Saskatchewan campus for the main training camp. On the eve of our departure my initiation into prairie life continued when almost a foot of snow fell. While I was no stranger to snow, having it in that quantity at that time of year was a new experience.

The rookies and equipment were transported in two large buses while the veterans were permitted to make their way to Saskatoon in their own vehicles. This concession to the veteran players has been an on-and-off tradition over the years, subject to the whim of coaches and management. In 1982 the vets took cars. An optimistic highways department had apparently put away much of the snow-clearing equipment in anticipation of what is known in many parts of the country as spring, and so only one lane had been plowed on the highway between Regina and Saskatoon. The trip took well over three hours, and I remember thinking what a long, boring drive it was. Of course, I would soon discover that football fans in Saskatchewan make this and many longer trips to attend Rider games. At the time, however, the culture shock of prairie travel was particularly acute for me. In Great Britain a drive of fifteen or twenty miles is considered a journey of some consequence.

When we finally arrived in Saskatoon, I was immediately struck by the beauty both of the city, which is set along the North Saskatchewan River, and the campus of the University of Saskatchewan, which reminded me of the University of Toledo. The buildings are old and full of character on both campuses and most are of the fieldstone and sandstone construction that seemed to characterize schools that sprang up during the early decades of the century.

The buses came to rest next to the building that would serve as our dorm for the main camp, a quaint, delightful structure called Qu'Appelle Hall. (It was, and still is, one of the regular student residences during the academic year.) Most of the rookies were carrying a lot of their belongings with them, not surprising since each was hoping to be employed in that part of the world for at least several months. As we made our way toward the dorm, we were greeted by a strange sight. At the bottom of the steps leading into Qu'Appelle Hall stood a 6' 5", 265-pound giant dressed in cowboy boots, jeans, a lumber jacket and Stetson, with a guitar strapped to his back. I recall thinking how considerate it was of the team to have arranged a little entertainment.

I didn't have it quite right although it turns out the guy who was standing there is a pretty good picker and singer. He was shaking the hand of each rookie as we passed. When I got to him he laughed, stuck out a hand the size of Yorkton and said, "Hi, I'm Bob Poley."

Another coincidence. The first two veteran players I encountered in my rookie year were Stew Fraser, whom I'd met on my way to Regina and who would be my first holder, and Bob Poley, who would be my center for nine seasons. I might have considered this a good omen except that as he introduced himself I had no idea who the hell Bob Poley was. What made his gesture unique was the fact that rookies are typically treated with something a long way from cordiality and at times with outright contempt at training camps, particularly by the veterans. His being there to greet us was typical of the man known to his teammates as Polecat.

The rooming arrangements were set according to the prevailing pecking order among the players. The bottom two floors were reserved for veterans, the top floor for rookies. There were four kickers in camp, three of us rookies. The other two, Kevin Rydeard and Regina Rams' graduate Dave Badowich, and I were assigned to the fourth floor, a problem in that Qu'Appelle Hall had only three floors. It was some time before I discovered a turretlike structure at one end of the building. Inside was a winding wrought iron staircase leading to three rooms, which, since they were higher than every other room in the place, were designated as the fourth floor.

The single advantage to being on the fourth floor was sharing a bathroom with only three others. This was vastly superior to the situation on the lower floors where there were often a couple of dozen guys sharing a bathroom. That would be fine except that a lot of football players see Oscar Madison as their role model when it comes to the issue of tidiness.

The main disadvantage to the part of Qu'Appelle Hall that was to be my home for the next few weeks was its isolation. At night the place was quiet as a cemetery. If I were ever write a novel in the tradition of Stephen King and Dean Koontz, I would have the first body discovered in one of those spooky turret rooms. I admit now, long after the fact, that after a few nights in the new quarters I decided it would be best, except in emergencies, to make all trips to the bathroom during daylight hours.

Sleep is an important part of the training camp process, and many players develop special strategies to deal with it. In Montreal I had been amused to learn that time was set aside for the players to take a nap. I soon changed my attitude toward nap time and like most of the players took advantage of that and every other opportunity to get a little extra sleep. In my case naps were necessary because I wasn't getting a lot of sleep at night. I can break down my time in bed as follows:

11:00 P.M.	*Curfew*
11:00 P.M. – MIDNIGHT	*Read*
MIDNIGHT – 4:00 A.M.	*Worry about making the team*
4:00 – 5:30 A.M.	*Sleep soundly*
5:30 – 7:30 A.M.	*Sleep restlessly*
7:30 A.M.	*Wake-up call*

The wake-up ritual at training camp is not the highlight of the day. Whether sleep ends with heavy pounding on the door, a coach's whistle, an air horn or the imitation of a rooster crowing (Mike Samples' personal favorite during his tenure as assistant coach) its chief purpose appears to be to make the start to the day as unpleasant as possible. In Samples' case revenge was exacted each year near the end of camp when one morning was designated for the annual water ballooning of the rooster.

Meals were mandatory, which, because I am not a breakfast eater, meant throwing on sweats and a pair of flip-flops, hustling to the dining center, getting my name checked off, grabbing a juice and racing back to the dorm for a final half hour in the sack.

The first days of camp are especially nerve-wracking for rookies. While the veterans are joking and kibitzing around in a reunionlike atmosphere, the rookies spend most of their time making sure they aren't late for a practice or meeting and doing everything possible not to offend veterans.

The first team meeting of the 1982 season was held in the dining hall. As Coach Faragalli stood to address the assembled players, I noticed several prominent veterans sitting together at a nearby table. Among them were Mike Samples, Ken Clark, Eugene LaRoque, Ken McEachern, John Hufnagel and Lawrie Skolrood. At this moment the door opened and in strode Lyall Woznesensky, he of the famous *Woz-tusi* sack dance, and, as I would learn, one of the genuine characters in the game. Woznesensky strode across the floor toward the single vacant chair, which happened to be at the table of veterans. As he took his seat the players sitting there, on cue and without a word, got up and walked away with mischievous smiles playing across their faces. Woz, never to be outdone, made quite a show of getting himself comfortable and sat there alone through the entire meeting.

One of the veteran players I was able to talk to during the course of training camp was punter Ken Clark. He'd already had a great career, having played in the 1980 Super Bowl with the Los Angeles Rams and earlier with Toronto and Hamilton in the CFL. He was a great team player and one of the most respected men on the ball club. As camp progressed Clarkie became the guy I most wanted to model myself after.

Too often the specialists on football teams are outside the mainstream of the team. They will be set apart or will set themselves apart in the stereotypical role of the flaky kicker that has become the norm of American college and pro football. I wanted to distance myself as much as possible from the image of a short, fat, European tie salesman who has never before kicked a ball that wasn't round. The famous Alex Karras quote comes to mind. When he asked a kicker what he did, the reply was, "I *keek* touchdowns." Having Ken Clark as a teammate in those early years of my career was a great learning experience for a young place-kicker wanting not just to make the team but to be a genuine part of it.

As I've noted the practices themselves were not particularly strenuous for the kickers simply because it is not practical to kick a couple of hundred footballs in a practice. More often than not this will just tire the leg. Pretty soon the kicker finds himself altering his style to compensate for the fatigue, which is completely counterproductive to the process of developing as a kicker. So for kickers practice tends to be a fairly social occasion.

Which isn't to say no work gets done. At that first training camp we practiced by splitting the four kickers in pairs on opposite sides of the field and simply kicking back and forth to one another. About three days into camp we were standing along the sidelines when Ken Clark turned suddenly to Kevin Rydeard and said, "Come on, let's go kick." I'm not sure whether it was rookie nerves or what, but as Kevin headed off after Kenny, the kid's nose virtually exploded into one of the worst nose bleeds I'd ever seen. Kenny turned to Kevin, who by now had blood covering much of the front of his jersey and said, "Jeez, kid, I didn't want to compete with you, I just wanted to kick a few."

The atmosphere in my first Roughriders' training camp was for the most part relaxed. In fact, some members of the sports media were critical of Coach Faragalli on this point. Their view apparently was if players lived in barren living conditions with few if any creature comforts, they would have nothing to think about but football, and this would somehow translate into a better team. They seemed to take particular exception to the idyllic setting for the camp. The University of Saskatchewan campus, with its tall trees and manicured lawns, was not nearly Spartan enough for that segment of the media.

Joe's response to the criticism of his training camp methods was to say he was a football coach, not a prison warden. Joe tended to treat all of his players as adults, expected them to behave as professionals and saw his coaching staff as teachers. He wanted to create an atmosphere in which the players could learn. This didn't mean the camp was one big lawn picnic. Far from it. Joe worked us hard and, as a matter of fact, our practices lasted longer than anyone else's in the league, which meant being on the field for over five hours a day working on fundamentals and execution.

My feeling was that Joe was very much a players' coach despite being under tremendous pressure along with everyone else associated with that year's team. The whole province of Saskatchewan was starved for a winning team, and everyone was under intense scrutiny from media and fans alike. Nevertheless, I don't think I could have begun my professional career under a more understanding coach, and I believe he played a large part in my having a successful rookie season. Joe was able to successfully combine his role as boss with his natural inclination to be a friend. It was particularly helpful for me as an insecure rookie to have a person like him to talk to. To me and all of my teammates he became Papa Joe.

My confidence received a big boost early in camp when after the first few practices Joe told me that during the kicking drills involving the kicker, the holder and the long-snapper, most of which took place after regular practice, he wanted me to work with Stew Fraser and Bob Poley. Knowing that the coach had designated me as the place-kicker to work with the "regulars" made me feel pretty good, but I was still keenly aware of the need to do the job in a game situation.

I also realized my fate was at least in part out of my hands. The coaches would have to decide whether to keep one kicker such as Rydeard, who could both punt and place-kick, or go with Ken Clark as the punter and the best place-kicker from among the other three. The CFL had entered the age of roster limitations, and a number of clubs were going with a single kicker; Bernie Ruoff, Gerry Organ and, of course, Lui Passaglia were proof the one-kicker system could work. This caused me more than a little concern as I waited to see if I would win a spot or get another apple and road map.

One concern I did not have was that Ken Clark would be called upon to do both jobs. The one field goal I saw Kenny attempt during the camp gave an indication of the confidence other players had in his ability as a place-kicker. As soon as the ball was snapped all the offensive linemen, in a classic put-up job, threw themselves face first on the ground, the message being that they didn't want to risk being hit in the back by the ball. Kenny was laughing so hard he almost fell down on his approach to the ball. That one abortive attempt and a field goal Kenny actually did kick in 1983, after I had thoughtlessly decided to tackle someone and spent the rest of the game at

Pasqua Hospital, were the last two place-kicks Ken Clark attempted as a Roughrider.

A *Regina Leader-Post* report gave me further reason for hope. The story stated that my power and accuracy had "flicked on lights in Faragalli's eyes." The same piece quoted Joe as saying, "He has more of a leg than the others, and he's quicker getting the ball off . . . he's the guy you'd have to beat right now."

About the time I was getting a little puffed up on all the praise, the story took a turn. The writer noted that Faragalli "was not yet ready to hand the job to Ridgway. 'It's like everybody else up here,' Joe said. 'You get guys who are doing well in camp, who are showing some good stuff, but you don't know how they're going to perform once the lights go on'." This part of the story brought me back to earth in a hurry.

The other concern I had was that General Manager Jim Spavital was taking some heat from the media about the Roughriders' performance at recent CFL drafts. They had not for the most part produced many players who could make the team and contribute. I reminded myself that Kevin Rydeard was a draft pick and that his making the team just might make Jim Spavital's life a little easier. That was just one of the things running through my mind during those midnight to 4:00 A.M. worry sessions.

My list didn't end there. It's amazing how preoccupied my mind became as training camp progressed and how it blew small things all out of proportion. One of these was being assigned sweater number 79. Because kickers are not normally given numbers in the seventies (Ottawa's Gerry Organ wore number 71 but he also played as a receiver for part of his career) I was worried this might be a hint the club had decided to cut me. Who gives a damn what sweater the guy wears, right? Being a rookie brings out a lot of insecurities.

As training camp continued, the tension, particularly among the younger players, increased in quantum leaps. We were aware that in order to have a legitimate shot at making the team, we had to show well in the preseason games. It was crucial to be chosen to dress for one or both of the road games. This was in the days of four preseason games before the league decided there was more revenue to be had by dropping two of the exhibition contests in favor of more games in the regular schedule. This is undeniably true, but I'd hate to be a coach having to make tough roster decisions after just two games.

Making the traveling roster for exhibition games is not the only stress factor in the lives of rookies as training camp winds down. There are in the CFL specified days on which all teams have to be down to a specified number of players. These cut-down days are undoubtedly the most difficult times of the entire training camp for players and coaches alike. The coaching staff on most teams does all it can to make the releasing or cutting of players as considerate and discreet as possible. With the Riders this is often done by quietly rousing the player at 4:00 or 4:30 A.M. He is told to take his playbook and report to the coach. The reason for the early call is to allow the player to leave without the embarrassment of having to see his teammates. Most football players I have known, upon learning they have been cut, have appreciated the club's courtesy and have taken the opportunity to slip away as quietly as possible.

The final cutdown after the preseason games is made even more difficult by the fact that any player who has made it that far is likely a very good athlete. He may even be capable of playing at the professional level, but for whatever reason not with that particular team at that particular time. On a number of occasions throughout my career, just prior to the final cutdown, the coach has asked for a show of hands of all players who have ever been cut during their careers. The number who raise their hands is astonishing. I'm not sure if knowing that makes a player feel any better when he gets that dreaded 4:00 A.M. call, but I've always felt it was a nice gesture to help young players realize that even some of the best have been cut at one time or another.

As I had hoped I got the call to dress for the first preseason game against the Stampeders in Calgary. I can recall, thirteen years later, almost every detail of the game from the flight into Calgary to the bus trip to the hotel to the sleepless night before the game and finally to sitting in front of my locker in McMahon Stadium. (Norm Fong has assigned me that same locker for every game we've played in Calgary since that exhibition contest in 1982.) I particularly recall Ken Clark sitting opposite me, telling me to relax and to just keep doing the things I'd been doing throughout training camp.

It turned out to be a tremendous football game as we beat the hometown Stampeders under Jack Gotta. Victory wasn't secured until 13:58 of the fourth quarter when quarterback Steve Alatorre snuck in for a two-point conversion. Final score: Saskatchewan 33, Calgary 32. I went 3 of 3 in the game and hit from 37, 20 and 23 yards, not particularly long field goals, but given the pressure I was feeling going into the game, 10-yarders would have been tough. It helped a lot that the first one I kicked was the longest. Had I missed it, it's hard to imagine how the rest of the night and maybe my career might have gone. Rookies get few chances to prove themselves in game situations.

Among the players who made an impact in the game were rookie quarterback Joe Adams, veteran quarterback John Hufnagel and rookie import defensive back Fran McDermott, who picked off two passes and looked like a definite threat to take some veteran's job. Ken Clark was amazing. With a slight wind at his back in the second quarter, he pounded singles of 76 and 85 yards to bring his punting average for the day to an incredible 56 yards. More than ever I was glad the guy couldn't kick field goals.

After the game the visiting team showers had no hot water, and some of our coaches were convinced it was Jack Gotta's doing. I don't know if Gotta had the authority to shut off the water, but I can say, having played for him a few years later, it was the sort of thing he might do.

Gotta was quoted after the game as saying, "We're going to make our quarterback position solid with [Gerry] Dattillio and [Bruce] Threadgill. I wouldn't trade them for the guys we just played against, I'll tell you that."

I learned early that Gotta didn't let facts get in the way of his opinions. The trio of Rider quarterbacks—John Hufnagel, Joe Adams and Steve Alatorre—went 15 of 24, 8 of 12 and 8 of 11 respectively for a total of 31 completions in 47 attempts for 409 yards and three touchdowns while our defense managed to intercept five Stampeder passes. Still, I can understand Gotta's expression of solidarity, if that's what it was, toward his quarterbacks.

In the locker room after the game, Ken Clark came up, offered his hand and said, "Congratulations, rook, you just made the team." I appreciated the compliment, especially coming from Kenny, but I knew there were still three exhibition games to go. When I reminded him, Kenny shook his head and said, "Trust me, you have made this football club."

When we got to the Calgary airport I phoned my father (collect as usual) to tell him the news. He was ecstatic to hear how I'd done but very quickly said, "Okay, now that's gone. Don't think about it and don't dwell on it because you've got to go out and do the same job next week." It was a reaction typical of my father: truthful and straight to the point, but not always what I might have wanted to hear.

If my father's cautionary words hadn't been enough to keep my feet fixed firmly on the ground, the stories in the papers over the course of the next few days would have done the job. Though most applauded my performance some made THAT mistake. It was then I first realized that if I did manage to stay in the league, I'd better get used to seeing my name spelled Ridg*e*way with an *e*. I've lost count of the number of times I've cursed that *e* and still after years in the league it pops up like an unwanted relative at family dinners. Sort of gives a guy that Rodney Dangerfield feeling.

The following week we played the Edmonton Eskimos in my first game at Taylor Field. The game ended 34–27 in our favor, and although it was preseason and didn't count for anything in the standings, all the players in green and white uniforms and the 24,732 fans (a record preseason Taylor Field crowd at the time) were delighted to knock off the team that was then and still is today the one every other team most enjoys beating. Coach Faragalli, a former Edmonton assistant coach, said, "Beating the Eskimos at tiddleywinks is worth something."

Once again victory came late in the game as quarterback Joe Adams snuck into the end zone from the one-yard line to provide the winning margin with eight seconds left on the clock. The game marked my first time going up against legendary Eskimo place-kicker Dave Cutler, and although I managed to hit 2 of 2 from 13 and 37 yards, I spent most of the game in awe watching him kick. It was also my first time seeing Edmonton quarterback Warren Moon in action. Though his stats weren't especially impressive that night, it was impossible not to recognize his enormous talent.

Our third preseason game took place only seventy-two hours later as we faced the B.C. Lions. I had never been to the West Coast of Canada before and was stunned by the beauty of the city of Vancouver. I thought then and still think today that with its ocean on one side and mountains on the other, Vancouver has to be one of the most desirable places to live anywhere in the world.

The game was played at old Empire Stadium, a horseshoe-shaped facility that provided a spectacular view of the distant mountains through the open end of the stadium. It was a night game and I remember standing in the end zone after our warm-up staring up at the lights of Grouse Mountain and being in something akin to a trance as the beauty of the setting swept over me. I was also aware of the illustrious history of the place including, of course, the Miracle Mile of the 1954 British Empire Games with Roger Bannister and John Landy. Yes, football players do occasionally think about things like this.

Before the game Paul Watson, the place-kicker from the previous year and a Vancouver native, came by to see the team, the cast still on his injured leg. I was intimidated by his presence there and in particular at seeing how popular he was with his former teammates. All the guys rushed over to him to see how he was doing. While it was the most natural thing in the world, I felt uncomfortable being the place-kicker who was replacing Paul.

Whether the brevity of the time between games was a factor or not, we were beaten 43–39 by the Lions. Our late-game heroics came up short this time, but we did make things interesting by scoring two touchdowns in the final minute. I got to be a part of the excitement in a way I was not accustomed to. Joe Adams had capped off a late drive with a 10-yard touchdown pass to wide receiver Joey Walters, then threw for a two point convert to Dwight Edwards. At this point, with 19 seconds showing on the clock and the score 43–33, the kickoff team was told to go onto the field for the onside kick.

The onside kick employs a very different strategy in Canada than in the U.S. college football I had known. On the narrower American field the object is to have the ball skitter along the ground and take a last big hop just about the time the kicker's teammates reach the vicinity of the ball. In Canadian football, with our wider playing field, the idea is to loft the ball like a lob shot in tennis from the hash mark in the direction of the opposite sideline. The ball must travel more than 10 yards, but coaches like it to go no more than about 14 yards with lots of hang time to allow the other members of the kicking team to get into position to outjump or outscramble the opposing players during the mayhem that normally follows. The rule in Canadian football is that possession is awarded to the team of the last player to touch the ball before it goes out-of-bounds.

I had practiced the kick during training camp but was far from comfortable as we lined up for the attempt. As it turned out Fran McDermott, who had been having a brilliant training camp, came up with the ball. Joe Adams then teamed up with Joey Walters for a couple of completions that led to a touchdown, which at least made the score more respectable.

We came home for our final preseason game against the Winnipeg Blue Bombers, and in front of another large and boisterous crowd lost 25–16. I went 3 of 5 in that game, hitting field goals from 19, 14 and 45 yards out but missing from 30 and 47 yards. This left my preseason record at 9 of 11, which I was happy with, especially since I had attempted only eight field goals during my entire final season of collegiate ball.

Preseason and training camp came to an end, and as they

did it occurred to me that I was still with the football club. No longer were there sixty or seventy guys at the practices and meetings. Now there were only forty-five and I was one of them. Still, I didn't allow myself to believe it until I heard Joe Faragalli speak the words that to this point in my life were about the best I figured the English language had to offer. They came during the first team meeting after the final cut-down. Joe entered the room, looked at us for a time and said, "I'd like to welcome the members of the 1982 Saskatchewan Roughriders football team."

There was little fanfare and no brass band or high fives around the room, but I do know there was a place-kicker in that meeting who was grinning so hard his face hurt.

CHAPTER 4

The Green and White

Got to believe in yourself, kid. The only difference between you and the major league ballplayer is that they believe they belong there. —TALENT FOR THE GAME, 1991

THE SASKATCHEWAN ROUGHRIDERS began the 1982 regular season as a team that had not made the playoffs since losing the 1976 Grey Cup game to Ottawa. The natives, as they say, were restless.

We had been relatively successful during the preseason, and expectations were high although fan and media optimism was tempered by the cold reality of the previous five seasons. For the players, once the uncertainty of training camp was over, the feeling of pressure was felt almost immediately; we knew we were expected to turn things around; it was *demanded* that we turn things around.

The early line on the 1982 Riders was that after the previous season, which had seen the team live and die by the pass, we had further improved our receiving core with the addition of Ron Robinson out of Utah State to go with incumbents Joey Walters and Chris DeFrance. The pundits felt as well that our offensive line would show the maturity of another season together and that John Hufnagel, solidly entrenched as the number one quarterback, would do a capable job. The media experts pointed to the running game as the big question mark on offense heading into the season. There was some concern that the resurrection of Jimmy Edwards might not be enough to shore up this weak spot.

The biggest improvement was thought to have taken place in the defensive secondary where Marcellus Greene on the corner and Fran McDermott inside both had excellent training camps. I was happy to note that the media felt the kicking game had been improved because Ken Clark had recovered from the hamstring problem that had hampered his punting the year before and because I had shown promise during training camp as a place-kicker.

Our coaching staff was headed, of course, by Joe Faragalli, who had put together what I felt was an outstanding group of assistant coaches. Mike Murphy was the defensive coordinator and defensive line/linebacker coach; Gerry Hart coached the secondary; Steve Buratto was in charge of the offensive line; and Monte Charles handled the offensive backs and receivers. They worked hard and asked the players to do the same, but they were also a fun group of coaches to play for. During one early season practice, Coach Hart was standing a little way off watching me kick field goals when he suddenly yelled out, "Dan Simrell." This took me by surprise. The last thing I expected to hear in the middle of practice was the name of one of my former University of Toledo coaches.

I spun around and asked, "You know Dan?"

Gerry replied that he did and was aware that Dan had been coaching at Toledo when I was there. He went on to relate a story about coaching against Toledo when Dan was still a player. Dan, a quarterback, had been knocked out early

The Green and White

in the game and had to have a number of stitches in his face. He came back later to lead the University of Toledo to victory. Gerry told me he figured Dan was one of the toughest quarterbacks he'd ever seen.

The conversation between Gerry Hart and I was no big deal, I suppose, but to a rookie it went a long way toward relieving some anxiety. Looking back on it now, I believe this was the coach's intent.

Monte Charles, on the other hand, was one of the funniest guys I have ever been around. One of his favorite ploys was to stand near Kenny or me whenever the media was hanging around during practice. While we were kicking, Monte would assume a watchful pose as if he were actually coaching us. He never said anything, probably because he didn't know a damn thing about kicking, but there he'd be looking wise as all get out. It got to the point that if the media asked Joe about one of the kickers, he'd direct them to Monte. One day I asked Monte if he had any pointers for me. He grinned and said, "Kid, just don't go into a slump because I won't be able to get you out of it." Whatever Monte did or didn't do that year, it must have worked because both Kenny and I were Western Conference and League All-Stars.

Monte looked like a cowboy right out of a John Wayne movie, with a gruff, rugged exterior but a thoroughly likable interior. One of his favorite lines, usually said to shock a group of rookies, was: "You know my wife is such a slob. Every time I go to piss in the sink there's dirty dishes in there." Invariably it would break up everybody in the room. I was genuinely sad when I learned that Monte passed away a couple of years ago. He was a good coach and a fine person.

Steve Buratto was the coach of what was becoming a very good offensive line. It consisted of Don Swafford, one of the last American offensive linemen to play in the league prior to expansion, Bob Poley, Roger Aldag, Neil Quilter and Gerry Hornett. The line had improved dramatically from three years earlier when it blocked for Tom Clements during his brief stopover in Saskatchewan. Clements had almost been killed playing behind our O-line, but under the tutelage of coach Buratto, we now had one of the solid units in the league. Mike Murphy was on the defensive side of the ball and as a result I didn't get to know him as well as the others.

As for Joe Faragalli, he was a coach who liked to be involved in every aspect of the on-field running of the team and had a pretty good knowledge of each. He was tremendously fair with his players and provided the kind of leadership that made players feel they would go to war for him.

I recall how during his pregame talks he never asked for the proverbial 110 percent; he'd simply ask each guy to give the best he had in him that day. During our warm-up on the field prior to a game, Joe made a point of going to every player, shaking his hand and making some remark, often humorous, to loosen him up. Joe never deviated from the ritual, and I know we all appreciated his taking the time to demonstrate his personal concern for each of us.

On July 9, 1982, I played in my first league game in the Canadian Football League. We met the Blue Bombers in Winnipeg. My eighteen-hour tryout with the Bombers the previous year was still fresh in my mind. While I didn't bear any animosity toward Bomber Coach Ray Jauch, who really had no control over what had happened, I nevertheless wanted to show him what he *could* have had. The Blue Bombers also had figured in my childhood from the time my father had worked in Manitoba. He had sent back to my brothers and me a number of packs of CFL football cards. I remember very well from this first exposure to the Canadian Football League that my favorite team, probably based on something very scientific—like the name—was the Winnipeg Blue Bombers.

In 1982 the Bombers still played in the Western Division of what was a nine-team league. Any game within one's own conference was of particular importance, especially since only three of the five teams in the West qualified for post-season play.

This didn't stop us from losing 31–21 in a game in which we simply did not play well. I went 2 of 2, and although I was disappointed about the loss I was happy with my own performance. The truth is that what a player does in preseason is soon forgotten; it's what happens when the first whistle is blown for regular season play that really matters, especially for rookies.

Our second game of the 1982 season was at home against the B.C. Lions, who were coming off a 51–34 thrashing of the Hamilton Tiger-Cats. The starting quarterback for the Lions, Joe Paopao, was hurt early in the game and Roy DeWalt came off the bench to have a great outing against the Ti-Cats. When he heard the score of the Lions' opening game Joe Faragalli quipped, "I couldn't score 51 points in basketball."

Many people had picked B.C. to succeed Edmonton as the power of the Western Conference that year, and with their size and speed they weren't a bad bet. They came into Regina, and when they left we were 0 and 2 in the young 1982 season. It was a great ball game played before over twenty-seven thousand fans, and it was one we could have and probably should have won. We kicked a 42-yard field goal with 2:03 left in the game to take a 24–23 lead. This field goal was really my first pressure kick in professional ball. I felt good as I watched the ball sail through the uprights.

Unfortunately for us DeWalt then led the Lions downfield on a drive that involved two successful third-down gambles. The drive ended at our one-yard line and Lui Passaglia kicked a 12-yard field goal with no time left on the clock to give the Lions the win.

Punter Ken Clark again compiled unbelievable stats. He had kicks of 80 and 84 yards among his eight punts for 403 yards and over a 50-yard average. Those numbers I would discover were typical of what we could expect from Ken.

Our third game of the season was already one of those "must games" the media likes to talk about. If we had any serious designs on a playoff spot, we really couldn't afford to go to 0 and 3 to start the year.

Over thirty thousand people crowded into Calgary's McMahon Stadium for the start of that game, but a rainstorm struck in the fourth quarter and only about two-thirds of the faithful stuck around for the final gun. Of those who stayed, a surprisingly large number were clutching green and white pompoms. It was my first encounter with the phenomenon known as Rider Pride. In virtually every Canadian city expatriate Saskatchewanites come out in large numbers to cheer us on. It is one of the things that has made the wearing of the Green and White for over thirteen seasons very special.

We got our much-needed victory, prevailing over the Stampeders 25–19. Rookie quarterback Joe Adams came into the game with just under eleven minutes remaining and the Stampeders ahead 19–10. He got some help on play selection from John Hufnagel and the coaches, and brought us back for our first win. It wasn't the last time Joe was to display the talent that could have made him one of the all-time great CFL quarterbacks had he been able to conquer the demons that ruled his private life.

The Green and White

I kicked three converts, a single on a kickoff and a 27-yard field goal in the game. Another field goal attempt from 53 yards out was blocked by Stampeder linebacker Danny Bass, who would eventually move on to the Edmonton Eskimos and have an outstanding career.

The Toronto Argonauts provided the opposition on week four of the 1982 season. We embarrassed ourselves in a sold-out Taylor Field, losing 44–22 as we turned the ball over seven times. It was the worst loss the team had suffered during the tenure of Joe Faragalli, and it could have been even worse as we trailed Toronto 41–8 going into the fourth quarter before we were able to put up a few points against the Argonauts' second stringers.

Joe, not surprisingly, wasn't happy. After the game a reporter asked him if we were overconfident going into a game against supposedly weak opposition. Joe replied, "How could we be overconfident? Who are we, the Edmonton Eskimos? What have we done except play lousy?"

We headed off for our next game against the Rough Riders. (Only in the CFL could there be two teams with the same name while another, the Baltimore whatevers, goes through an entire season with no name at all.) With a record of 1 and 3 one quarter of the way through the season, we faced another must game.

I'd had a terrible week of practice leading up to the Ottawa game and was so upset that I phoned my father the night before the game. He told me not to worry, that I had done okay to that point in the season and that I just had go out and do what I had been doing. While his words reassured me they were more than offset in the dressing room immediately before the game when lineman Bryan Illerbrun came up, pointed a finger at me and said in as nasty a way as he could muster, "You better kick good today, you son of a bitch."

ROBOKICKER

The remark was typical of Illie's attitude, especially in the pregame locker room and in particular toward rookies, but his timing couldn't have been worse. Nevertheless, I went 4 of 4 and had my best game to date. I credit my father's words more than Bryan's with giving me whatever help I got that day.

Once again we came up with a pressure effort and knocked off the eastern Riders 26–19. Joe Adams made his first start at quarterback and put up very good numbers in going from opening kickoff to final gun. In fact, although the score was close our team improved with every quarter, and by the end we had things pretty much under control. My last field goal came with four seconds to go and meant that even a successful "Hail Mary" pass on the last play could do no more than tie the game for Ottawa. The last-play heroics didn't materialize and we left Ottawa having improved our record to 2 and 3. The win moved us into a fourth-place tie with the Edmonton Eskimos and left us four points out of first place.

I phoned my father again after the game and we had a pretty good long-distance celebration. Five games into my first season I was 8 of 11 in field goals and sat sixth in the Western Division scoring race.

Hamilton supplied our next Taylor Field opposition. The game marks one of the weirdest and most exciting of my early career. On that Saturday, August 21, the weirdness was provided by the stadium lights going out just prior to half-time, resulting in an intermission of seventy-six minutes. The playing of the game took a total of three hours and forty minutes. There was some talk during the delay that it might be necessary to play the balance of the game on Sunday. I found this a ghastly thought. I was still adjusting from a college schedule of eleven games in total. Here I was in my tenth game, only the halfway point of the professional season, and they were thinking of splitting one game into two. Nobody was happier than I when SaskPower got the lights back on in Taylor Field.

Bob Hughes, then covering the Riders for the *Regina Leader-Post*, and always good for some excellent one-liners when the opportunity presented itself, wrote, "There are massage parlors, I am told, in some of the darker recesses of Regina, that have better lighting than the Riders had Saturday night.... For over an hour during the longest half-time in Canadian Football League history, people sat in the stands wondering whose hand was on whose knee.... It could have been worse, how would you have liked to be the guy in the can when the power went out?"

Hamilton led 9–1 when the lights went off and 12–7 after three quarters. Bernie Ruoff added a 28-yard field goal early in the fourth quarter, his fifth of the game. Joe Adams had not been having a good game to this point and hadn't been helped by our repeatedly coughing up the ball. Even Joey Walters had uncharacteristically lost the ball twice. However, after Ruoff's fifth field goal, the two Joeys got it together and combined for a touchdown to bring us to within two points of the Tiger-Cats. Joe Adams then hit Chris DeFrance with a two-point conversion and the game was tied.

Hamilton quarterback Tom Clements took his team down the field to our 21 where our defense held. After the game the media dubbed the Rider defenders the "poplar defense" because several times they were forced to bend but not once did they break. Ruoff missed a 31-yarder after the late Ti-Cat march and we took over the ball on our 17 with 1:56 left to play. A 12-yard pass to DeFrance and a 30-yard run by fullback John McCorquindale got us close enough for a Ken Clark punt to the end zone that was returned by Howard Fields to the Hamilton two-yard line.

Our defense held again and Ruoff, after a controversial time violation against Hamilton, punted from his end zone. Tom Schulz, one of our linebackers, got a hand on the ball as it was being kicked. As a result Fran McDermott was able to run the short kick out-of-bounds at the Hamilton 35 with two seconds to go. I was 2 of 3 to this point, but Joe elected to send Ken Clark out to try to kick for a single. Hamilton called a time-out and during the break in the action, Joe asked if I thought I could make it. I nodded yes and Joe brought Ken off and sent out the field goal team. The kick was good to make the final score 18–15. The win was a big one for us in the standings, but it also was important to a young place-kicker trying hard to build his confidence and find his place on the team.

After the game Joe was asked about the change of heart and said that during the time-out he recalled I had been kicking them through from 50 yards in the pregame warm-up and simply decided to go for the field goal.

I wish I could say I was calm and confident as we lined up to try this field goal, but the truth is I was so nervous I could actually feel my knees shaking as I waited for the snap of the ball. It reminded me of the feeling I had for my first pressure college kick. The good thing about a field goal is that it only takes a second and a half to perform the necessary actions to get the ball into the air. This doesn't leave a lot of time for thinking and worrying once the signals are called. I remember that I didn't follow through in my normal fashion, but fortunately I hit it cleanly and it stayed true.

We were playing .500 ball after six games, and fans and players alike were giddy at the prospect of ending our long playoff drought. We figured if we could stay even for the entire year we'd have a pretty good shot at post-season play.

Our seventh game of the season took us into Edmonton to

play the four-time Grey Cup champions. The Eskimos' roster had changed some from the previous year but still read like a Who's Who of the Canadian Football League: Warren Moon, Dave Cutler, Dan Kepley, Larry Highbaugh, Hank Ilesic, Leo Blanchard, James Parker, Hec Pothier, Waddell Smith, Tom Scott and on and on it went. Going into Commonwealth Stadium and getting out with two points was like breaking into Fort Knox and sneaking out with the gold.

In front of a record crowd of 59,273 the upstarts from Saskatchewan got away with the gold and our third straight victory. The game followed a different script from our previous wins. This time it was the almost-forgotten John Hufnagel who came off the bench in the second half to play the hero's role. The final outcome was 32–25. Joe Faragalli called the win over his former team the biggest of his life.

I've already made the point that the team everybody in the league takes the most satisfaction in beating is the Eskimos. As near as I can figure there are two reasons for this. One is the extraordinary success the Eskimos have enjoyed year after year in the CFL. They are Canadian football's New York Yankees and Montreal Canadians rolled into one. They have a tremendous organization and even in their rebuilding years they are usually formidable. The second reason teams take great pride in beating the Eskimos may be connected to the first. Edmonton teams and their fans have what others have described as "an attitude." While I understand that the great success of the Eskimos and Oilers over the years has made Edmonton residents feel they are justified in being a little arrogant, it nevertheless makes everybody else want to shove it down their throats. And when we are able to do it—when little David from the Saskatchewan stubble can ring one off Goliath's swelled cranium—we enjoy the hell out of it. Unfortunately this hasn't happened nearly often enough during the course of my career.

The next highlight of my rookie season was the annual Labor Day game with the Winnipeg Blue Bombers. This was my first exposure to what is known as the Labor Day Classic, and I had no idea of the importance attached to the game by the fans, the media and the veteran players. The Saskatchewan Labor Day contest is one of three games that have become over the years annual renewals of rivalries within the league, and all three are very much a part of what makes the CFL special. The league's detractors, who are continually pointing to the NFL as a symbol of excellence, will find no rivalries more intense than the Calgary–Edmonton, Toronto–Hamilton and Saskatchewan–Winnipeg wars fought on Labor Day in Canada every year.

The game was played before a record number of 30,621 fans who had sardined their way into Taylor Field. I had played in front of large crowds before. When the University of Toledo had traveled to Tempe to be pummeled by Arizona State there were more than 78,000 people at the game. Commonwealth Stadium often drew crowds of 50,000. But there is a difference in Regina. When 30,000 people are packed into a stadium as tiny as Taylor Field it is an impressive sight. And the fans really do play a part in the game. There are always tremendous numbers of fans who travel in from opposition territory for all three Labor Day tilts. The 1982 game in Regina was no exception as a huge contingent of Manitobans helped give it a festive atmosphere second only to the Grey Cup itself.

The game lived up to its advance billing. The Bombers beat us 36–35 in a game that featured six lead changes. The Bombers' running back Willie Miller had a brilliant day with 143 yards rushing and 70 more on four pass receptions. But as was often the case in those days, it was Dieter Brock, the Win-

The Green and White

nipeg quarterback, who made the difference. After I had kicked a field goal to increase our lead to 35–30 with 8:27 remaining on the clock, the Bombers got the ball back on their own 49. Brock went to work and nickel-and-dimed us down the field for the winning touchdown, which he appropriately scored himself on a two-yard sneak after first eating up an incredible 6:05 on the clock.

I went 4 of 4 on the day including my first-ever kicks that traveled 50 yards or more, one of 50 and one of 53 yards. That made me 6 of 6 against the team that had cut me after one practice the year before. What wasn't so great was the fact that on a day when the wind was a major factor we were reticent to use a normal kickoff and twice tried squib kicks, neither of which worked. On both occasions Winnipeg wound up with excellent field position and went in for touchdowns.

In addition to losing the game we also lost defensive end Lyall Woznesensky, who went down with torn fibers in the ligaments of his knee. The Woz was a tremendous leader on our ball club and his injury was a blow to our stretch-run at the playoffs.

Following the game the *Leader-Post* broke out our stats for the year to date and compared them to the same period for the previous year. For example, the punting average for 1981 was 44.9 yards per kick; in 1982 it had soared to 48.2, which gives an indication of the year Ken Clark was having. In 1981 Paul Watson had been successful on 14 of 27 field goals to that point in the season for 52 percent. In 1982 I had been successful on 19 of 24 kicks for 79 percent. I was surprised at my success in my rookie year and was hoping I could stay somewhere close to those numbers for the balance of the season.

The next week we flew to Montreal, a city I really enjoyed visiting despite having been released the year before. In 1982 the team had been renamed the Concordes and could only be described as very bad. They were good enough, however, to beat us courtesy of a Don Sweet field goal of 51 yards with 32 seconds on the clock: Concordes 16, Riders 13.

Don Sweet, by the way, is one of the nicest guys I have ever played against. A couple of years later, during the 1984 season, I was mired in what I felt was a miserable slump. I bumped into Don before a game in Regina. We chatted for a while and when I told him I wasn't happy with my kicking he suggested we meet after the game for a chat. Don sat with me and talked about kicking for about forty-five minutes until the Montreal team bus had to leave for the airport. It meant a great deal to me because he took the time to help an opposition kicker and because what he had to say was comforting to a guy who was only in his third year in the league. All the same I wish he'd missed that damn kick in 1982.

The loss to the Concordes was devastating. We had been 4 and 4 going into the game while the Concordes were 1 and 7, having scored only 95 points in eight games. This game marked a downward turning point in our season. Afterward Joe Faragalli was quoted as saying, "We made mistakes and lost, and it's my fault, my [bleeping] fault. . . . When we had to come up big, we didn't. We didn't cover one guy on a pass and he went for a touchdown, we let a quarterback run for 50 yards on second and ten with two minutes to go. That's dumb football and it's my responsibility." That was typical of Joe. He rarely used the media to point the finger at players for mistakes made on the field. He would be all over us in practice to get us to straighten up, but he didn't cut us up in public. Instead he took the blame himself.

The media didn't need any help from Papa Joe in chewing us up. The *Leader-Post* asked, "What has sixty-eight legs, is

The Green and White

green and white and lives in the basement? If you answered the Saskatchewan Roughriders, you have the potential to be the next general manager. . . . Their fumbling, bumbling, unimaginative, couldn't-care-less performance on the weekend in Montreal . . . has been attributed to, of all things, lack of intensity. Losers always haul out that description, they have to use it; the description which follows 'lack of intensity' is *not good enough*. . . . To make the playoffs now would take almost a miracle. . . . Some think it will take six wins in their last seven games. . . ."

Bob Hughes also wrote a piece after the Montreal loss and headed it, "Roughriders Lose to Worst Team in North America." His article concluded: "[the Riders] fell flat on their collective faces and in a race as torrid as the one in the West, it will be losses such as yesterday's which could spell doomsday in the end. What's next? The B.C. Lions, that's what's next. Circle the wagons."

We went to Vancouver the next week and lost another close one, this time 36–32. Roy DeWalt completed his first 10 passes for a total of 268 yards before he threw an incompletion, and the Lions led 33–13 at half-time. Joe Adams threw two late touchdown passes to Ron Robinson, who made circus catches on both to let us get out of town with a shred or two of dignity. The problem was that dignity didn't show up in the standings and we were running out of time. Bob Hughes summarized our play that week as "auditioning for a role in *Ship of Fools* . . . . They are letting the whole province down." For the first time I began to realize that the fortunes of the Green and White really did have an impact on people all over Saskatchewan. Bob was right. A lot of them were mad as hell at us.

We faced Ottawa the following Friday at Taylor Field. The headline following the game pretty well tells the whole story: "Next Year Here Already." This was a refrain we were to hear a lot during my first seven years with the team and one we all got awfully sick of. The score was 30–19 and marked our fourth loss in a row.

Bob Hughes wrote: "They [the western Riders] don't get beat, they surrender. They think the national anthem means the game is over. They've folded so many times this month, somebody should stick a stamp on their foreheads and mail them someplace. They've reached the point where right after the opening kickoff, time becomes a factor. . . . They should have paid to get into Taylor Field last night. . . . If they showed up in full uniform and padded to the hilt, helmets neatly in place, as guests on *What's My Line,* they'd stump the panel."

Our next outing was at home to Calgary. Prior to the game John Chaput wrote an article in the *Leader-Post* in which he quoted Joe Faragalli on a range of issues. "Was I too easy on them last year? How come I did the same things last year and won and now the same approach is questioned? . . . They said I was Coach of the Year last season and I said, 'Baloney, the players win the games.' Now that we're losing do I go home and look at my trophy and say, 'Hey, I'm Coach of the Year, it's not my fault, it's the players'? You could live to be a hundred and fifty and you won't see me doing that."

The NFL was on strike at the time and NBC was coming to Regina to televise the game. John Brodie, the one-time 49ers' quarterback, Bob Trumpy and Don Criqui would be telling the rest of North America about the Canadian game as it was played in the prairie hinterland. We came out of our losing streak with a vengeance, beating Calgary 53–8 in front of over twenty-eight thousand faithful fans. Dwight Edwards caught a Joe Adams' pass and scampered 84 yards for a touchdown just after the two-minute mark of the opening quarter and the slaughter was on. The 56 points were the second highest total in Rider history, surpassed only by a 56–8 rout of the Edmonton Eskimos back in 1964. Man, would I have loved to play in that one!

I had a career day that afternoon against the Stampeders, hitting on five converts and six field goals from 47, 42, 32, 33, 31 and 47 yards. The last field goal came with less than two minutes left in the game, and before I went out to kick it, Joe Faragalli turned to me and laughed. "If I send you out there now, Jocko will never speak to me again. On second thought, go kick it." The 23 points moved me to the top of the Western Division scoring race and even had the *Leader-Post* touting me as a candidate for the Riders' Rookie of the Year. It was a great day.

In those days in the CFL, Rothman's Tobacco Company gave out weekly awards, one each for the top offensive and defensive players and the other for the top lineman of the week. The award included a cheque for five hundred dollars, an Inuit carving and a Rothman's carry bag. After the Calgary game I was named the Rothman's Offensive Star and was the first kicker to win the award that year. We swept the awards that week as Billy McBride won the defensive honor and Bryan Illerbrun got the lineman award. We had a tradition on the team that when anybody won the award he'd have chicken and pizza delivered to the locker room one day after practice the following week as a treat for the rest of the guys. It was a nice tradition and a good way for award winners to salute the people who had made it possible.

The following week we were headed for Hamilton, and I was pretty excited as it marked a homecoming of sorts for me. My father was still working in the area, which made the trip just that much better. I was also excited about seeing old high school pals Dennis Montford and George Evans, who had been very supportive of my dream of one day playing professional football and who would undoubtedly be at the game.

It was played on a Monday afternoon and ended in a 24–24 tie, this being before the advent of overtime in the CFL. It was a wild game as both teams had chances in the final minute. We blew ours when we lost five yards on a running play from the Hamilton 43 on second down. This left us with the prospect of a 54-yard field goal into a breeze. My attempt was right down the middle but fell four yards short. It was one of those kicks I could stand and watch because the ball had to travel so far. I felt sick when it missed.

Tom Clements then marched the Ti-Cats down the field to our 38 with two seconds to go. Bernie Ruoff had been having an awful day with three missed field goals, a fourth attempt blocked and a fumbled snap on a punt. Hamilton Coach Bud Riley decided to punt for the single.

I was sent into the end zone with punter Ken Clark and Stew Fraser. Ruoff's punt went to Stew (thank God!) and he shanked it out of the end zone and out-of-bounds at the five-yard line with no time left on the clock. I think of this game when I hear Canadian fans saying we should eliminate the single point in Canadian football. I hope they are aware we would lose one of the most exciting and uniquely Canadian plays in football—the last-second kick for the single point followed by the scramble to kick the ball out where it may be kicked back in and so on.

Bob Hughes wrote another of his highly entertaining articles the following week. This one had to do with Joe Faragalli's ritual of going to each player during the pregame warm-up with a handshake and a few quiet, encouraging words. Hughes speculated, tongue in cheek, about what was said during those little chats: "To Joe Adams—'Your sweater is green today so don't throw the ball to anybody who isn't in a green sweater like yours' . . . To Stew Fraser—'You've got good hands, Stew, now give me my watch back' . . . To John Hufnagel—'Have we met?' . . . To Ken Clark—'If I catch you watching the cheerleaders one more time' . . . To Ken McEachern—'You make more money than I do' . . . To Dave Ridgway—'Do you know who Jack Hill is?'" The reference to Jack Hill was significant because after the Hamilton game I had collected 141 points on the year and was only four back of Jack's all-time Roughriders' season scoring record established back in 1958.

The Montreal Concordes were our next opposition. Going into the Taylor Field contest we had recorded five wins, seven losses and a tie. With only three games left we were five points out of the final playoff spot and would need divine intervention to qualify for post-season play.

I managed to collect 13 points during our 25-20 win in Montreal to surpass the previous Riders' single-season scoring record. But mine wasn't the only record set in the game. Joe Adams completed 29 passes to tie Ron Lancaster's 1977 record for most completions by a Rider quarterback in a single game. John Hufnagel also completed two passes, giving our quarterbacks a total of 31 completions in 50 attempts, both single-game team records at the time.

Stew Fraser returned a punt 78 yards for a touchdown, and while this wasn't a record it was one of the highlights of the game for me. By this time Stew and I had become close friends, and I was thrilled to cheer for him as he danced down the sidelines all the way to the end zone.

Another highlight was provided by team management. They had arranged to bring in Jack Hill from his Utah home in the event I broke the record. I didn't know anything about the plan going into the game, and it was very special to be given the ball by Jack after I broke the record. I was disappointed that it was set on a single point off a missed field goal. Actually I didn't have one of my better days that afternoon—I went 3 of 5 in field goals—but it was my first professional record and I was glad to have set it. Later I learned that I had set another record that day. I became the highest scoring rookie in CFL history, passing Dave Cutler of the Eskimos by a single point.

After a 41–36 loss to Toronto we met the Edmonton Eskimos at Taylor Field in our final game of the 1982 season. We were hammered 46–22 in a contest that saw Warren Moon become the first player in either the CFL or NFL to pass for over 5,000 yards in a single season. The win, their eighth in a row, also gave the Eskimos first place.

Joey Walters caught 10 passes for us that day, and his season total of 101 catches was a CFL record. This was about the only bright moment for us. Dave Cutler had a big day and passed me to win the scoring race for the year.

My first season in the Canadian Football League had required a major transition from college ball. I'd had difficulty adjusting to the number of games and amount of travel. In team sports, generally speaking, athletes are required to play half their games on the road (the exception being the 1994 Las Vegas Posse) and this means travel. A simple thing like flying to games marked a significant change from my college years when most of our road trips were made on buses. This change I would not by the way categorize as an improvement. My fear of flying is real and in fact has grown worse through my years in the CFL. This is no doubt due in part to Glen Suitor, who sat next to me throughout most of my career and who never failed during takeoff to remind me that *it* is the most critical moment in any

The Green and White

flight. Then on landing he would turn to me and say that he was mistaken earlier and that *this* is the most dangerous point.

Kidding aside, travel is, in my opinion, one of the real drawbacks to playing professional sports. Regina's winds, which have made for some interesting departures and arrivals, only exacerbate the problem. I am not alone in my distaste for traveling on machines that leave the ground. Bob Poley and Roger Aldag were also noted for their discomfort in the air. I suppose there is always in a recess of my mind a reminder that one of the most tragic moments in CFL history involved four members of the 1956 Saskatchewan Roughriders who were among those killed in a plane crash while returning from the All-Star game in Vancouver. As the league continues to expand farther and farther south, the time we have to spend in the air continues to grow.

There is, I'm sure, a feeling among sports fans that travel must be exciting. To be honest I would describe that part of being an athlete as a chore. After a couple of seasons in the league, the glamour of going on the road is replaced by boredom. Most of the time now, after thirteen seasons, my preference is to get comfortable in the room, order room service and dial up a movie on the TV. I think the majority of veteran players probably feel the same in wanting to get there, play the game and get home to a familiar bed and home-cooked meals.

Those aren't complaints; they are simply the realities of playing pro sports. Of course, back in my first year, every part of the game with the exception of flying was exciting. The dream I'd harbored of playing professional football—a dream that had been such an important part of my life in high school and college—was coming true.

CHAPTER 5

1 - 800 - Phantom

Henry, don't take this game too seriously because one day it's gonna be over. —ROOKIE OF THE YEAR, 1993

THE LIFE OF A ROOKIE at a professional football training camp revolves around the never-ending pursuit of two goals. The first is the obvious one familiar to every fan: to earn a spot on the roster. The second, not as well known but almost equally important, is to avoid incurring the wrath of the Phantom.

The identity of the Phantom is unknown to rookies except that he is a veteran or group of veterans who dispense justice, often in sinister fashion and under cover of darkness, to offending rookies. Rookies need to be very visible on the field in order to impress evaluating coaches, but off the field they are expected to act like the well-behaved children of a bygone era. Rookies who come to camp with a cocky attitude do so at their peril.

Most veteran players share the belief that rookies are placed on the planet primarily for veterans' entertainment. At mealtimes the tinkling of spoons, wedding-reception style, signals that rookies must perform, usually by telling a joke or singing their school fight song or a popular TV theme. The audience is demanding and critical, and the performer whose effort fails to measure up to an unwritten standard may bring down upon himself, his room or his locker a visit from the Phantom. This is a foretaste of the annual event known as the Rookie Show, an evening when all the newcomers are called upon to perform songs and skits for a discriminating audience of veterans.

Occasionally rookies go to considerable lengths to keep their dignity intact. Some adopt the strategy I used in Montreal in 1981 and again in Saskatchewan in 1982: get to the dining room as quickly as possible, shovel down the meal and get the hell out before the veterans filter in. This ploy may spare the rookie the dubious honor of being one of the day's performers (as it did me through two complete training camps) and is apparently acceptable, probably because rookies aren't in short supply. But there is no way short of outright refusal to avoid the Rookie Show. Rookies who rebel have committed a grievous error. They have just invited the Phantom to pay a visit.

One such rebel was Rennick Tuck, a rookie defensive back attending our 1985 camp. In addition to displaying an attitude that was universally thought to be lousy, he committed the cardinal sin of refusing to participate in the Rookie Show.

One of our veteran defensive linemen at that time was Al Johns, whose girlfriend worked in a Regina restaurant called Bartleby's. One of the establishment's specialties was the medieval smorg, complete with a pig's head, apple in mouth, adorning the buffet table. Even festively appointed pigs' heads eventually exhaust their usefulness so Al arranged to have his girlfriend bring along one of the outdated heads on her next visit to our Saskatoon training camp.

By the time she arrived the pig's head had been in a plastic bag in the trunk of her car for a few days. Its condition had not improved, not even a bit. The smell coming from the trunk of the car was unbelievable. Not one of the players on the team—and these are men who put their bodies on the line on the playing field—could summon the courage to open the bag.

The following morning, just after Tuck had left for practice, the Phantom somehow got hold of a passkey and entered Tuck's room, which was located on the third floor of Qu'Appelle Hall. The Phantom removed the pig's head from the plastic bag and slipped it under the covers of the rookie's bed.

When we returned to the dorm after the morning practice, the smell from the third floor had permeated the entire building. The veterans took up positions on the first and second floors and waited for word from a posted sentry that the rookie was en route. When word was received the two lower floors instantly became library quiet as grinning veterans waited to hear the reaction from the room above. The silence was hardly necessary. For at least five minutes a stream—no, make that a torrent—of vividly blue vocabulary gushed out and down from the rookie's room.

At this point the story takes an unfortunate turn. Rennick Tuck lost it, and in his rage he made a serious error in judgment that compounded his problem. He rushed down the stairs into the room of Joe Paopao, one of the best-liked and most respected veterans on the team. I happened to be in Joe's room when Rennick Tuck burst in and began itemizing what he would do if Joe had been responsible for the Phantom's raid. I can't quote his comments verbatim, but he threatened to use his martial arts skills to kick Joe's ass.

Joe, in typical Paopao fashion, said very quietly, "Son, the worst thing you can do right now is to go around threatening veterans."

I have no idea if Rennick Tuck had much talent as a

ballplayer; in the early years of my career I was too preoccupied with ensuring my own position on the team to worry about anybody else's, but I can say this: he did not make the team. I don't know if the Phantom's visit or the kid's reaction to it played any part though frankly I doubt it. I've often thought about him and what he remembers of the incident, and I hope he now understands why it was done.

It is important to realize there is a serious side to the Phantom's sense of humor. It has to do with a word badly overworked by the sports media, but it is an important part of building a winning football team. The word is *chemistry*. It is a fact of football life that teams, on the one hand, are made up of players who have worn a particular uniform for a period of time, sometimes a long time, and, on the other, of guys who have never played a down for the team. Melding the two together into a cohesive unit is a challenge facing coaches and players alike.

The rookie who swallows his pride and submits his ego to a tabletop rendition of his school fight song and performs in the Rookie Show will almost invariably win acceptance and respect from his veteran teammates. And this is the point.

True professionals never make hazing an excuse for hurting people. I have read accounts of hazings of rookies in high school, collegiate and university sports that get completely out of hand. In professional sports hazing is used as a device to build camaraderie and should be fun for everybody involved, including the rookies. The Phantom only strikes after action has been deemed a necessary last resort by the majority of veterans and only after the rookies have been forewarned. Players like Gary Lewis or Don Narcisse would preface Phantom activity with a warning: "If you refuse to perform for the veterans somebody's gonna dial 1-800-Phantom." And sure enough, if the rookie in question failed to heed the warning. . . . At some training camps, the most recent in 1995, the needed chemistry was already in evidence and the Phantom didn't need to pay a single visit.

My first venture into the world of the Phantom was in 1986, my fifth training camp with the Riders. I became involved because the target was a kicker, and it is generally Phantom policy that veterans handle situations involving rookies at the same position. Offensive linemen handle rookie O-line candidates, defensive backs take care of incoming DBs and kickers Phantomize kickers. Outside help is permitted and even welcomed.

The rookie in question was a kid named Tony Brown. He was from Vancouver and had played his college ball at San Jose State. Several veterans approached me to say, "He's your rookie and he's a problem; you gotta do it." Tony had clearly managed to alienate a lot of veterans very quickly, which if you are a kicker is both difficult and stupid. Kickers don't get beat up in the same way as most of the other ballplayers. This being the case it's best to be as inconspicuous as possible during camp in order not to irritate the guys who are taking the pounding.

I was what could be called a virgin phantom so the first thing I did was seek a little instruction. It turned out offensive lineman Neil Quilter was preparing to mete out a little Phantom justice of his own. We decided to pool our creative resources. Neil's creative resources were contained in a body that stood 6' 3" and weighed 270 pounds. Though his nickname was Tubby he was, in a word, solid, a description that also fits his character.

One of the academic features of the University of Saskatchewan is that it offers degrees in agriculture. Situated conveniently between our dorm and the football practice facility is a working farm with all the buildings, corrals and animals one finds on a Canadian mixed farm. Tubby and I decided to make use of some of the by-product of the livestock operation.

We arranged to pay a twilight visit to the corrals that housed some of the university's cow herd. Neil had made plans to head off after the raid to one of Saskatoon's nightspots with some of the other offensive linemen (a country bar, naturally) and he was dressed for a night out. He was wearing cream-colored dress pants, a natty dress shirt and white running shoes. We took up our positions in a field containing a bumper crop of cow patties. The very dapper Neil decided that not just any old cow pies would do and began surveying the area for perfect specimens. He accomplished this by taking a stick and delicately turning over various droppings in order to find those with just the right consistency.

We loaded the preferred samples into plastic ice bags we had borrowed from Ivan Gutfriend's training room and made our way to the equipment room. Norm Fong was there as he often is during training camp when he puts in long hours keeping up with the endless work. As we entered the room Norm knew immediately that skullduggery was in progress and uttered the words I have often heard from him over the years. In perfect Sergeant Schultz staccato (of *Hogan's Heroes*) he said, "I see *nussink* . . . *NUSSINK.*" What Norm pretended not to witness was Neil and I tampering with the two rookies' lockers and placing the cow dung in the places where we felt it would do the most good.

I began by filling Tony Brown's white kicking shoes with the unpleasant ooze. Then I smeared the inside of his wristbands. And finally—the *coup de grace*—the helmet. But I didn't just fill the helmet; this would have been too obvious. Instead I carefully worked the stuff in behind the padding on the inside of the helmet. What was left I hung inside the kid's locker in the fashion of a hangman's noose with a note attached that said, "You've got a horseshit attitude for a rookie." (Although the offending substance was of bovine origin, as a city kid I didn't think the exact source was the issue.)

The next morning the shit literally hit the fan. When the rookies came into the locker room a number of veterans, including me, were on hand to see the results. The first thing Tony encountered was the bag hanging directly in front of him. He merely sneered at it, probably thinking if this was the best the Phantom could do it was no big deal. He disposed of the bag and note and went on getting dressed for practice.

He became noticeably more unhappy when he got to the wrist bands (not exactly required equipment for a kicker) and discovered they had been . . . uh . . . soiled. They followed the bag and note into the garbage. Next he reached under the bench for his kicking shoes and at this point became genuinely irate. I was sitting three lockers down from him and for reasons I'll never understand Tony turned and glared at me. I looked back at him, shrugged and said, "Hey, don't look at me, I didn't have anything to do with it." (Hell, nobody said the Phantom can't lie.)

Then Tony Brown made a huge mistake not unlike Rennick Tuck's. He took the shoes to the equipment office, set them in front of Norm Fong and yelled, "Clean these." He then grabbed another pair of shoes, picked up his helmet and headed out to the practice field. As soon as he left, Norm looked at us, laughed and tossed the shoes into the garbage. Out on the field, as was customary, we gathered for calisthenics on what happened to be a hot Saskatchewan morning.

Soon Tony Brown was working up a sweat. Some of my night deposit trickled down his forehead. He removed his helmet, looked inside and without a word stomped off the field and didn't return for the remainder of the practice.

To his credit, Tony, who had a very good leg, said no more about the incident. He did by the way spend a lot of time practicing on his own from this point on, taking time out to occasionally remind us he was good enough to be playing in the NFL. Tony Brown didn't stick around very long that year.

One of the busiest years in the Phantom's career with the Roughriders came in 1988. This training camp brought the worst bunch of rookies in terms of attitude that had ever come together at one time during my years with the Riders. Because the cow patty caper had worked so well in 1986, we decided to resurrect it, albeit on a grander scale. So after fortifying ourselves in Louis's, the campus pub at the University of Saskatchewan, it was off once again to the farm. This time the Phantom's persona consisted of Tom Burgess, Jeff Fairholm, Ray Elgaard and me.

Luck smiled on us in spades (make that spadefuls). The University farm crew had just that day cleaned the cow barns, leaving us an ample supply of attitude modifier. Unfortunately we had made one oversight in the planning end of the operation. While we had remembered to bring bags for transporting the product, no one had thought to bring along anything with which to get the stuff into the bags. At this point Elgaard announced he was prepared to make the ultimate sacrifice for the good of the team and offered his ball cap, which was then pressed into service as a scoop.

The hat was brand new and bore the California Angels' logo. The rest of us were surprised to see Ray using the inside of the peak to ladle fresh cow pies into bags. After a very short time the hat was ruined. Phantom or no Phantom, this seemed a mighty high price to pay to discipline some rookies, and one of us finally said, "Boy, how can you do that to such a great hat?"

Elgaard threw the hat on the ground and replied, "No problem, it's Illie's."

This cast a whole new light on the situation. Bryan Illerbrun, Elgaard's roommate, was not known as one of the really congenial guys on the team. Still it was hardly proper to return the guy's hat to him in that condition, so the four of us formed a circle around the hat and . . . well . . . sort of rinsed it off. (Illie, if you read this, believe me, I faked it—actually I aimed wide right.)

Then it was back to the locker room where we deposited our cargo in the selected helmets, this time filling them to overflowing. The next morning the room was ripe with a foul smell and foul language.

But the change in attitude was total and immediate. The same rookies who had earlier replied that they wouldn't do shit if they didn't want to were now leaping to their feet and begging for permission to sing if a veteran even dropped a spoon.

While visits from the Phantom are largely reserved for rookies—wayward rookies at that—practical jokes take just as great a toll on veterans. One of the classic practical jokes was perpetrated on punter Mike Lazecki and the culprits, I modestly admit, were Glen Suitor, a legendary prankster, and me. Lazecki was himself one of the most fun-loving and goofiest guys it's been my pleasure to have as a teammate. His highly creative spliced inserts to special team game films probably didn't improve our on-field performance, but they certainly lightened up some of the film sessions in ways the Saskatchewan Censor Board would not have approved.

One day after practice, Suitor and I noticed Lazecki giving a tour of the stadium to a group of family friends. Never ones to overlook an opportunity we headed straight for the parking lot to find Mike's vehicle. At one time it had been a Chevy Blazer, but now it was so covered in rust that it was almost unrecognizable. The removable roof was absent winter and summer, and there was a similar problem with floorboards—there weren't any.

As Lazecki was orchestrating his tour of Taylor Field, Suitor and I raced to the equipment room and borrowed a pair of pliers from Norm Fong who as always knew *nussink*. Then we hustled out to the Blazer, lifted the hood, removed the battery and hid it in the equipment room. While this was going on, the CBC, in preparation for filming the game the following day, was just wrapping up a news conference in the President's Lounge.

Suitor and I stumbled into the news conference giggling like a couple of school kids and alerted everyone to what was going on. Because the President's Lounge overlooks the parking lot there was now a pretty good audience for Lazecki's arrival at the Blazer. And sure enough, a few minutes later we watched him stride across the parking lot with a boy of about ten or eleven years old in tow. They got into the Blazer; Mike turned the key in the ignition and got nothing.

Mike, ever resourceful, jumped out of the Blazer and flagged down a motorist in hope of getting a boost. The driver pulled his car into position in front of the Blazer. Mike lifted his hood and without so much as a glance underneath, went around to the driver's side of his vehicle and got back inside. The other driver, in the meantime, had lifted his hood and attached the booster cables to his battery.

By this time Suitor and I had made our way out to the parking lot and were out of sight around the corner. We could hear Lazecki calling instructions to the helpful motorist to hook up the cables to the Blazer's battery. And the guy tried; he really did. We saw him finally look around the hood and inform Mike there was no battery. Lazecki got out of the Blazer, went around to the front and looked under the hood. Not seeing the battery he got down on his knees to look underneath. I don't know why he did this—maybe the thing had a history of sinking batteries—but I do know that Suitor and I were in serious danger of having to send our trousers to the laundry as we watched the goings on.

Eventually it occurred to Mike that the battery wasn't there and that he may be the victim of a prank. Suitor and I hustled back into the equipment room and were there when he came in to ask Norm where his battery was. Norm denied all knowledge of such a cruel thing so Lazecki turned to us. Somehow Suitor and I were able to pull ourselves together, and we replied with poker-straight faces that we also knew nothing about it. Then we headed off to the President's Lounge where the TV crew had been enjoying the whole escapade.

Finally we took pity on Lazecki—actually on the kid who had been with him for the tour and was waiting for a ride home from his football hero. We told Mike where the battery was, and after we all shared a great laugh he went off to reinstall it. What he didn't know was that we still had the necessary tools. Lazecki jockeyed the battery into place and headed back to the equipment room to gather up his young friend for the long-awaited ride home. As soon as Mike entered the clubhouse Suitor and I sprinted out another door, headed back to the Blazer, got the battery out a second time and managed to return to our previous hiding place before driver and passenger reemerged from the equipment room.

Like a television replay Mike and the boy got into the car,

the key went into the ignition and again nothing happened. At this point Lazecki put his forehead against the steering wheel in that classic gesture of futility. Later we were to find out that as they were walking across the parking lot for the second time, the kid had said to Mike, "You don't think they would have taken it again, do you? Maybe one of us should have stayed with the car." (Which says something about the wisdom of eleven-year-olds as compared to that of punters.) Mike raised his head from the steering wheel, climbed back out and raised the hood one more time. He stood there with his hands on his hips and laughed for a long time. Then, in a voice that could be heard over most of the parking lot, he yelled, "Okay, you bastards, where is it this time?"

Practical jokes are very much a way of life on a football team. They are a means of dealing with the pressures of being a professional athlete. These pressures are real. Very few players can be certain from one season to the next that their jobs are safe. Or for that matter from one game to the next. Every year management acquires through recruiting and trades players whose goal in life is to take veterans' jobs. The better management does its job the more intense the competition for positions. Then there are injuries to think about, some of them the career-threatening variety, and if that isn't enough there is the pressure associated with the team's success or failure. I know of very few players who simply collect a pay cheque and give no thought to the on-field fortunes of their team. And in the CFL, unfortunately, there are those teams that have more than on-field success to consider. There is all too often the very real concern about the team's survival, and to think that doesn't weigh on players' minds is to deny reality.

So, yes, practical jokes are important. It's not overstating the case to say they play an important part in players being able to survive mentally while playing the game. Which may be why it's a rare day when somebody doesn't "get" somebody else. Defensive tackle Gary Lewis, for example, added a new twist to the old pie-in-the face prank by enlisting the aid of a local TV station. The unsuspecting victim was being interviewed (or so he thought) in the locker room in full view of his teammates. At a critical moment in the interview, the cream pie was administered. The prank became an annual event and Big Lew's trademark.

Birthdays and other special occasions receive special treatment on football teams, at least on the Riders. Often the celebrant will be found fastened in some manner to the goalposts. There are variations on this theme as befits the occasion. During the mideighties rookie fullback David Conrad was tied naked to a lamppost in the middle of the University of Saskat-chewan campus while Ray Elgaard sat and tossed pebbles at him.

On the Friday of the 1989 Grey Cup week Glen Suitor celebrated his twenty-seventh birthday. The team acknowledged the auspicious event by taping him from head to toe to one of the goalposts just beneath Windows, the SkyDome patio restaurant. Glen's teammates then gathered around to sing "Happy Birthday," and in a moment of uncharacteristic Toronto spontaneity the patrons leaned over the railing and sang a second chorus. Big Dan Payne then capped off the event by dumping one of our Gatorade containers over the birthday boy. The photograph of the event went across Canada on the CP Wire Service. I'm pretty sure Glen was deeply moved by the whole tribute.

Prank playing will be extended outside the ranks of the teams' players if the situation warrants, as it did when one of Coach Ray Jauch's sons, Joey, came to visit training camp. While Ray's other son, Jimmy, is quiet, laid-back and extremely nice, Joey, the second of the Jauch-o-motion boys, is the complete opposite—right out of the Mike Lazecki school of raising hell. Joey took delight in getting under everybody's skin. Finally, nerves raw, the team had endured enough of Joey's shenanigans and decided to tape him to the goalposts.

This was a goalpost caper with a difference. Instead of taping Joey to the vertical goalpost they secured him to the crossbar. It was suggested it might be a good idea for me to kick a few field goals. Never one to miss an opportunity to practice my craft, I headed out to about the 45-yard line and rained footballs over, under and around the crossbar.

An important and somewhat disturbing point is that I have not personally escaped the pranks of the Phantom. Among those who seem to take special pleasure in making me the victim are Norm Fong and locker room assistant Lorne "Shorty" Mitchell. One of the classic capers was a Norm Fong production with a supporting cast that included General Manager Alan Ford. We had just acquired defensive lineman Stew Hill from B.C. Stew had worn sweater number 36 throughout his career and let it be known when he joined our team that he would like to continue the tradition. I have also worn number 36 throughout my career, and naturally when I was asked what I thought of the idea, I replied, "No damn way."

Enter Norm Fong. After first making sure the issue was kept front and center around the locker room for some time, Normie sewed Stew's name on sweater number 36 and mine on number 39 and hung the two jerseys in our respective lockers. When I saw my new sweater I went ballistic. I charged into Alan Ford's office and told him I didn't know who would be doing the place-kicking that day but it wouldn't be me. If Alan hadn't started laughing I might still be in his office yelling. I didn't think the prank was all that funny then, but now a couple of years later I can see the humor even though it runs counter to my philosophy about practical jokes: it's better to give than to receive.

Which is why I didn't think it was particularly humorous when our trainer, Ivan Gutfriend, and Shorty teamed up to get me. This one occurred about three weeks before training camp in 1993. I had twisted my ankle while running as part of my get-in-shape program leading up to camp. The next day I went down to Taylor Field to get some treatment. It turned out Ivan was on his way to a trainers' symposium and would be leaving shortly. I went into his office and said, "Ivan, you have to take a look at this."

Ivan, who has been known to be testy on occasion, growled, "Damn it, Ridge, I can't. I have to leave right away. Just throw some ice on it and I'll look at it when I get back." These instructions didn't exactly thrill me. The ankle was swollen to twice its normal size and was an ugly rainbow of purples, yellows and blues.

I did as I was told and put some ice on the ankle while I watched Ivan bustle in and out of the training room getting ready to leave on his business trip. After about five minutes he suddenly rushed back in, and with one eye on me said to Shorty, "Okay, I've just got time for one more game of crib before I have to leave for the airport."

While many pranks are perpetrated in the familiar surroundings of Taylor Field, road trips are by no means safe havens for potential victims. In 1994 rookie Dallas Rysavy, a fine athlete from Moose Jaw, made our football club. Our fourth game of the season was in Sacramento, and we had traveled to California the day before as is standard practice in the Canadian Football League. Glen Suitor and I started our day with a visit to the Arden Park Mall, located not far from our hotel. Glen had won about eight hundred dollars at the blackjack tables in Las Vegas when we played the Posse a couple of weeks earlier. He decided to spend some of it on gifts for his family back home. Suitor, by the way, is not a good shopper. We've all seen and heard whining kids being dragged along on a shopping junket by their mothers. Glen is one of those kids, complete with the pitiful wails of "I'm tired, I wanna go home, my feet hurt," and all the other standard complaints of a five-year-old.

On this occasion, however, Glen was a shopping fool, and he kept at it until the mall closed its doors at nine o'clock that evening. We had worked up an appetite and chose to eat Italian at an Olive Garden restaurant, one of our favorite spots.

After dining we collected our bill from the waitress and asked if she'd call a cab to get us back to the Sacramento Hilton. The waitress said, "What a coincidence. I had two other gentlemen in here earlier, and they're also staying at the Hilton." She went on to say that one of the earlier diners was "just so gorgeous" and had thoughtfully given her his room number at the hotel.

Suitor and I figured this magnificent male specimen might just might be another player. The waitress confirmed this when she said the guy's name was Dallas and he'd left his address and phone number in somewhere called Moose . . . uh . . . Moose Jaw, Sask . . , aaatch . . . ooo . . . wan. This started our wheels turning. Glen and I asked the waitress if she could get us a piece of Olive Garden letterhead, and, bless her heart, she was only too happy to help out.

We wrote a note to our love-struck teammate that read: "Dallas, it was nice meeting you this evening. I would like to get to know you better, but I don't want to come up to your room because I don't want you to think I'm a football groupie.

I am waiting downstairs in a blue Chevy and hope you might like to go for a ride. –Gina."

When we got back to the hotel we recruited the assistance of a bellboy and had the note delivered to Dallas's room. Suits and I went out to the hotel parking lot so we could observe the glass elevator on the side of the building as it came down with our quarry. By this time it was 11 P.M., the time of our unwritten but nevertheless widely observed curfew.

It wasn't long before the freshly scrubbed rookie entered the elevator and began his descent to his date with destiny. Suitor and I headed for the entrance to the hotel, timing our arrival for the moment Dallas would appear at the door. We met the departing lothario on the steps. We asked him where he was going, and after first claiming he was just stepping out for a breath of fresh air, he sheepishly produced the note and let us read it, which was not easy to do with a straight face. We, of course, were all over Dallas with suitable references to his masculine qualities and Saskatchewan charm. We kept it up for quite a while, during which we couldn't help but notice he was spending a lot of time looking past us, trying no doubt to spot the blue Chevy. Being responsible teammates we reminded him of curfew and of how it wasn't a good idea to let rookie hormones interfere with his duty to the team.

Finally, as Suitor and I headed for the hotel door, Glen turned and said, "By the way, Dallas, about that note—she isn't going to show up. Ridge wrote it." We laughed our way into the lobby where we ran into a couple of players and Greg Marshall, one of our coaches. As we were telling them the story, Ray Jauch, our head coach, came along and we informed him of the prank. He too enjoyed it. Later Dallas tried to deny there was anything amorous in his intentions, to which Suitor and I replied in unison, "Bullshit!"

1 – 800 – Phantom

The following week lightning struck the young man from Moose Jaw a second time. Normally, on charter flights the prevailing dress code rules are relaxed, but on commercial flights Coach Jauch wants players to dress professionally. On this occasion we were flying commercial into Edmonton. The coach reminded us of this fact. I was among the first players to arrive at the airport that morning. Not long after, Dallas trooped in wearing sneakers, shorts and a tennis shirt. I pointed out this flagrant breach of team policy to several players who made a point of conveying to Dallas the seriousness of the offense. We speculated on the size of the fine that would no doubt be levied.

Rookies live in constant fear of missing a flight or being late for a team meeting or practice or doing something that will get them on the wrong side of management. Now here was the kid's third official road trip as a member of the Saskatchewan Roughriders and he had made a major blunder. When Suitor arrived he joined the chorus without missing a beat. Dallas is a free safety, as was Glen, which meant he was "Suitor's rookie." Glen made it clear to Dallas that this breach was not only an embarrassment to himself personally but brought shame on the whole free safety fraternity.

Once we were in the air we enlisted the help of one of the flight attendants. It wasn't long before she presented a copy of a bogus Air Canada fax to Alan Ford, general manager of the Roughriders, stating that one Dallas Rysavy had failed to adhere to the team dress code and may not be permitted to board future team flights. Later Glen and I wrote a note and another flight attendant read it over the aircraft's public address system. The announcement instructed Dallas to proceed to the back of the aircraft where he would be presented with a map detailing the locations of all Zellers' stores in Edmonton.

Dallas handled it pretty well, but it's interesting that since that fateful two-week period in 1994, he has been appropriately dressed for all team flights and not once has he violated curfew for an evening with a waitress driving a blue Chevy. And who knows . . . in a few years when he's a grizzled veteran and has a rookie of his own to hassle, he'll think altogether differently about the hazing of fuzzy-cheeked rookies. Hell, he might even turn out to be a pretty good Phantom.

CHAPTER 6

The Long, Lean Years

Rock, someday when the team is up against it, and the breaks are beating the boys, ask 'em to go in there with all they've got... —KNUTE ROCKNE: ALL-AMERICAN, 1940

THERE'S A SAYING ON THE PRAIRIES: *This is next year country.* During the mideighties the Saskatchewan Roughriders were a next-year team. The annual air of optimism was in evidence as my sophomore season approached in 1983. Although 1982 had been a disappointment as we slumped from a near-playoff record of 9 and 7 in 1981 to a dismal 6–9–1, there were solid reasons for confidence as the new season approached. Joe Adams, Fran McDermott and Mike Washington were coming off excellent rookie campaigns, and we had placed six players on the Western All-Star team and five on the All-Canadian team, the most since the Riders' 1976 Grey Cup appearance.

The front office was particularly excited about the new season. In 1982 we'd recorded five sellouts, set a single-game attendance record and established an astonishing attendance average of 102 percent of capacity. However, despite the optimistic feeling surrounding the team, the seeds for the further decline of Rider fortunes had actually been sown the year before. Halfway through the previous season General Manager Jim Spavital had jumped to the USFL. What followed was a long period of turbulence and turmoil in team management.

After Spavital's departure team president Dick Rendek took over as general manager. He simply didn't have a sufficient football background to fill the post. By December Rendek had hired John Herrera, late of the Oakland/Los Angeles Raiders where he was reputed to be one of Raiders' owner Al Davis's whiz kids.

We got off to a decent start with a 2 and 2 preseason record, but it quickly became clear that the 1983 Riders hadn't turned any corners insofar as the team's on-field success was concerned. After beating the Montreal Concordes to start the regular season, we were dissected in our home-opener 50–19 by the Hamilton Tiger-Cats.

Our third game of the young season marked our first appearance under the dome at Vancouver's B.C. Place. Nice place—bad game. The Lions rolled over us 44–28. B.C. Coach Don Matthews elected to start the game with an onside kick. Lui Passaglia's chip shot came down in the arms of Lions' receiver Mervyn Fernandez and the Lions never looked back.

Our fourth game of the season was another ugly affair before a Taylor Field crowd of almost twenty-six thousand. The Toronto Argonauts laid a pretty good licking on us, 40–21, and almost before the lights were turned out at Taylor Field that night, the murmurs had begun—murmurs about changes. That there would be changes was not in doubt. The only questions were when and how the shakeup would happen.

It was clear that John Herrera was eager to put his stamp on the ball club, and it was just as clear that Joe Faragalli wasn't going to be part of it. Herrera had for some time made a habit of coming onto the field during practice and, from a position just behind the offense, watching every move Joe made. It had to be unnerving to coach under this kind of scrutiny, but if it bothered Joe he never let on, at least not to the players.

Our next game took us to Edmonton, which in my experience has never been any picnic even for a good ball club, which we obviously were not. The Eskimos put it to us 36–21 in a game that saw the two teams combine for over one thousand yards of offense. During the game Eskimo kicker Dave Cutler established an all-time professional football scoring record by bringing his total to 2,003 points, eclipsing the former mark held by George Blanda of the Oakland Raiders.

We pounded the final nail in the Faragalli coffin the following week by dropping our fifth game in a row, this one at home, again in front of over twenty-five thousand Taylor Field fans. The loss was doubly damning as we blew a 20–3 second-quarter lead in succumbing 36–28 to the Calgary Stampeders.

What followed came as no surprise. Our terrible start had given John Herrera more than enough ammunition to implement his agenda, one that had as its first item the firing of Joe Faragalli. The year had to be bitterly disappointing for Joe. Only two years before, the Riders had been a team whose star was rising and Joe had won Coach of the Year honors. Now here we were, only two seasons later, a floundering team. Nevertheless, while most players and fans expected Joe to be let go, when it finally happened many of us deplored its graceless handling.

Herrera demanded that Joe fire defensive coordinator Mike Murphy. Joe refused, which was the excuse Herrera needed to axe Joe *and* Murphy. Monte Charles made it a hat trick when he resigned after being told he wouldn't get a shot at the head coaching vacancy. In addition to the three coaches Herrera also dumped quarterback Joe Adams, fullback Jim Manz, lineman Don Swafford and defensive back Andre Jones and ushered Mike Samples into retirement. Mike became an assistant coach.

It was the first time I had witnessed a front office bloodletting, and I found the experience disturbing. I have since been through enough coach dismissals that, although I still find some of them painful, I am better able to accept them and the trading of teammates as an inevitable part of the game.

The players designated this period of Roughrider history as The Great Purge of 1983. Bob Hughes coined the phrase "The Night of the Long Knives." Bob was particularly critical of the firing of Joe Faragalli, writing, "It lacked class, showed no sense of decency and, in fact, was cruelly done. They have no conscience. They stuck him on a spit last Sunday night following a 36–28 loss to the Calgary Stampeders, their fifth straight defeat, and left him spinning on it until yesterday when they finally got around to telling him he was fired. It made you want to puke . . . Trickless [team president] Dick Rendek and the shaky seven [directors] in backroom concert with general manager John Herrera, let out little bleats of concern all week, palmed the bumps on their foreheads, read their private collection of tea leaves . . . slid their sabres from their belts and slashed away at their easiest target." What bothered Bob Hughes was not the firing of Faragalli, whom he saw as not tough enough to win, but the manner in which it was done.

The man who replaced Joe for the final ten games of the 1983 season and remained with us through 1984 was Oklahoma oilman Reuben Berry. Reuben reminded me very much of Jimmy Johnson, who took the Dallas Cowboys to two Super

Bowls and is now a television commentator and analyst. The resemblance in terms of appearance, mannerisms and even the cemented-in-place hair style was uncanny. I got along well with Reuben, which was a little surprising considering that I was of a mind that not even my own father could replace Papa Joe.

Reuben coined the phrase "Saskatchewan Tough," which became popular during his tenure. And he believed it. He would often point to Bob Poley as the kind of player he wanted around him—a guy who "in October would bare his chest to the north wind," he'd say. I can't say I ever saw Bob actually doff his shirt in the dead of winter, but Ruben was probably right in thinking Polecat loved his team enough to do it. He was also crazy enough.

Old habits die hard and we lost our first game under our new coach, dropping a 36–15 decision to the Argonauts. But we came back to win the Labor Day Classic as we nudged our arch rivals, the Blue Bombers, 32–30 on a last-play 41-yard field goal by—wait for it—Ken Clark.

The week before Labor Day Ken had gone home to attend the funeral of his mother and arrived back in Regina just in time to suit up for the game. I got dinged on an early kickoff return by the Bombers' Nate Johnson and spent the second half in the hospital. Ken came off the bench, and not having kicked a field goal since training camp a couple of years before, booted the winning three-pointer with no time on the clock. During post-game interviews he dedicated the field goal to his mom and said that wherever she was he was sure she had watched him make the kick.

Our next game took us to Ottawa. We won 29–28 by capping a 13-play, 90-yard drive with a Greg Feiger one-yard touchdown with 16 seconds left in the game.

Not used to the dizzying prosperity of a two-game winning streak, we returned to form for our next two outings, losing to Edmonton and Winnipeg as they ran up 46 and 50 points respectively. In both games, as was often the case that year, our defense could best be characterized as charitable.

Then came a game I'd prefer to forget. We lost at home to Ottawa 24–23 as I missed three field goals, one from 22 yards, one from 17 (off the upright) and a last-minute attempt from 35 yards.

After the game John Herrera announced that Ken Clark had been traded to Ottawa, citing as the reason Clark's reputation as a clubhouse lawyer. The timing could hardly have been worse, coming so soon after Ken's selfless Labor Day heroics. His game-winning kick, instead of being a special moment in Rider history, became a bittersweet reminder that professional football is a business and that some people in the business could use a course in ethics. Above all Ken Clark was not a clubhouse lawyer. He was a veteran player younger guys counted on for advice. Several of us sought him out from time to time when we were having trouble on or off the field, and we all appreciated his wisdom and sincerity.

After the trade Norm Fong refused to assign Ken's number to anyone else for a couple of years. (Norm repeated the gesture when I was traded, something I've always appreciated.) Norm believed Ken Clark would one day come back to our team, and when he did his sweater would be waiting for him. Unfortunately Ken never did return to Saskatchewan, but many of us remember him as a great punter and a hell of a human being.

The trading of Ken Clark was more than just a public relations disaster. As bad as we had been all year, we were worse after the trade. We were demoralized and dispirited, and it showed in our play. The only positive result was an irony: it marked the beginning of the end for John Herrera. Rider fans can be especially loyal to the men who don the Green and White, and if the point was ever in dispute, the outcry from fans after Ken Clark was shipped out put all doubt to rest. Any long-term career plans John Herrera had were clearly not going to be realized on the Canadian prairies. The fans' ire eventually boiled over, and they hung Herrera in effigy from the west-side upper deck of the stadium. It was a nice ceremony.

We did manage to win our last two games of the season, knocking off the Lions and the Stampeders. The Calgary game was significant because had the Stampeders won they would have made the playoffs and kept the Edmonton Eskimos from post-season play. The day before the game Tom Krebs of the Eskimos stated, "If anybody can blow it to Saskatchewan, Calgary can."

Krebs was right. We knocked off the Stamps, and the Eskimos made the playoffs while Jack Gotta's Stampeders joined us on the sidelines dreaming about next year country. Kreb's prognostication, however, was probably based more on his dislike of Gotta, his ex-coach, than a legitimate evaluation of the talent on the respective teams.

We finished 1983 at 5 and 11, and it was clear we simply weren't good enough. Many of us doubted whether the team's front office was capable of providing the direction needed to lead us out of the wilderness. In order for any team to be competitive there needs to be competent and consistent recruiting of talent, not simply a never-ending airlift of more and more bodies to fill sweaters.

John Herrera, in his year-end assessment of the ball club, said, "It's not rebuilding any more. It's just plain building.

We're going to work with what we have." He then announced that import slotback Sammy Greene, who had been claimed from B.C. ten days earlier, and import defensive end Willie Jones, the former Oakland Raider who had been working on a 21-day trial, had both signed three-year contracts. "These are two major additions, without any question. We're talking about two productive, high-caliber players. We're very pleased to have signed them."

Neither amounted to much. Sammy, when his head was straight, was an average player, not much more. Willie is best remembered for a hamstring injury so bad that he forgot which side it was on and actually had the wrong leg taped for a game against Ottawa.

The year wasn't a good one for me. Whether it was the sophomore jinx or the endless distractions supplied by head office, my numbers weren't what I had anticipated after my rookie season. I was anxious to get things turned around the following year.

From the outset of the 1984 training camp a new pressure was placed on me. Herrera had resurrected the idea of having one kicker do both the punting and place-kicking. He told me to learn to punt or risk being replaced by a dual-purpose kicker.

Our second game of 1984 took us to Ivor Wynne Stadium in Hamilton. With less than two minutes to go we had a 27–13 lead, but the game ended in a 27–27 tie. I missed a 30-yard field goal with a little over five minutes left in the game.

I'd be the first to say those are kicks I have to make. But the upshot of my miss was that in a game in which we committed six turnovers and took sixteen penalties I was made the scapegoat for having let a win slip away. In the very next game, which we lost to the Montreal Concordes, I missed another field goal. The general manager's trigger finger became itchy, which shouldn't have come as a surprise since Air Herrera was making more flights than prairie mosquitoes on a summer night. Punter Dave Badowich had been released, linebacker Larry Wruck, who went on to become a perennial CFL All-Star with Edmonton, was swapped for punter Paul Hickie, defensive back Leroy Paul came, defensive back Steve Dennis went and, in what was easily the most bitter pill for me to swallow, Paul Watson was brought back once again to compete for the kicking job.

The following week we were going into Lansdowne Park in Ottawa. In order to determine whether Paul or I would start the game, Coach Reuben Berry came up with the novel idea of a head-to-head kicking tournament with the winner getting to dress against Ottawa. Each day following practice during the week leading up to the game, Paul and I started at the 15-yard line with Reuben charting our hits and misses until we were all the way back to midfield. The week was one of the most stressful of my career. As the incumbent in the "duel to the death" I had everything to lose while Paul had everything to gain.

Looking back on it now, I believe my career might have ended had I not won this competition against Paul Watson. Fortunately I did win, probably as a result of my experience with Saskatchewan wind. During my first two seasons with the Riders I had learned to adapt my kicking style by using a lower trajectory in order to counter the prairie breezes. At least a couple of days that week were windy, and it was then I either made up ground on Paul or pulled ahead. Finally, the day before we were to leave for Ottawa, I won the right to dress for the game. It had been a bitter and emotionally exhausting week.

ROBOKICKER

The day of the Ottawa game was designated Gerry Organ Day. Gerry was one of several outstanding CFL kickers when I came into the league. In his thirteen seasons he had amassed 1,462 points and was certainly deserving of the honor the Rough Riders were giving him. Gerry was also a tremendous person, kind and generous to a fault. We talked before the game and I told him what I had gone through during the course of the week. As he was walking away, Gerry, who is deeply religious, turned and said, "I'll say a couple of words for you." I knew what he meant and I appreciated it.

That afternoon in Lansdowne Park I kicked eight field goals to set a Canadian Football League record. I was 8 of 9 and made kicks from 41, 30, 21, 27, 20 and 40 yards and tied the previous record of seven (held by Bob Macoritti of Saskatchewan and Trevor Kennerd of Winnipeg) with a 50-yarder. When we lined up for my seventh field goal, one of our offensive linemen, Gerry Hornett, spoke across the line to Ottawa's Greg Marshall, who was Gerry's friend and is now a defensive coach for the Riders. Gerry told him this kick would tie the CFL record.

Later I got the chance to break the record. With time running down on the clock we made a large gain and got into Ottawa territory. Reuben sent me onto the field for a 46-yard attempt. Greg Marshall, who was making his way back to the line of scrimmage after the previous play, came up behind me, patted me on the arm and said, "Good luck. I hope you get it." It was a decent thing for an opposing player to say and probably did more to relax me than anything anybody else could have done.

I am not superstitious nor am I a kicker with a lot of eccentric rituals. However, I remember very well how on the way to the airport to depart for the Ottawa game I had inadvertently run over a cat. I felt awful about the incident, and it stuck in my mind for most of the weekend.

The Long, Lean Years

After we won the game 46–24 and I established a new CFL record, I got to thinking about omens and good luck charms and the like. The next week, in preparation for a home game, I left the house four hours early and drove up and down the back alleys of Regina looking for another cat—at least that's how I tell it on the banquet circuit.

The last game of the 1984 season symbolized our year. The Eskimos blitzed us 52–7 to leave our record at 6–9–1. The bright spot in the season had been a 5 and 1 stretch that momentarily had us in the hunt for a playoff spot, but by season's end we had reverted again to playing losing football much to the disappointment of our long-suffering fans and everyone associated with the team.

One of the things I remember about the mideighties is how the players came together not necessarily as a team but as small groups. We began to draw on one another. I guess that's not uncommon in bad times and make no mistake—those were bad times. The media was eating us up and with good reason. We were terrible. This isn't to say there weren't talented guys on those teams who played their hearts out. But we could not, no matter the individual sacrifices, put a winning team on the field.

Though the Ottawa game was the highlight of my season, 1984 wasn't particularly good to me. But if I thought I had reached the low point of my career I was wrong. That was just around the corner.

The end of the season brought with it the firing of both Coach Reuben Berry and General Manager John Herrera. Jack Gotta, a three-time recipient of the CFL's Coach of the Year award, was hired to replace Reuben while Bill Quinter took over the general manager's reins. Excitement bordering on exuberance took hold of the team. Jack Gotta had put together a solid record of success in the CFL, and few doubted he could turn things around and take us at last back into the playoffs. I was as enthusiastic as everybody else to learn we had Jocko coming on board. I was sure the Riders, and Dave Ridgway personally, were about to see the good times roll. I was wrong on both counts.

The two seasons Jack Gotta spent in Saskatchewan were the longest of my career, and several times I contemplated quitting the game of football. Previously it was unimaginable to think anybody could ever make me stop playing the game I had loved since high school. But during 1985 and 1986 I not only didn't enjoy football, I began to hate it.

Gotta came to Saskatchewan under admittedly difficult circumstances. Our club had been labeled "a graveyard for coaches" by Bob Hughes and this wasn't an exaggeration. We'd missed the playoffs for eight consecutive years prior to Gotta's arrival, and there had to be tremendous pressure on whoever took up the head coaching duties.

I learned early I was in trouble when Gotta told the *Leader-Post* he too preferred to have one kicker perform all the kicking duties. He went on to say that all he wanted from me was "dependable place-kicking and adequate punting. He doesn't have to be Lui Passaglia or Bernie Ruoff. I'd be happy with a Gerry Organ."

Typical of Gotta's media pronouncements he found a way to disparage even when he complimented. Gerry Organ was a hell of a kicker. But the bottom line was that the old one kicker-two jobs scenario had reared its ugly head one more time. That year in camp we had Paul Hickie, the punter we had traded for the previous year; Terry Leschuk, whom Gotta had used in Calgary when J. T. Hay was hurt; Colum Armstrong, a rookie out of Acadia University; a free agent signing, a kid named Pierre Deschamps. And me. If it sounds like I was just

The Long, Lean Years

a footnote, that's certainly how Jack Gotta made me feel. Not that I was in any way unique in this regard. Gotta was unfeeling with most players, particularly those he didn't like.

Jack was skilled in dealing with the media and as a result was very popular with them. Unfortunately the witty quip and quotable thirty-second sound bite don't have much to do with putting a good team on the field or providing leadership for the guys in uniform. After he'd been released by Saskatchewan, Paul Hickie failed his medical with Ottawa because of a suspected heart murmur, and Jack, always ready with the one-liner, said, "Heart murmur? Every time he went on the field, he gave me a heart murmur."

Our preseason began that year in Winnipeg, and for the first time in my career I wasn't on the roster for our first exhibition game. It is not a good sign to be left behind when the team makes its first preseason road trip, and I'd be lying if I said I wasn't deeply concerned about my future. The Riders won the game 9–7, and Terry Leschuk, who had made the trip to Winnipeg, went 2 of 3 in field goals and punted five times for a 43.6 yard average. I listened to the game on the radio and confess to hating every minute of it.

I dressed for our second preseason game when we met the Eskimos at Taylor Field. We won 28–25 and I kicked the winning field goal, a 45-yarder, with 11 seconds showing on the clock. It was the second year in a row I had kicked a late-game field goal in our preseason matchup with Edmonton. After the game I was quoted in the *Leader-Post* as saying, "Now people can say that Ridgway has still got it or that he's never lost it. What made me happiest this week was that all the veterans were really behind me."

Later that day General Manager Bill Quinter strode onto the practice field, newspaper in hand, sort of jabbed it at me and said, "What the hell do you mean making a comment like that?" We called Quinter the Hat because of the assorted cowboy hats he loved to wear, and he was so incensed as he spoke that the hat jiggled up and down. I'll never know for certain what he found so offensive about my remarks to the newspaper, but maybe he was overreacting to the stress of the deep and very rancorous rift forming between him and Jack Gotta.

Paul Hickie played half of one game during the preseason. After our last preseason game Gotta was asked if Terry Leschuk had beaten out Hickie for the job. The ever-sensitive Gotta replied, "Oh yeah, Hickie hasn't been in the race for weeks." Paul learned he had been cut from reading the newspaper. A lot of veterans on the team felt this was unnecessary and cruel.

As the regular season began the team's management continued its efforts to replace me by bringing in Lance Chomyc on a twenty-one day trial. Lance and I didn't get along. I'm not sure it was anybody's fault. The Riders released him, but to his credit he eventually developed into a very good kicker. Probably because of that three-week period in 1985, he is one guy I enjoyed playing well against.

Our first game of the regular season was especially memorable for me. Not only did we trounce Ottawa 46–22, but I chalked up the one and only fumble recovery of my career. The big play came on a kickoff. After the Ottawa returner had brought the ball back to their 45, he was hit and fumbled. The bounce brought the ball right to me. I grabbed it and the thought that immediately ran through my mind was: *Here we go—seven points, baby!*

Two steps later I almost had my head taken off. Suitor had been right beside me when I grabbed the ball; in fact I actually bumped him off it. He has never let me live this down, the reason being the incentive clause he had in his contract for turnovers. My own feeling is that if Suitor had bothered to throw a block instead of standing there pouting, I probably could have gone in for the major. At least in my dreams it goes this way.

In our sixth game of the season Terry Leschuk went down with a knee injury and we were once again in the market for a punter. The club brought in Gerry McGrath, or Lumpy, as he came to be known on the ball club. I had met Gerry in 1981 at the Montreal Alouettes' training camp, and we became good friends when he came to the Roughriders. He was a good punter with a great sense of humor. And best of all, while he was with us, he didn't kick field goals.

We were 4 and 4 for the first half of the season, but things really went into the tank in the second half. We lost the next four in a row and the dispute between Jack Gotta and Bill Quinter reached the boiling point. The two men handled the dispute very differently, however. Gotta began sniping at Quinter through the media, which was one of his favorite tactics, while Bill never discussed his differences with Jocko publicly.

The season wound up as pretty much a disaster for both the team and me. I was 23 of 38 that year, a 60.5 percent success rate, my worst numbers ever. There was no excuse for my personal performance, which was admittedly disappointing, but I believe the lack of continuity in our on-field personnel hurt our over-all team performance in 1985. Our troubles began as early as May of that year when Gotta traded Gerry Hornett, Bob Poley and Greg Fieger to Calgary for Willie Thomas, Kevin Molle and Ken Moore. The message was crystal clear. Jocko wanted to clean house, even if doing so meant disposing of well-liked, solid players, two of whom were Saskatchewan boys. Gotta chose in favor of his own people. While this is not in itself necessarily a bad thing, many of Gotta's trades certainly didn't improve the performance of our ball club.

The three players who came to us were not under any illusions about what it meant to be Jocko's boys. On one occasion, after he had been teased about being one of Gotta's sons, Willie Thomas told the taunter, "Let me tell you something. Jocko would stab me in the back just as fast as he would anybody in this room."

I got a taste of what Willie was talking about at the end of my first season under Jack Gotta. It is customary for players to meet with the coach at the end of the year, one on one, to discuss the season and often to receive what amounts to a report card. I was disappointed with how I'd performed, and when I went in to see Gotta I asked him point-blank how he felt about my year and what he'd like to see me doing differently. I expected him to tell me to get my act together and start making more field goals. Instead he had nothing but good things to say and indicated he was satisfied with how I had kicked and would be content with a similar season from me in 1986.

I left the meeting feeling confused but thinking maybe Jocko and I could work together after all. The next player to talk to the coach that day was Joe Paopao. When he came out Joe told me that for most of his meeting, Gotta had talked disparagingly about me. He had basically said the team couldn't win with "that idiot" doing the kicking. I was shocked but was learning more about the Jack Gotta way. It was easier for him to criticize someone to a third party, as he often did through the media, than speak directly to the person. But it was obvious the writing was on the wall as far as my future with the Riders was concerned.

This was the cloud I was under as the 1986 season got underway. I had not kicked well for the previous three seasons

The Long, Lean Years

and was well aware of the need to have a big year. Added to this was the knowledge that the team's coach either didn't like me or didn't have confidence in me—or both. I was feeling anything but comfortable as we headed to Saskatoon for training camp.

The new season saw one change to the team staff. Gerry Hart returned for a second tour of duty as an assistant coach. Gerry, for my money, was a tremendous coach and a long way from the Jack Gotta mold. It came as a pleasant surprise when he was brought back.

The training camp also saw the Gotta–Quinter power struggle come to a head. During the first team meeting, which is also the first time the veterans and rookies come together (some ninety-five of us in those days) Gotta entered the room wearing what we had dubbed his Terminator sunglasses and walked on stage to welcome everybody to camp. But that wasn't all Jocko had to say. He stunned us into silence when he announced, "I run this team, not that idiot over there in the hat." As he pointed to the building in which Bill Quinter's training camp office was located, he went on to say, "You got a problem, you come to me. You don't go to him." We were dumbfounded. We were hoping to get the season off to a positive start and this sure as hell wasn't the way to do it.

The general manager wasn't Gotta's only target as we stumbled our way toward the starting gate. A *Leader-Post* article stated rather prophetically, "Gotta is not totally satisfied with Ridgway and that may be understating the matter. This relationship between coach and kicker is not a match made in heaven. Will 1986 be the year that brings divorce?"

The team brought two other kickers to camp: Terry Leschuk, coming back from the knee injury of the previous year, and Tony Brown, a fourth-round draft pick out of San Jose State.

Our second game of the year is etched in my memory. In front of almost twenty-seven thousand patrons in Winnipeg we endured the worst drubbing I have experienced in professional football. The final score was 56–0. Tom Clements was 20 of 23 in passing for 274 yards and four touchdowns in just one half of football. It was a horrible experience for all the Rider players and staff, and not even Jack Gotta deserved it.

Despite that inauspicious beginning we were 3 and 2 going into our sixth game of the season against the B.C. Lions, a game we lost. Darnell Clash of the Lions returned 7 punts for 201 yards. This was reason enough for Jocko to put the blame and the boots to punter Gerry McGrath, who was let go after the game. George Brancato, our special teams' coach, was aware, as we all were, of the threat Clash posed as a returner. Instead of instructing Lumpy to kick it away from Clash, Brancato's pregame orders were to kick it to him and we would cover it. Clash ran all over us and Gerry McGrath lost his job for following orders. Another ex-Stampeder, Mike McTague, had been brought in about a month earlier and took over the punting duties after Gerry got the axe.

We lost our next game 23–21 to Hamilton, and I missed a 47-yard try with 17 seconds left in the game. In a situation like this I accept responsibility for missing a kick that is not a shoe-in but is certainly makeable. Nevertheless, at the halfway point of the season, I had made 17 of 22 attempted field goals, which I felt was an acceptable ratio.

I wasn't the only kicker to have a bad day in the Hamilton game. Mike McTague averaged only 38.4 yards per punt. The result was that the following week we were joined in practice by Stan Gelbaugh (later of the WLAF's London Monarchs and NFL's Seattle Seahawks) and Zenon Andrusyshyn (formerly of a lot of places).

The Long, Lean Years

Our eleventh game of the season was a rematch with Hamilton, this time at Taylor Field. Once again I supplied Jack Gotta with a target at whom to aim the blame for not winning. The game ended in a 21–21 overtime tie, the first overtime game in CFL history, and I was an abysmal 4 of 8 that afternoon. Even though I scored 15 of our 21 points, I missed four field goals, two of them in the last four minutes of regulation time, either of which could have iced it for us. I did kick a 19-yarder after a Bobby Johnson touchdown was called back on a holding call to Nick Hebeler. Shortly after this field goal, Paul Osbaldiston hit one through the rain and wind from 51 yards out to give Hamilton the tie.

After the game Gotta was quoted as saying, "Full marks to that kid Osbaldiston. We couldn't make the chip shot and he comes in and kicks it 51 yards under duress. The ball was waterlogged and heavy and the guy kicked it right down the middle."

We ended the year with four straight losses, the last a 42–14 defeat to Edmonton, to bring our 1986 record to 6–11–1. The season finale was played on a sunny but bitterly cold afternoon before a sparse Commonwealth Stadium crowd. It was a season we all wanted to forget. Morale was so low that a number of the American-born players had packed their cars with their belongings and left them at the Regina airport so they could leave immediately after we got back from Edmonton.

There was plenty of speculation swirling around the club at season's end and the betting was about even as to whether Jack Gotta or Bill Quinter would be fired. There were even pretty good odds for both of them getting the sack. Team president Keith Critchley sealed the fates of both when he publicly expressed confidence in the jobs they were doing and extolled the merits of stability in the organization. Having a senior team official offer support for a coach is like having a Mafia boss kiss you on the mouth. You know you're dead, you just haven't quit breathing yet.

One thing I'll say about Gotta—he went out with guns blazing. When asked about his possible firing and the booing he'd received from the fans in our final home game of the season, he said, "They crucified Christ—you think they're not going to get a goof like me?"

At the end of the 1986 season I was at a crossroads. I sat down with my wife, Nancy, and we talked for a long time about whether I should continue to play. I was no longer enjoying the game and for the first time began thinking about life without football. When I bounced these thoughts off my father he went through the roof. He couldn't understand how I could even consider quitting the life of a professional athlete.

Over the course of these discussions I realized for the first time that I had been playing football for my dad. We all want to succeed in life in order to make our parents proud, but in my case it had gone beyond the typical. My father wanted me to be an athlete, and I was doing everything in my power to make *his* dream come true. It was during the off-season between 1986 and 1987 that I made one of the biggest discoveries of my career: I still loved the game of football, but if I was to continue playing, from that moment forward the person I would be playing for was me.

I had turned a corner. If I divide my career into two parts, the first beginning with my entry into the CFL and the second beginning in 1987, the statistics are quite astounding, at least to me. Up to the end of 1986 I was a 68.5 percent kicker. Since that time I have been successful on 82.7 percent of my attempts. The reasons for the difference are many and varied, but the most important is the decision I made to take my career into my own hands from that point on.

The big question remaining was whether there was going to be a career at all. One person I had not talked to about my future was Jack Gotta. Though both Gotta and Quinter had been despatched at the end of the 1986 season, Jocko had left me something to remember him by. Before he was fired he traded me to the Edmonton Eskimos.

If seeing friends released and traded was tough it was a cakewalk compared to being traded myself. The trade came on the heels of four years of turmoil for the team and for me. I've always suspected the trade occurred after the final season game at Edmonton when we stopped at a Wendy's so the guys could have something to eat before getting on the airplane. Hugh Campbell, the Eskimos' general manager, happened to be there with his family. Jocko joined them for maybe forty-five minutes. The deal involving my going to the Eskimos may have been done there over a Wendy's Single with cheese.

I learned about being traded from Bill Baker—not Jack Gotta—and I didn't find out until March of the following year. Nancy and I were in Portland, Oregon, holidaying with Al and Donalda Tingle. I found out that Bill, who succeeded Bill Quinter in the general manager's chair, was in town to look at some prospects with Pokie Allen, who was coaching at Portland State. Nancy and I went down to the stadium and then out to dinner with Bill, Pokie and some of his staff. Following dinner, Bill informed me I had been dealt to the Eskimos. I was speechless. A few months earlier I had attended an I-Survived-the-Jack-Gotta-Era party. Turned out the celebration was premature in my case. For the second time in my career, my worth as a player had been called into question.

Here was something new and completely unexpected to

consider in making the decision about my future in football. I was no longer a Saskatchewan Roughrider. But before I could even get used to picturing myself in the green and gold of the Eskimos, I learned I had been traded again, this time to the Montreal Alouettes, who had recently hired Joe Faragalli. The equation had once again been drastically altered. If I decided to play I would do so under the coach who gave me my first opportunity in the league, a man for whom I had enjoyed playing and with whom I had enjoyed success.

The realization that I wanted to begin living my life for me and the prospect of being reunited with Papa Joe Faragalli helped me decide that I wanted to go on playing football. When I flew into Montreal a few months later I was on something of a high. I had phoned Joe and received permission to report a few days early with the rookies so I could get in a little extra work. I had an extremely positive attitude, and I was in excellent shape. Life was good and the future again looked bright—for about five weeks.

Montreal's 1987 training camp was staged at St. Mary's University in Halifax, Nova Scotia. I found it odd at the time for a team with an identity crisis to remove itself even farther from its hometown fans. I suppose it's possible we were a bit of a test market commodity to see if the CFL could generate interest in an area that had long been rumored as a potential franchise site, but that's pure speculation on my part.

I enjoyed the Alouettes' training camp. St. Mary's was a wonderful facility and the city of Halifax was full of rustic charm and friendly people. Our first preseason game that year was memorable in that it was played in St. John, New Brunswick, and labeled the St. John Bowl. I rang a convert attempt off the crossbar as Hamilton beat us 14–13 in a driving rainstorm.

The Long, Lean Years

I made the ball club, beating out the incumbent kicker, Roy Kurtz. Nancy came up and we found a studio apartment just a few blocks from the Montreal Forum. About a week later we were preparing for our first regular season game against the Argonauts in Toronto. Center Willie Thomas, who would later author a book chronicling his experiences in the CFL, punter Terry Baker and I had stayed on the field after practice to work on some things. When we got to the locker room it was buzzing with rumors. The word was that we should stick around, that something was coming down from management but nobody knew what.

I had been in the process of renegotiating my contract with General Manager Bob Geary. I stuck my head into Joe's office and asked if he could get me an appointment to see Bob. Joe said he would when he got the chance, but he was tied up with a couple of things at the moment.

After a half hour or so, no news was forthcoming. Joe came out and told us we might as well go home. He'd see us in the morning. The next day we were to head for Toronto. I got up, put on my traveling clothes and waited for Terry Baker, who was to share a ride to the airport with me. There was a knock at the door and when I opened it Terry was standing there in shorts and a T-shirt. I laughed and said, "That isn't going to cut it on the plane." But Terry wasn't laughing. He looked shocked. "I just heard on the radio that the team has folded," he said. "There's a meeting at the stadium in an hour."

I didn't believe him. Being the eternal optimist I still didn't believe him as we pulled up to the stadium. In fact I went to the meeting still dressed in the clothes I was sure I would need for the flight to Toronto. We milled around in the locker room for a while and finally Norm Kimball came in, and with little emotion and no apology told us he and his partners had decided to cease operation of the football team due to a lack of fan interest. He turned and walked out of the room.

The place went very quiet. After a while some of the guys began shuffling around and getting ready to leave. Joe asked if we'd be seated for a minute, that he'd like to say a few words. We sat back down. As Joe spoke he was fighting back tears. He felt bad for all of us but was also disappointed because we had the makings of a very good football team that year. We had an excellent mix of youth and experience, talented people at the key positions and good coaching all the way down the line. It was the kind of team every player hopes to play on at least once in his career. To see this opportunity snuffed out in Norm Kimball's terse and cold announcement was hard on everybody.

The other and I suppose even tougher part of the team's folding was being suddenly unemployed. The team paid us one game cheque and told us there would be a league dispersal draft that might see some players going to other teams. But as one of the guys who suddenly had no job I found cold comfort in those words. On my way out I went into the office area to say good-bye to the coaches and Joe pulled me into his office. "If you don't get picked up in the draft, I'll get you a shot in Buffalo with Marv." Marv was Marv Levy, a former CFL coach and a long-time friend of Joe's.

I thanked Joe and told him I was sure he would surface somewhere and to call me if he should happen to need a kicker. I went back to the apartment on which we had paid a hefty first month's rent and security deposit, and when I got there Nancy was as shocked as I was.

We talked for a long time. Remembering the game cheque in my pocket I told Nancy to get ready, we were going out. That's exactly what we did. We cashed the cheque, went out for a long lunch, then shopped and finished the day with din-

The Long, Lean Years

ner and cocktails ... a lot of cocktails. We got home after midnight having spent every dime of my one and only Montreal Alouettes' pay cheque.

When we opened the door, a bit of a challenge in the shape we were in, we found a dozen or more messages slipped under it. Most were from an old friend, Dan Rambo, the director of player personnel with the Roughriders. He had somehow found out where we were living and had spent much of the day trying to get word to me to call him immediately, no matter when I got in.

So at about 12:30 A.M. Montreal time, slightly inebriated, I reached Dan back in Regina. His message was simple and brief—catch the first plane out of Dorval and get back to Saskatchewan right away. He told me the Riders had cut a deal to take me in the dispersal draft, and they wanted me in the lineup for the upcoming game against B.C. The first plane out was at 6:00 A.M., just five and a half hours later. We didn't have much time to get sober, get packed and get ourselves and our two cats to the airport.

The night was harried. Yet despite the tight timelines, everything went well but for one detail. Before we left the apartment we gave each of the cats a tranquilizer for the flight. Though they were chalking up frequent flyer points at an astounding rate, neither liked being on airplanes any more than I did. When we arrived at the airport and looked down at the cats in their cage, we noticed that one had spit out its pill, which was now lying on the floor of the cage. The problem was how to determine which cat had taken its pill and which had not. The situation was a little like Russian Roulette; if we guessed wrong we'd have one cat awake and yowling all the way to Regina while the other would be in a coma for about a week. So there we were in the airport, tired and feeling the effects, Nancy on her knees trying to get the selected cat to take its pill like a nice kitty while a good crowd gathered to enjoy the scene. It had been a hell of a night.

Two days later I was again a Roughrider, under new head coach John Gregory, and en route to Vancouver for the game against the Lions. The upshot was that I had been traded twice, drafted once and had only missed one league game with the Green and White. My first game back I accounted for all the team's scoring, which was no big deal. We were beaten 44–1 by B.C. and I kicked my single point on a wide 49-yard field goal attempt.

My return to the Riders was not without incident. Our next game was at home, and, of course, we all wanted to make amends for the B.C. debacle. Historically our practice on the day before a game has been held in the morning. In the hustle of doing all the things required when one moves—fun stuff like having the power and gas turned on, the telephone hooked up and purchasing a car—I somehow managed to forget we had a morning practice. Here I was, having just rejoined the team under a new coach and general manager, and I missed, for the first and only time, a practice. The team had tried to reach me but had been unable get in touch because we had no phone. At about 10:30 that morning the wife of defensive back Dave Singh/Sidoo knocked on our apartment door and informed Nancy that practice had begun a half hour before.

In a huge panic, convinced John Gregory would soon share Jack Gotta's opinion of me, I raced through the shower, jumped in a cab and headed for the ballpark. As we pulled up in front of Taylor Field it was about 10:50, and I could see the players out on the practice field. By the time I made it onto the field there was very little time left in the practice.

Mike McTague had been kicking in my absence, and as

The Long, Lean Years

soon as I ran onto the field, he backed out and I rushed into place. My first attempt was from the left hash about 40 yards out. Glen bobbled the snap and it was falling off the tee as I kicked it. I caught the ball with the end of my toe and drove it into the back of Roger Aldag. Roger, who was already unhappy with me for being late for practice, turned and gave me a look that said, *Do that again and I'll tear your face off.* I looked down at Suitor, thinking he would jump up and say, "Hey, Rodge, it was my fault, I muffed the snap." Suitor, my team buddy, said nothing. To this day Roger doesn't know the ball rolled off the tee. But Suitor sure does.

The next day we played Toronto to a 33–33 tie. I kicked a 32-yarder into the wind on the last play of regulation time to force overtime. On the final play of overtime we tried a 46-yarder into a stiff breeze for the win. I was instructed, because of the wind, to aim wide and we'd try to get the single point by tackling the returner in the end zone. Or failing this, we'd be in one of those classic CFL kick-it-in, kick-it-out situations. I agreed with John Gregory's strategy, but unfortunately the ball landed about four yards deep in the end zone and bounced straight up in the air. The Toronto returner was able to scramble out to the one-yard line. Had we got a decent bounce on the kick I think we would have won that game.

Game six of that season we lost 38–28 to Edmonton, which took our record to 1–4–1. I kicked four field goals, which gave me a career total of 161, a team record, one more than Jack Abendschan. This milestone was dramatically overshadowed, however, as the game was played only twenty-four hours after the terrible Edmonton tornado claimed a number of lives and resulted in millions of dollars in damage. Prior to the game there had been some discussion about it being canceled because of the tragedy Edmontonians had endured only hours earlier. I remember looking out the window of the hotel the day before the game and remarking to Glen that I had never seen a sky so black or wind and rain so fierce. It was only later we learned of the horror other parts of the city had suffered.

As the season wore on it was evident that the team under John Gregory was faring no better than it had for his predecessors and that we were destined to finish out of the playoffs one more time. The media and fans were unrelenting in their attacks on the "relapse Roughriders."

More serious than the team's on-field woes was the announcement in early June that the team might not have enough money to get through the remainder of the season. What followed was another example of Rider Pride in action as fans rallied around their beleaguered team by supporting a lottery, a telethon and several other fund-raising campaigns. Bob Hughes of the *Leader-Post* summarized the attitude for all: "Who cares if you win as long as you're around to lose?"

The year went well for me personally as I put together consecutive strings of 17 and 19 field goals, which were my best to that point in my career. Unfortunately I had one miss sandwiched between the two streaks. It was my first attempt of the Labor Day game, a contest we lost 29–25. I wound up with five field goals that day, but I remember two kicks particularly well. The first was that early miss, a 35-yarder into a strong wind. I hit the ball really well and right down the middle, but it hit a wall of wind and died at about the five-yard line. The second memorable kick that day was a successful 60-yarder, this time with the wind. This established a CFL record for the longest kick, nudging out Paul Watson's record of 59 yards. I didn't realize as we were lining up just how far out we were, but as I bent down to get ready it occurred to me that the 55-yard line

The Long, Lean Years

was up there another five yards. I hit the ball as well as I've ever hit one in my life, and as we were going off the field one of the officials said it would have been good from another 10 yards back. I was more than happy with 60 and, yes, I am willing to acknowledge the wind as a factor. In fact it was so strong it was pushing me forward as I lined up for the kick. My guess is that if and when the record is broken it will be by another wind-assisted kick . . . maybe even in Taylor Field where such wind is not uncommon.

In game twelve of the season I went 7 of 7 and dedicated my performance to my recently deceased cat, Church (from Stephen King's *Pet Sematary*). Those who are into stats in a big way will note I am 15 of 15 while mourning departed felines.

I told the *Leader-Post* after the game that one of the major factors contributing to the kind of year I was enjoying was having a coach who believed in me. And it was true. It was a lot more pleasant coming to the sidelines in 1987 than it had been in the two previous years.

In our fourteenth game of the season we beat Hamilton 23–20 in Kent Austin's first game as a Roughrider. Kent went 15 of 24 for 292 yards and threw for one touchdown and two interceptions. It was obvious from the outset that in Austin and Tom Burgess we would have a hell of a tandem at quarterback if we could keep them both happy.

Our last game of the year was another loss, 34–14, to the B.C. Lions to leave our season record at 5–12–1. I entered the game sitting at 47 of 50 for the year with Lui Passaglia at 50 of 62. The CFL record for most field goals in a single season at the time was 50, set by Dave Cutler in 1977. Clearly Lui was poised to break the record and I had an outside shot. I went 2 of 3 in the game while Lui went 2 of 4 to break Cutler's mark and at the same time establish a single-season points record.

When that announcement was made to the crowd, I heard one fan yell, "Hey, Ridgway, you're a bum. Look what Passaglia has done."

I was content with my year. I was voted to the Western and CFL All-Star teams and received two Schenley nominations, one for Most Outstanding Player and one for Most Outstanding Canadian. The downside was missing the playoffs for the eleventh straight year. I began to wonder if I would ever see post-season play.

The 1988 season began on a different and, for me, very pleasant note. The league staged an All-Star game pitting the CFL All-Stars against the defending Grey Cup champions, the Edmonton Eskimos, at Commonwealth Stadium in Edmonton. Jackie Parker coached our team to a 15–4 win. I kicked two field goals that day and we failed to get a third one off as Matt Dunigan had trouble with the snap from center. But what I enjoyed most about the game was the opportunity to meet players who up to this time had been adversaries and about whom I had drawn conclusions that in many cases were wrong.

There have only been fourteen All-Star games in the history of the league, the first in 1955 and the last, the one I played in, in 1988. Since then the reluctance of coaches and general managers to expose their best players to injury has overruled whatever marketing benefit might be enjoyed from the staging of all-star games. That's understandable. Where hockey all-star contests are often no-hitters this is not an option in football, and the chances of injury remain virtually as high as in any other game of the season.

Nevertheless, I enjoyed the game and especially enjoyed playing for Jackie Parker, arguably the greatest player in Canadian football history. He demonstrated that he was a fine coach as well, keeping things simple and designing an offense

The Long, Lean Years

and defense that would allow the talent and in some cases the egos of the players to be showcased. With only five days to prepare the team, developing a workable game plan was not easy, but Jackie and his staff accomplished it and still managed to let the guys have some fun. During one practice, after we had done our stretching and some running, Jackie called us together in a circle and, head down and in a slow drawl, asked, "Does anybody know where Ray is?"

We looked around and at one another and realized Ray Elgaard was nowhere to be seen. A couple of guys snickered a little but said nothing. Jackie said again, "Does anybody know where Ray is?"

Nobody knew where he was, and Jackie looked at us and then at the sky and said, "Aw, what the hell, take it in." Just like that, after only fifteen minutes, the practice was over. I guess Ray was an integral part of the offensive plan and without him Jackie felt the practice would be a waste of time. I never found out where Ray was, but I think some of the guys were out the night before and my guess is the evening had taken its toll.

The Riders' training camp that year was the first one in my career at which I did not have competition for the place-kicking position. The lack of pressure during camp contributed to the success I was to enjoy that season.

Our second game of the year was a big one for me as I once again managed to kick eight field goals and surpassed Jack Abendschan's team record for career points at the same time. At the conclusion of the game I had 873 points, 10 more than Jack. I remembered how, when I came into the league in 1982, I'd thought it would really be something to stay in the CFL long enough to break that record while at the same time thinking it wasn't likely to happen.

We met the Eskimos in our fourth game of the year. Before the game Terry Jones wrote a story in the *Edmonton Sun* that was titled, "Rider Kicker Can't Miss." Going into the game I was 16 of 16, which was the best start I'd ever had. I dinged my first attempt of the game off the right upright from the 22 to put an end to Terry Jones' claims of perfection on my part. The Edmonton fans were only too willing to remind me of this fact as we suffered our first loss of the season, 43–27.

Everyone on the team was aware of Coach John Gregory's volatile temper, the legendary "Wrath of John." In game five we were beaten by the Stampeders in Calgary 48–10. Following the game John closed the dressing room door with enough force to damage the frame and shatter the glass. The outburst certainly put an exclamation point on his displeasure.

Just after the halfway point in the season, the cat came back. Bob Poley, one of the victims of Jack Gotta's purge, was reacquired by the Roughriders. Polecat had been released by Lary Kuharich, whose performance while in the CFL made Gotta look like Gandhi. It happened just a week after the Stampeders had axed J. T. Hay in one of the bloodier moments in league history. Hay had missed a 42-yard attempt, which is far from a chip shot, and was first slammed by the media, then cut by Kuharich. Polecat reacted to the handling of the whole affair by taking members of the media out to the 42-yard line to show them how narrow the posts look from there. Kuharich was enraged and ran Bob out of town. Much to the delight of many people in Saskatchewan, including me, Polecat headed back to Regina.

It was about this time I acquired the nickname Robokicker. The title of this book notwithstanding I have never been entirely comfortable with it. While I realize it is intended as a compliment there are several reasons I don't like it: first, it adds pressure to an already tough enough job. The notion of robot-like precision suggests action without the possibly of error. This is unrealistic. Second, I feel the designation Robokicker tends to trivialize the contribution of the eleven players in front of me. Every place-kick involves a number of precise movements that have to be performed by a lot of people. If even one of these movements is not performed quickly and correctly the chances for success are limited. This is a very human game, and I don't like to think of myself as any different from the other people who play it.

My nickname is Ridge. It was my father's nickname, and it was also the name he called my mother and my grandmother. It is a name I am much more comfortable with than Robokicker. Occasionally I am asked to sign autographs as Robokicker, and I always decline because of my discomfort with the name. As for this book's title I was overruled by my co-author and publisher, who maintained that more people would recognize the book with the Robokicker title. I disagreed; we argued; they won.

In game fifteen of the 1988 season we beat the B.C. Lions 28–25, and for the first time in twelve years the Saskatchewan Roughriders made the playoffs. It was a tremendous relief to all of us and a well-deserved feather in John Gregory's cap. In the previous game I had passed the 1000-point plateau, which was a nice personal milestone, but it was easily overshadowed by our venture into the uncharted territory of playoff football. Both events, exciting as they were, were eclipsed in importance on September 26 when my first son, Christopher Dallas, was born.

Our last game of the year was a 46–11 win over the Ottawa Rough Riders. I entered the game 14 points away from Lui Passaglia's season point record of 214. With nine minutes left in the game, I had tied Lui's record. With 3:43 remaining our backup quarterback, Jeff Bentrim, tossed a 13-yard scoring pass to Tim McCray. I went onto the field to attempt the convert. We were 41 of 41 for converts to this point in the season. There was by the way a stiff wind at my back. Robokicker couldn't miss, right?

When the ball was snapped Glen Suitor did something he almost never did—he bobbled it and we never got the kick off. I got a second shot at the record on the ensuing kickoff. In the huddle Ray Elgaard said, "Go for it. Kick the hell out of it and we'll nail 'em for a single." I took his advice and hit one that cleared the heads of the Ottawa return men, Orville Lee and Derrick White, and bounced around crazily in the Rough Riders' end zone. I was holding my breath, hoping the ball would not roll out of the end zone because no single point is awarded in this instance. However, the ball did sneak out the back of the end zone, and I figured my shot at the record was gone.

I was to get one last opportunity. With sixty-two seconds left on the clock defensive back Eddie Ray Walker blocked a Tom Dixon punt and another defensive back, Mike McGruder, scooped up the ball and ran it in for a touchdown. This time our convert try was successful and I had my 215th point. After the game Suits told the media that if I had missed out on the record because of his bobble, he never would have forgiven himself. I told him he wouldn't be the only one, but only in jest. I as much as anyone know records are made to be broken. A new mark would be set at 236 points in 1991 by Lance Chomyc.

We had the home field for the 1988 Western Semi-Final, a situation that has not repeated itself since. Unfortunately, on a frigid afternoon the B.C. Lions came into Taylor Field and manhandled us to the tune of 42–18. It was a tough loss to take, particularly for the veterans. We had worked so hard for so long to finally get into the playoffs only to have our butts kicked. Of course, we had no idea that we had taken an important step toward ensuring a very different result the following year, a point John Gregory rather prophetically made in post-game interviews. John told reporters we had learned a lot from our brief playoff experience and would put those lessons to good use the following year.

CHAPTER 7

A Few Good Men – The Early Years

Dunlap: You cheap son of a bitch, are you crazy? Those guys are retards.
McGrath: I got a good deal on those boys. The scout said they had a lot of promise. —SLAPSHOT, 1977

During those difficult and often frustrating times that were the 1980s for the Saskatchewan Roughriders, I learned an important lesson. While I was already aware from my high school and college days of the bonds between teammates, it was during my first years in the CFL that I came to realize it is the people, not the games, I will remember when I leave football. The laughter and the pain of all the times we shared together are what has made my journey through football the greatest ride imaginable.

Papa Joe *(Joe Faragalli)*

I suppose it's unusual for a player to include a coach among the people he counts as his closest friends. But that's the way I feel about the man who was my first professional football coach.

I'm grateful to Joe Scanella, not only for being as good as

his word and recommending me to a prospective employer but also for choosing Joe Faragalli, fellow Italian and paisano, to be the recipient of the information.

Joe told me early on that what he wanted from a place-kicker was the ability to consistently make the field goals that he should make, particularly those Joe called "money field goals" from inside the 40-yard line. That's a very realistic expectation for any coach, and it has been a continuing goal throughout my career.

Once I had met Joe I quickly came to realize why the media, the players and Saskatchewan fans referred to him as Papa Joe. He was one of the kindest, most sincere people I have ever known in or out of football.

Coaches, like players, have their detractors. Joe was often criticized in the media for allowing—in fact encouraging—players to play soccer on the day following a game. Apparently the media wisdom (which was shared by John Herrera when he became general manager) was that especially after a loss players should be out there kicking some butt around the practice field the next day. All Joe wanted from the guys on the day after a game was for them to do some running to keep their muscles from stiffening up. Soccer was the ideal way to achieve this, and it was also useful in helping Joe and the rest of the coaching and training staff determine who was injured and how badly. Lastly it was something that most of us really liked doing, and Joe was not opposed to having his players enjoy themselves once in a while.

In 1983, although I was coming off a rookie season during which I was named to the Western and CFL All-Star teams, the Roughriders brought Paul Watson, the place-kicker from 1981 back to training camp. Paul had missed the entire 1982 season with an Achilles tendon injury, but he had lost none of the strength and velocity that were his trademarks in 1981. He was one of the strongest kickers I have ever seen and for a while held the record for the longest field goal in CFL history at 59 yards.

On one of the practice fields at the University of Saskatchewan was a chain-link fence about 30 yards on the end zone side of the goalposts. Paul and I would head out to the 35- or 40-yard line to kick field goals. Paul consistently kicked balls over the fence while my efforts would land 10 or 15 yards short and roll up to it. Paul could kick for distance, there's no doubt about it.

During the camp, whenever Joe was watching, I found myself competing with Paul for leg strength. I was trying to beat the hell out of the ball, and my kicks were going everywhere. Joe called me over one day and said, "What's going on out there? You're missing kicks that you should make."

I said, "Well, you know, I'm just trying a few things."

Joe said, "I don't want you to try some things. All I want you to do is kick like you did last year. You can't compete with Paul's leg so quit trying. Go about things like you did last year and everything will be fine." It was good advice and I took it to heart. I quit trying to outkick Paul for distance and before long was back in my groove.

People often underestimated Joe's toughness. One example of how tough he could be took place in 1983 and involved me. We went into Ivor Wynne Stadium to meet the Tiger-Cats. After a first quarter touchdown we lined up for the subsequent kickoff. I did everything the way I'm supposed to, head down, good follow through, not hurrying to look up—it was a textbook kick. The only problem was that one of Hamilton's big guys, Henry Waschuk, started running at me the instant the referee blew the whistle. By the time I looked up from kicking the ball, the big palooka was on me and busted me one right under the chin. (This by the way is the same Henry Waschuk who now hosts a fishing show on television. I've seen the show a few times and have noticed Henry sporting a Grey Cup ring as he goes about his host duties.)

Well, he landed the big one that day in Hamilton. It was a regular slobberknocker and I went down for the count. Trainer Ivan Gutfriend came out and helped what was left of me off the field. When I got to the sidelines Joe asked me what had happened. I told him all I knew was I had been shmucked by what felt like a Kenworth. Joe asked one of the other guys who told him Waschuk had nailed me just after I got the ball off.

Two or three series later Joe said to me, "Watch this." Hamilton was punting on third down and Joe sent one of our guys in with instructions to hit punter Bernie Ruoff. Joe told our player it didn't matter if he got flagged, but to get Ruoff. Our guy did as he was directed and hit Ruoff as hard as Waschuk had hit me. As it happened Joe was looking directly across the field and waving his arms at Hamilton Coach Bud Riley. Riley nodded and gestured back at Joe in effect saying, "Okay, you leave our guy alone and we'll leave your guy alone."

It was the first time I had ever encountered such a situation and I appreciated what Joe did. It isn't that kickers aren't supposed to get hit in football, but no team can afford to lose its specialists to cheap shots. This was the message Joe sent to his counterpart on the other side of the field that day, and Bud Riley got the message.

Joe chewed tobacco, which, of course, made him a big hit with the offensive linemen, affectionately known as hoggies. For the uninitiated, chewing is the act of placing wadded tobacco either in the lower lip or "between the cheek and gum" as the ads used to say. The by-product of this activity is a great deal of spitting. Ken Clark had warned me early in 1982 never to stand downwind of Joe. At first I wasn't sure why this was important, but I was soon to learn that those Saskatchewan winds have the same effect on tobacco juice that they have on footballs.

I was to cross paths with Joe again in 1987 in Montreal where he had taken over as coach of the Alouettes. Joe ran a great camp in Montreal and in my estimation had the franchise survived, we were going to be a hell of a football team that year. In Montreal my competition for the kicking job was the incumbent, Roy Kurtz. I was a little worried about the situation and early in camp talked to Assistant Coach Kevin Gilbride, who eventually would become the quarterbacking coach of the Houston Oilers and was involved in the infamous sideline altercation with Buddy Ryan in 1993. During the conversation I expressed concern about my future with the team and the fact that my wife, Nancy, was back in Cleveland waiting word on whether we'd be residents of the city of Montreal in 1987.

Not long afterward Joe cornered me after practice and we had a chat. As we talked it became clear that Joe and Kevin had discussed my situation. Joe asked me point-blank if I was worried about winning the kicking job. I told him I was damn worried about it. Montreal wasn't my town, I had no history of kicking there and I was competing against a two-year veteran. Joe laughed, put his hand on my shoulder and pointed to a phone booth. He said, "Why don't you just go over there and call Nancy and tell her to pack her things and come on up to Montreal." We hadn't even played a preseason game to this point, but Joe, as he had done in Saskatchewan, was telling me to relax and do the things he knew I was capable of.

A Few Good Men – The Early Years

The only bright spot out of the whole trade nightmare that followed the 1986 season was the fact that I eventually wound up on another team that was coached by Papa Joe. Of course, neither he nor I had any idea just how brief our time together would be that second time around.

Stewie *(Stew Fraser)*

I've already mentioned that the first member of the Saskatchewan Roughriders I met en route to my first Riders' training camp back in 1982 was Stewart Fraser. I couldn't have picked a better guy to be my first close friend in professional football.

Stew would be the first person to say that he was not a gifted athlete in the true sense of the word. He was, however, a *good* athlete and a great team player who would do whatever was asked of him to benefit the ball club. He was an excellent possession-receiver, a dependable kick-returner and, most important to me, a very good holder on place-kicks.

Stewie had a knack for lifting the spirits of the other guys on the team when we were having a bad practice or suffering a losing streak. He'd often do this with a spectacular, diving, fingertip catch or by making some other impossible play when it really wasn't necessary to put out that kind of effort, especially in practice. But in almost every instance players and coaches alike would respond to Stewie's example and the tone of the practice would turn upbeat.

Special team players—long-snappers, holders, punters, returners and place-kickers—are always the first to go onto the field for pregame warm-ups because they need most of the field to do what they do. This is also the time I invariably begin to get nervous about the upcoming game. Maybe this was the reason Stew's pregame ritual drove me crazy. He was seldom ready when the time came for us to go onto the field.

Stew liked to spend an inordinate amount of time in the bathroom prior to each game. To Stewie, the john was a social place, a place where, for example, he could wad up a piece of toilet paper and play volleyball with the guy in the next cubicle.

Stew liked to sit in there with the door open so he could converse with anyone who happened to be around. During the forty-five minutes or so he was encamped, he would put on his equipment piece by piece. Then he would finish his preparation by brushing his teeth. I always meant to ask Stew if that was a New Brunswick thing or just a Stew Fraser thing, but I never did.

I wasn't the only one upset about Stew's penchant for hanging out in washrooms. It used to drive Roger Aldag crazy. Roger was always dressed and ready to go four hours ahead of the opening kickoff. As game time neared he'd storm up to me and yell, "Get that Newfie sonofabitch out of the can. Get him out of there!"

To which I could only shrug my shoulders. Stew was Stew. The result of Stew's fastidiousness was that we never got onto the field as quickly as Roger and I would have liked. But, by God, when we got there Stewart Fraser was the most relaxed and best-groomed player on the field.

Maybe the most important thing in Stewie's life was his love for all things Maritime. He loved to talk about the Miramichi and about hunting fiddleheads back home. Every year he would arrive at training camp with the latest game or some other paraphernalia currently popular in New Brunswick. His love for playing the spoons and for listening to the bagpipes drove his teammates nuts. His talent with spoons was not limited to making music. He could also hang a dozen or so from his face. I was never sure just how he did this, but it had something to do with getting a little condensation on the spoon and then cupping it against the part of the face he wanted it to hang from. Even as I write about it now, long after the fact, it sounds weird.

One of the other joys of Stew's life, which he was only too willing to share with unappreciative teammates, was Stompin' Tom Connors. Stew loved Stompin' Tom's music and could remember every song his hero had recorded. I personally have nothing against Stompin' Tom's talents, but after you've heard "The girls are playin' bingo and the boys are gettin' stinko" three thousand times or so, it begins to wear a little thin. But it never wore thin for Stewie. In fact it wouldn't surprise me if he starts his physical education classes at Salisbury High School in Moncton, where he now teaches, with a few laps around the gym to the strains of Stompin' Tom.

Stew's parents used to take the train into Montreal to watch him play, and I had the privilege of meeting them and other members of his family. In 1990 I visited the Maritimes to speak at a banquet, and I renewed acquaintances with Stew's mom and dad. It was great to see them again. During my stay Stewie took me around to the places he had talked about when we were teammates, and I finally understood why it meant so much to him. The country around Moncton has to be some of the most beautiful anywhere. He took me to one of his favorite places, which happens to be one of the holes at a local golf course. Though it was the off-season and the course was closed, Stewie had thrown a couple of clubs and a dozen or so range balls in the back of his car. He was right. It was one of the most spectacular holes I had ever seen. We drove golf balls from the tee-box at the top of a bluff onto the fairway far below. While we were hitting down to the fairway, a huge elk trotted out of the bush and across our field of vision. It was a moment that said a lot about the kind of person Stew Fraser is.

In 1985 Stew was traded to Ottawa. I was devastated at the prospect of losing one of my best friends. There's a tradition that calls for a traded player's teammates to take him out on the town for a little farewell party, the idea being to help the departing player forget his troubles. On this occasion we went to Bartleby's, one of the places frequented by the team in those days. After several hours of serious forgetting Stew was barely able to walk and I said to the guys, "Hey, I gotta get him home, you guys are gonna kill him." This, as you might guess, was greeted by a chorus of boos (and booze) but I got Stew out of there and we headed for his place where his wife, Patty, was hosting a little farewell party with the wives. When we got there and Stew had managed to get himself together a bit, he came over and put his arms around me and we both shed some tears. Only one other time in my career, when Coach John Gregory was fired, did I react as emotionally as I did when Stewie left the Riders. If there's a heaven for people who have played this game, Stew Fraser, the overgrown kid from the Maritimes, will be guaranteed a spot, believe me.

The Woz *(Lyall Woznesensky)*

The Woz was the personification of the wild man athlete. During most of the time he played in Regina, he was single and all the stories one hears from time to time about the off-field antics of football players were probably true in the case of the Woz and in some cases likely understated.

I only played one year with Woz but I remember him, along with Mike Samples and Ken Clark, as three of the truly free spirits of the game. With Woz around the fun never stopped. Even during our warm-up prior to a game it wasn't unusual to hear him suddenly yell, "Hey, Samps, will you tell Janet [Mike's wife] to quit phoning me, and by the way I'm tired of your kids calling me dad."

During our 1983 training camp Woz was caught sneaking out after curfew. He had someone pull into the University of Saskatchewan grounds near our dormitory and was creeping along the wall of Qu'Appelle Hall trying to be invisible as he made his escape. One of the coaches, Monte Charles, spotted him and yelled down from his room, "Hey, Woz, you should tell her to turn the lights off while she's waiting." Which sent the Woz slinking back to the dorm, sorry only that he'd been caught. I'm not sure it would have worked anyway because we also had bed check during camp. The Woz, instead of stuffing the bed with pillows to give the illusion he was in there, placed four cardboard boxes in the bed and pulled the covers over them. This was Woz's way. He wasn't a big believer in team rules, and the boxes were his way of saying, "Hah, gotcha again."

The Woz bounced around from team to team during his career, and I have no idea if that was due in part to his craziness off the field. I do know this: nobody enjoyed the game more than the Woz.

Clarkie *(Ken Clark)*

If I were to attribute the longevity of my career to one person, this individual would be Ken Clark. His counsel, his patience in showing me the ropes of professional football and his attitude toward the game and life were invaluable to a young place-kicker trying to find his way.

I was quoted during my rookie season as saying that when I was in high school, Ken Clark had been one of my heroes. Ken made out that he was upset by the remark because it suggested he was old, but my statement was absolutely true. Ken had a splendid career, which included a Super Bowl appearance with the L. A. Rams, and he was plain and simple one of the best kickers in the game. I was on the sidelines when he unloaded the 101-yard punt that still stands as a Rider record. Ken was stationed just outside our end zone and I was at about midfield. When that ball passed me it was still climbing. His 45.6-yard career punting average stands as a CFL record as does his single-game average of 60.2 yards per kick.

Early in the 1982 season, after I had made the team, Ken saw me punting a ball to a teammate during practice. He came over and said, "Hey, let's make a pact to keep two guys employed. I won't place-kick and you won't punt." It was a wise suggestion and one I have since made to more than one punter on the team.

Later that year while Kenny and I were standing on one side of our practice field, one of the coaches called for a ball. I took one out of the bag and punted it to him. Kenny walked over, picked up my kicking tee and a ball and headed onto the field to kick a field goal. Then he walked back and without a word returned the tee. I got the message and this was the last time I ever punted a ball in practice while Ken was with the team.

Ken was among the most prolific and creative practical jokers to ever come through this or any other league. He dared to take on the hoggies, who for the most part could best be described as . . . well . . . rednecks. One of their trademark practices—before the Surgeon General began making pronouncements on its threat to the health—was to dip, or as the practice is also known, to chew.

A Few Good Men – The Early Years

During my rookie year Ken and the hoggies were at each other almost constantly. Ken finally had tolerated all he could of Bob Poley, Lawrie Skolrood and the others and decided to exact a little retribution. So he dug up a bunch of fat, wiggly worms and a few dozen ants. These he diced and deposited in the tobacco pouches of Messrs. Skolrood and Poley and waited for the fun to begin. It almost worked. Skolrood pulled a wad out of its satchel and had it almost to his mouth when he noticed an odd smell, as one might expect from a rotting compost of dead worms and ants. Skolrood detected the tainted substance just in time, but I never found out if Poley discovered the switch or not. My guess is it wouldn't have mattered a hell of a lot to Polecat anyway—he would have gone on chewing and enjoying it.

Another of Ken's coups took place after practice one night. On this occasion he was aided and abetted by the usually angelic Norm Fong. Clarkie got hold of Poley's pants and stitched up one of the legs. When we got back to the locker room after practice, Ken, whose locker was next to mine, leaned over and whispered, "Don't leave. You gotta see this."

When Poley got to the pants he stood, inserted one leg and then tried the other. When the second foot reached the obstruction he hopped around for a while, then realizing he'd been had, fell over sideways, laughing all the way down.

I was Ken Clark's victim more than once, and one of those pranks was a classic. After the 1982 season I went back to Ohio, and Nancy and I were married in Cleveland. The USFL was in operation, and I received a phone call from the head coach of the Chicago Blitz, who told me I had been scouted by their team and they were interested in signing me. I was all ears. Not that I didn't love playing in Saskatchewan, but the USFL was reportedly throwing around some serious money, and if they wanted to throw some of it my way I was at least ready to listen.

I pointed out to the coach that I had signed a three-year deal with the Riders. He indicated they could get me out of my deal with Saskatchewan if I were interested in playing in Chicago. He told me they were willing to pay me one hundred thousand dollars a year. I told him, yes, I would play for the Blitz for that kind of money if they could get me out of my contract with the Riders.

At this point the voice on the other end of the line said, "Ridge, it's Clarkie." It was a few seconds before I was able to put together what had happened because the truth is, in my mind, I had already spent about half of my first year's salary with the Blitz. This is not a story I have told many people over the years, but I will now admit publicly that Kenny got me good. The son of a bitch.

Skullie *(Lawrie Skolrood)*

Most players in professional sports have nicknames. Some are fairly obvious like Suits for Suitor, Polecat for Poley, Ridge for Ridgway and so on. Sometimes, however, the nickname will make some editorial comment about the person it designates. Take, for example, Lawrie Skolrood, the offensive lineman who put in ten seasons in the Green and White. He had two nicknames: Skullie, the obvious one, and Wookie, maybe not so obvious. He was given the second name because he was as big as the Star Wars' character Chewbacca and because at times he was almost as hairy, having sported a beard from time to time.

He and his wife, Vicki, became close friends with Nancy

A Few Good Men – The Early Years

and I, and we spent a lot of time together, particularly once both couples began to have children.

During our 1984 training camp, Trivial Pursuit was the game of choice for passing time between practices. Almost everybody on the team enjoyed playing it and some guys had the game in their rooms. Athletes being athletes, the games were often very competitive. One evening after practice and the day's meeting several of us became involved in an intense match in one of the rooms on the first floor of Qu'Appelle Hall. Ken Clark, Stew Fraser and I were pitted against Skullie, Greg Fieger and Gerry Hornett. A little beer had been consumed to properly prepare our minds for the challenges that lay ahead. But what made this game especially memorable was its connection to an incident that had taken place earlier in the day.

That afternoon, as we were returning from practice, Stew Fraser had spotted a flower in the middle of a dense patch of green foliage. Not just any flower, mind you, but a lily of the valley, which didn't mean a hell of a lot to the rest of us but was a big deal to the eccentric kid from the Maritimes.

Stew dived into the bushes and picked the flower. So much for conservation. He was ecstatic about it. He went from player to player and held the flower under their noses so they could enjoy its beauty and fragrance. Later in the dining hall, while we were lined up to get our dinner, Stew repeated the performance, once again presenting the flower to different guys and saying stuff like, "Isn't it beautiful? Can't you just smell it?" To which most of us, not as cognizant of the joys of nature, replied, "Yeah, right, now get the damn thing out of here. I'm trying to get my food."

While we were eating Stew continued to pass the flower around. Eventually it was Skullie's turn to appreciate this example of Mother Nature's handiwork. Skullie took one cursory glance at the flower, stuffed it in his mouth and ate it. This put an end to the whole cosmic experience.

Later that night, after the Trivial Pursuit game had gone on a long time and everybody was tired and slightly inebriated, our opponents landed on the science category. It was Clarkie's turn to ask the question. He looked at the card and finally, without a hint of a smile, asked, "What flower, indigenous to the Maritimes, can trigger a hallucinogenic reaction if ingested?"

The other three huddled up and after considerable discussion offered an answer, something like the poppy. Clarkie flipped the card over as if checking the answer and said, "Nope, it's the lily of the valley." He then deposited the card back in the deck without anybody else seeing it.

At first there was no reaction and it wasn't until Horns (Gerry Hornett) was midway through asking the next question that Skullie, who had been leaning back and (I guess) thinking, suddenly bolted upright and in a panic-stricken voice yelled, "Hey, I ate one of those!" The look on his face matched the tone of his voice, and it was obvious he was trying to figure out if the flower's effects had begun to kick in. I don't think Skullie ever ate another flower.

This wasn't the last time the big guy and mind-expanding substances were to meet face to face with interesting results. The second incident took place during a flight back from Hamilton. Skullie had got up from his seat on the aircraft, a regularly scheduled commercial flight, and made his way to the washroom. It was occupied. While he was waiting a Regina businessman came and took his place in line behind Skullie.

Eventually the person in the washroom came out. It turned out to be Thomas Boyd, a linebacker on the ball club. Lawrie went into the bathroom but he wasn't in there long. A few seconds later he stormed out and headed straight down the aisle to where Thomas was sitting. Skullie was visibly upset and reached down and grabbed hold of Thomas and was doing a lot of close talking and finger-pointing—in fact everything short of hitting him. At this point Joe Adams got out of his seat and got into it by talking a lot of trash to Skullie, which didn't help to calm the situation. Bryan Illerbrun was next to get involved, and he grabbed Lawrie and pushed him back into his seat in an effort to play peace-keeper.

What had upset Skullie was that it was obvious the previous occupant had been smoking grass in the washroom. Skullie was angry that this would happen on a commercial flight because it was a given that one thing we did not do was embarrass the team in public. He was outraged that the gentleman next in line for the washroom might have concluded that Skullie was the guilty party.

When Skullie got back into his seat he was still very angry about the incident and proceeded to throw back a lot of beer. Eventually he got up and again went to Thomas Boyd's seat and this time got a little more physical with him. Illie took hold of Skullie a second time and pretty well threw him back into the row of seats where he had been sitting. Also sitting in that row were Al Johns and his wife, Lori. All 280 pounds of Lawrie Skolrood landed on Lori Johns, who was in the middle seat. At this point Al Johns was mad at Skullie. Skullie was mad at Illie and Thomas Boyd. Illie was mad at Skullie and Joe Adams, who had entered the confrontation again to defend Thomas, and suddenly we had a pretty good brouhaha taking place at thirty-seven thousand feet.

Eventually things became more or less peaceful, and I don't think any of the coaches or management ever found out what had been the root cause of the problem. The incident was indicative of how Lawrie Skolrood felt—as a lot of us have—about what it means to wear the uniform of the Saskatchewan Roughriders. Skullie was a damn good lineman and a damn good guy who cared about his team in every way.

747 *(Joe Adams)*

Not all my people memories are happy ones, particularly those of players with tremendous ability who for whatever reason never reached their potential. Maybe the saddest example of such a player was Joe Adams.

Joe came to the Saskatchewan Roughriders the same year I did—1982. The year before, the Riders had used the quarterbacking tandem of Joe Barnes and John Hufnagel. J.J. Barnagel, as the duo became known, missed by a whisker leading the team to a playoff spot. After the 1981 season Barnes was dealt to Ottawa, and to fill the vacancy at quarterback the Roughriders had recruited a rocket-armed kid out of Tennessee State. His name was Joe Adams.

A tall, tremendously athletic guy, Joe had the skills of a Warren Moon. Unfortunately this was where any comparison between the two ended. Warren Moon was intelligent, level-headed and a gifted leader. Joe was not. Had he been, I believe he could have had an outstanding career in professional football.

Joe's off-field activities were not the kind encouraged by a sports organization. He was arrested for shoplifting and also got into trouble for leaving a liquor store and a gas station without paying. In a close-knit community like Regina, where the spotlight tends to be very intense on high-profile people like athletes and entertainers, it's almost impossible to escape the public eye. Misbehavior that might not receive a lot of attention in Toronto or Vancouver is a very big deal in the Reginas and Saskatoons of the world. The glare of the spotlight is even more intense, I believe, for a black athlete in a community that has a very small black population and in fact where there is a good chance the black male encountered on the street is a member of the football team.

I can't confirm or deny the rumors rampant at the time that Joe Adams was heavily into drugs. I can testify he arrived for practice several times in what was clearly an altered state of consciousness. But what he had been doing or taking to get him to that point I can't say because I don't honestly know. One incident I do recall occurred late in the 1982 season. John Hufnagel had been hurt and Joey was to be the starting quarterback for the upcoming game. It was a perfect opportunity for him to really assert himself as a leader. Instead he showed up late for the morning practice before the game, and when he did arrive it was obvious he'd had a bad night.

On the first snap from center, Joe pulled back, howling in pain. It turned out he'd dislocated the middle finger on his throwing hand, and even though the injury put our quarterbacking situation into disaster mode, a lot of the guys were rolling on the ground laughing. The prevailing feeling was that Joe deserved whatever happened to him for showing up late and in bad shape for practice. Unfortunately the incident was a precursor of what was to come in Joe's brief and troubled stay in the CFL.

During the two seasons Joey was with our ball club the supporting cast around him was not the most talented group. Nevertheless, he showed flashes of brilliance. So much so that the coaches did not want to believe the stories becoming more and more abundant about the dark side of Joe Adams' life. But by early in the 1983 season it was clear to everybody that he was a liability and had to go.

It was sad to watch someone with his natural talent and one of the best arms the Canadian Football League had ever seen throw away a chance for almost certain stardom. And the time wasted on developing Joe Adams was part of the reason it took until 1987 (and coincidentally the arrival of Tom Burgess and Kent Austin) for the ball club to finally make a serious move toward respectability. Joe Adams could have been one of a few especially celebrated athletes. That he never achieved his potential is a tragedy.

Harley *(Ray Elgaard)*

Twenty years from now when people are discussing all-time Rider greats, I'm betting Ray Elgaard's name will come up constantly. Ray already holds virtually every team receiving mark as well as the CFL records for most career receptions and most career passing yardage.

Ray is a rarity. He is one of the few hits of the hit-and-miss Air Herrera years. He came to the Riders as a draft choice out of Utah in 1983, and we became friends almost instantly, partly because we had both played our college careers under Coach Chuck Stobart. I had played for him at Toledo before he moved on to Utah. Ray hadn't enjoyed playing under Chuck. The year before Chuck's arrival Ray had been an important part of Utah's potent passing attack. The new coach implemented a three-yards-and-a-cloud-of dust offense that didn't complement Ray's talents as a receiver, and he consequently became something of a forgotten man.

PHOTO: BILL DUBECKY, ROYAL STUDIOS

November 1989: The biggest kick of my life.

PHOTO: BILL DUBECKY, ROYAL STUDIOS

Suits pins the Cup. Dick Adams and Tuineau Alipate look on.

Glen Suitor lays on a massive hit.

Glen Suitor gets all wrapped in his birthday celebration, Grey Cup week, 1989.

Father and Sons: L-R: *me, John, Leonard and Neil.*

PHOTO: BILL DUBECKY, ROYAL STUDIOS

Two greats friends: Ken Clark (left) and Randy Pollock (center).

Bob Poley (left) discusses borrowing Bobby Jurasin's bandanna.

Team trainer Ivan Gutfriend–the witch doctor.

Ray Elgaard models the latest in fashion sunglasses.

Norm Fong holds court for Suits (left), Big Lew (center) and me.

The pride of Gull Lake, Saskatchewan: Mr. Saskatchewan Roughrider Roger Aldag, with the Grey Cup.

An early field goal attempt as a University of Toledo Rocket, vs. Ohio University, 1979.

A multiple-exposure action shot. The guy watching his fingers is Suits.

The worst moment of my professional career happened during the 1992 Western Semi-Final at Commonwealth Stadium in Edmonton. Elston's cartoon said it all.

The Saskatchewan Roughriders before the 1989 Western Final against the Eskimos.

The Saskatchewan Roughriders after the 1989 Western Final against the Eskimos.

TOP: *Quiet time with Drew (left) and Christopher.*
BOTTOM: *Yin and Yang try out some early football helmets.*

PHOTO: CHRIS TRIFFO, CSC

A Few Good Men – The Early Years

Ray had an excellent rookie year with the Riders. He came to us as a big, tough-looking kid almost in the biker mold and as a result was given the nickname Harley. He was quiet during his rookie camp in 1983, but that didn't keep him from giving one of the more dramatic performances in the history of the Rookie Show. Near the end of his act Ray called a few of the offensive and defensive linemen to the front of the room and after first giving a speech in praise of them asked each to spit into a glass, into which he had poured maybe an inch of beer. Ray swished the mixture around a couple of times and downed it. Several of us, including Coach Joe Faragalli, nearly became ill. For sheer impact nobody has equaled Ray's stunt. All the linemen gave the new kid their instant approval, and he was never hassled again during his rookie training camp.

I recall one of our trips to Ray's hometown of Vancouver not long after he joined the team. Ray hadn't seen his mom for a while, and as we were getting on the bus to go from the airport to the stadium, a lady suddenly ran onto the front of the bus, and in a high-pitched voice called, "Raymond . . . Raymond," as only a mother can. Ray sheepishly replied, "Over here, Mom." Instantly the camera came out and for several minutes she shot pictures of everybody on the bus while carrying on a conversation with her son. It was a touching moment and I think all the guys enjoyed it, including *Raymond*.

Ray reminds me of what I think the game was played like in the fifties and sixties when people like Jimmy Brown and George Reed were dominant forces in their respective leagues. He exudes the toughness of those guys, particularly in the way he carries the ball after he has made a catch. It almost always takes three of four tacklers to bring him down. Ray plays the game with reckless abandon and from the heart and is absolutely deserving of every record he holds.

ROBOKICKER

J. P. *(Joe Paopao)*

Joe Paopao had more heart and gave more of himself to playing this game and trying to win than anyone I have ever played with. I realize this is quite a statement to make, considering I have been fortunate enough to play with the likes of Elgaard, Poley, Aldag and a host of other dedicated people. Nevertheless, I don't think I'll ever meet anyone who cared more or gave more to football than Joe Paopao.

I'm certain most people have no idea of the tremendous character of Joe Paopao. Fans tend to focus on the win-loss record, and during the bad times it's often the quarterback who shoulders most of the blame. Unfortunately J. P., like Joe Adams before him, played in Saskatchewan during the mid-eighties when we were a pretty bad football team. He simply wasn't surrounded by the talent to help him get the job done. Joe by the way never shrunk from shouldering the responsibility for our lack of success.

One game that symbolizes the intensity and desire that was Joe Paopao took place in 1986. J. P. went into the game on a bad knee. That was also characteristic of this man who never took himself out of the lineup for an injury even though he was often hobbled, particularly later in his career. In this game Joe was sacked near the end of the first half. When he got back to the huddle, Joe had tears in his eyes because of the pain. Roger Aldag told him to take a knee and they'd get him to the sidelines. Joe shook his head. He wanted to continue. Finally, a couple of plays later, the guys on the field were able to convince Joe to leave the game.

Our young backup quarterback, Mike Kelley, came in and on his third play got hit and winded. The kid staggered back to the huddle and squeaked to his teammates that he didn't think he could continue. Roger grabbed the rookie by the jersey and snarled, "Listen, we've had a quarterback playing on one leg for half the season and you want out of here because you got winded? Shut the hell up and call the play." The kid decided he could continue after all. The incident was one of those that doesn't get written up in the game summaries, but it points out clearly the regard we all had for Joe.

After Stew Fraser left for the Ottawa Rough Riders and before Glen Suitor became our permanent holder for place-kicks, the coaches decided they wanted one of the quarterbacks to do the holding. As I'm a right-footed kicker the holder's job is to catch the snap from center and place the ball down with the left hand and spin it with the right so the laces are away from my foot on contact. It's essential that the holder get his right hand out of the way by the time my foot is coming through the ball. If he fails, his hand will slow the progress of the ball and he will likely end up injured. When I was in university a biomechanics class ran a test to determine the speed of one of my kicked balls. They calculated that as the ball leaves my foot it is traveling at a speed of one hundred and twenty feet per second (approximately eighty miles per hour).

During a practice, as Joe and I were working on our timing, he got his right hand out of the way as he was supposed to, but instead of bringing it toward himself he moved it forward and in front of the ball. The ball struck Joe's hand and I knew right away he was hurt. The incident was captured by a *Leader-Post* photographer who happened to be at practice that day. The picture showed Joe on his knees and in a great deal of pain. I felt terrible. To make matters worse it was his throwing hand that was hurt. Joe, as we had come to expect, played in the next game, but it was the last time he held for me.

Joe's competitive spirit isn't limited to football. During the off-season a few years ago, Nancy and I were visiting with Joe and Dottie at their home in Oceanside, California. Joe, a couple of his brothers and I decided to celebrate with a boys' night out. I made the mistake of trying to keep up with the Paopao boys. It was no contest. The result was that the next morning I declined to make the planned trip to Knott's Berry Farm, opting instead to put myself on the injured reserve list. Not Joe. He was up early and in fine form as he gathered everybody together for the day's excursion.

Joe was one CFL player who maintained a high profile in the United States. I recall on one of my trips back to Ohio that when Joe's name came up it was recognized by a number of people. I also remember a time in Los Angeles when Joe, Dottie, Nancy and I went to the Hard Rock Cafe. While we were eating, someone in the cafe recognized Joe. It was clear our "Throwin' Samoan" had fans on both sides of the Forty-ninth Parallel. He deserved them.

Joe Paopao was one of those guys you'd like your son to grow up to be like or your daughter to marry. He was a family man, a great team leader and in my opinion the definitive fierce competitor. In recent years J. P. has been considered for a couple of head coaching jobs in the CFL. I hope he will one day be a head coach in this league, and if his players give anything close to what he did when he played, they will be one tough team.

Polecat *(Bob Poley)*

I am proud to call Bob Poley a friend. When he was sent to the Stampeders it was a blow to our ball club and to me personally, and one of the happiest moments of my life was when Bob came back to the Riders a couple of years later.

A Few Good Men – The Early Years

After his return Polecat loved to needle me about Calgary place-kicker J. T. Hay. He was forever telling me what a great kicker and what a great guy J. T. was (he was right on both counts by the way) and whenever we went into Calgary he'd make sure I knew he was going out after the game for a couple of beers with his pal, J. T. I only hope Polecat spent just as much time bugging J. T. about what a good kicker and fine person Dave Ridgway is!

Polecat was very much the entertainer, and he was a pretty good one. He spent many hours picking the guitar and entertaining at training camp. Bob also loved to hunt, and one of his favorite pranks was to bring a dead goose to practice and keep it stuffed under his jersey until the coach indicated the time was appropriate for the caper. Bob would snap the bird to the quarterback, who was in on the joke, and he would hand it off to a rookie running back. The rookie would usually take a couple of steps before he realized what he was carrying. It was amazing what bad hands some of those guys developed when they looked down and saw what they were hugging to their bodies.

Another of Bob's favorites revolved around his bad knees. By bad I'm referring not only to the injuries they suffered over the years but also to their being unquestionably the ugliest knees on the planet. He is able to bend one of them at an unbelievable angle. Polecat loved to drive rookies nuts by making the knee form some abstract geometrical shape and limping up and down the dressing room like he was in agony. The guys who didn't know about the knee would cringe as they watched him and imagined the pain he must be feeling.

Over the years there have been some classic running feuds between guys on the team, feuds that ran the entire course of time they were teammates. These feuds were of the fun variety and featured a never-ending effort on the part of both guys to play the better practical joke on the other. That was the case with Bob and Ken Clark when they played together, and the results were often hilarious as they played prank after prank on each other. After the chewing tobacco and sewed-up pants incidents Polecat wanted revenge. He recruited a couple of the other hoggies to help him. One day after practice they picked up Kenny and carried him to the east end of our practice field, which at the time was a virtual swamp. They held Kenny upside down and swung him back and forth a few times before launching him into the middle of the slough. It wasn't what you would call a prank with finesse, but it was effective. Not to be outdone, Clarkie frolicked around in the goo for a while, doing the breast stroke and crawl like it was very pleasurable swim.

Bob maintains to this day that when we kicked the winning field goal in the 1989 Grey Cup game he had the most difficult job. And he's at least partly right. Without the snap being right on the money there would probably have been no kick. Of course, Suitor makes the same claim about his hold for that kick, and I'd like to think I had a small part to play in it myself. To hear Poley tell it though, it was a *damn* small part.

Bob Poley and linemate Roger Aldag were inseparable. Just as Suits and I took a lot of flack for always being together, Polecat and Rodge did too. They heard all the cracks about Mr. and Mrs. Poley. (Come to think of it they heard a lot of them *from* Glen and me.)

Glen and I were wrongly accused of putting one over on Bob when we were in Edmonton for the 1992 Western Semi-Final. It was a good prank though and to tell the truth I wish we had been responsible. Suits and I had just got back to the hotel after dinner and a movie and we were almost to our room when we heard a hushed, "Hey, you two shitheads, get over here."

A Few Good Men – The Early Years

We turned around to see Polecat standing in the hall, clad only in a pair of flowered boxer shorts and a T-shirt. He didn't look happy. We followed him into his room and Bob looked at us and said, "Okay, where's my bed?"

We looked around the room and saw that Bob was absolutely right. There was only one bed in the room, which was occupied by Aldag, who was already asleep. We started to laugh and Bob hushed us, saying, "Shush, you'll wake up Rodge." This, of course, made us laugh even harder, at which point Aldag growled, "Shut up, will you, I'm trying to get some sleep."

As we continued to look around the room we noticed over in one corner a metal foldaway cot, the kind that's about a three feet wide. (Bob is about four and a half feet wide.) Glen and I told Polecat we didn't have anything to do with the missing bed. Bob confided that the bed was not all that was gone—his clothes and shaving kit were also AWOL. Bob had phoned the desk of the hotel to tell them of his plight and they had accommodated by sending him the nice cot.

We finally managed to convince Bob we were innocent and headed back to our room. But the vision of Polecat trying to arrange his bulk onto that cot in something that resembled comfort had us laughing long into the night.

Bob Poley was one of the best offensive linemen ever to play in the CFL. He was an outstanding blocker and an excellent long-snapper. The Roughriders have, I think, been very good about honoring past players so I wish they had seen fit to retire Bob's jersey at the same time they retired the sweater of Roger Aldag. It would have been fitting, not only because of how close the two were, but also because of the enormous contribution Bob, like Roger, made to the Saskatchewan Roughriders.

ROBOKICKER

Rodge *(Roger Aldag)*

To the last couple of generations of Roughrider fans, Roger Aldag is Mr. Saskatchewan Roughrider. With his record of service to the club both on and off the field there is absolutely no doubt this is exactly the way it should be.

Rodge is one of only seven Rider players to have had his number retired, joining number 23 Ron Lancaster, number 34 George Reed and the four players who were killed in the plane crash in 1956, number 40 Mel Becket, number 55 Mario DeMarco, number 56 Ray Syrnyk and number 73 Gordon Sturtridge.

I know one of the big disappointments of Roger's career came when he just missed setting a CFL record for most consecutive games played. The mark of 254 was set by Dave Cutler and Roger had closed to within four of the record when he suffered the most serious injury of his career, a badly torn-up knee, and was forced out of action in game 250. Roger's ironman reputation was all the more significant for his being an offensive lineman.

One of the things a lot of people may not know about Roger is that he had a habit of vomiting prior to just about every game and often at half-time as well. Like Glenn Hall, the Hall of Fame NHL goaltender, Roger got so worked up before a game that he literally made himself sick.

Rodge, like a lot of ballplayers, had a few superstitious rituals he adhered to religiously. One was that he would allow only Norm Fong to pull his jersey on for him. And once again truth becomes stranger than fiction. For the game on which his consecutive-game streak ended at 250, Roger had someone else help him with his jersey.

Everyone who played with Roger had tremendous respect

for him as a player and as a person. At the end of my rookie season he paid me a compliment that I still remember very well. I had wandered over to the part of the dressing room known as Hoggy Heaven and Rodge looked up at me from where he was sitting and said, "If we'd had you on this team last year, we might have won the whole thing." I don't know if that was true, but I certainly appreciated hearing it, and I especially appreciated hearing it from the likes of Roger Aldag.

Roger won just about every award an offensive lineman can win, including several All-Star honors, but just as important was the leadership he provided every time he stepped onto the field.

I doubt if anybody on the Roughriders was more relieved and happy than the guy from Gull Lake, Saskatchewan, when we finally won the Grey Cup in 1989. Roger had been on the sidelines for the Grey Cup loss in 1976. He was nearing the end of his career in 1989, and I'm sure the thought must have crossed his mind that he might never get the coveted ring. But as glad as he was to win it I don't know if he could have been any happier than all of us were *for* him because no one deserved a Grey Cup any more than Roger Aldag.

CHAPTER 8

A Few More Good Men - The Recent Years

Now I might be a dumb jock strapper, but I do know this . . . I'm special just as long as I keep making touchdowns. When that's over . . . it's over.
—EVERYBODY'S ALL-AMERICAN, 1988

As I LOOK AT THE YEARS after our Grey Cup win I see a different attitude in Saskatchewan and the ball club. That old joke "Will the last person leaving Saskatchewan please turn out the lights?" is as outdated as *Gilligan's Island* reruns. And about as funny. Just as the province is a happier and more optimistic place in the nineties, the Saskatchewan Roughriders team approaches each season in a similar, upbeat way—not just hoping to win but believing it can. From general manager to ball boy, everyone associated with the team believes 1989 can and will be repeated. While we have yet to recapture the magic of that Grey Cup win, the despair and disillusionment of the mideighties are long gone. Both the players and coaches who have come to us in the nineties have helped ensure that Rider Pride is back to stay.

A Few Good Men – The Recent Years

John Gregory

I credit John Gregory with the resurrection of my career. At a time when my confidence was at a low John believed in me and helped me restore my belief in myself. It is no coincidence that my kicking percentages improved when he came to the Riders.

He also was one of only two men in the history of the Rider franchise to bring the Grey Cup to Saskatchewan. Just as important, he was absolutely tireless in his efforts to promote the Roughriders in all corners of the province and beyond. In a league that does not have an overabundance of good promoters, I was sorry to see John leave our team and more recently the Canadian Football League.

As the 1990 season got underway a triumphant John Gregory was still at the helm. Naturally there was the possibility and even the expectation we might repeat our Grey Cup victory of the previous year. The team had made some changes due to retirements and a few trades (notably Tom Burgess) going into the season. Nevertheless, the players felt we would be contenders at the very least.

What we didn't realize is that teams come out guns blazing when they play the reigning champs. We should have known this. After all, we had gone through a dozen seasons of gunning for the CFL champions. Even when our record was bad we had no trouble getting ready to play the defending Grey Cup winners. Yet for some reason we completely underestimated this phenomenon following our Grey Cup victory.

Though we slipped into a playoff berth with a 9 and 9 record, identical to 1989, we were speedily dispatched by the Eskimos in a snowbound Commonwealth Stadium. There were, however, some interesting moments that year both for the team and me personally. One such moment took place in game three of the regular season when a half hour before game time, our punter, Mike Lazecki, was nowhere to be found. We learned later that on his way to the game Mike had been pulled over by one of Regina's finest. The officer noticed an outstanding warrant for an unpaid ticket. He decided, incredibly, to take Mike downtown and put him behind bars. In Mike's absence the punting duties would fall to one Dave Ridgway, who prefers to kick balls from tees.

As it turned out the team arranged to have a judge brought in from his weekend off at Regina Beach. Mike was released and made it to the stadium minutes before kickoff. On the first punt of the night the snap went through the hands of an obviously shaken Mike. The ball struck him in the face mask and went straight up in the air. Though he got the kick off it wasn't a classic. I remember thinking, *They should have left him in jail. I could've done that much.*

Later that season we played the Toronto Argonauts at Taylor Field. The Argos at the time were coached by Don Matthews, and to put it simply I couldn't stand the man. I'm sure it had something to do with the reason I disliked Hugh Campbell when he was coach of the Edmonton Eskimos. These two coaches led teams that spent a lot of time kicking our butts. I now have much the same feeling for the Stampeders' Wally Buono for much the same reason.

The Toronto game was a great one. With 46 seconds left on the clock, the Argos scored a touchdown to close to within one point, 40–39. Don Matthews, who I would later learn is an on-the-edge kind of coach, elected to go for the two-point convert, which was successful and put the Argos up by a point. Our ensuing drive began on our 19 and was highlighted by a third-down Austin-to-Elgaard completion at the Toronto 40

A Few Good Men – The Recent Years

with three seconds left on the clock. The field goal attempt into a wind from the Toronto 47 was right at the outside limit, but I felt there was a chance I could make it. The kick was good and we won 43–41. A handful of field goals stand out from all of the others in my career. One, of course, was the Grey Cup kick, another was the 60-yarder to set a distance record and yet another was that kick against Toronto in 1990.

But while I'd had a decent year on the field there is no doubt that once again the greatest thing to happen to me in 1990 took place in a hospital not far from the gridiron. Our second son, Drew Bradley, was born, and for the second time in my life I was made aware that however much I love the game of football nothing will ever approach the joy and pride I felt with the arrival of each of my sons.

Our 1991 season started off badly. We lost our home-opener 34–25 to the Eskimos after blowing a 20–7 lead. What was worse than the loss of the game was losing quarterback Kent Austin, who went down with a separated shoulder on a hit by Larry Wruck. The loss of Kent proved to be disastrous as we went on to win only one of our first seven games. This period featured a couple of more-than-notable losses, one a 54–24 drubbing at the hands of the Eskimos and the other a 62–19 shellacking by Toronto at the SkyDome. After this loss in game six of the season, the cries for John Gregory's head could be heard on several fronts.

The Lions came into Regina the following week and we lost a 50–47 thriller. The game was won on a late B.C. touchdown and subsequent onside kick, which they executed successfully despite our practicing defending against just such a play the entire week before. As we were walking off the field after the game, Roger Aldag and I discussed the likelihood John would be fired and we agreed to take a players' vote of confidence to management in the hope we might be able to head off the move. In the locker room John didn't say much. I think he realized the game was likely his last as coach of the Saskatchewan Roughriders.

Before we even changed out of our uniforms Roger and I asked for a meeting with then team president, Phil Kershaw. Kershaw met with us in Norm Fong's office. Roger and I pleaded John's case, making it clear the players felt it was the loss of Kent Austin, which wasn't something the coach could control, that had led to the team's decline. I believe in retrospect the decision to dump John had been made a week or two earlier. This would explain why Kershaw made it very clear he didn't give a damn what we thought. He didn't want to discuss the issue, which in a way I can understand. No football team can allow the players to call the shots. But the majority of players on the team felt the same way Roger and I did—that our record that year was not a reflection of John Gregory's coaching ability. We didn't have sufficient talent at the backup quarterback position, which meant that when Kent went down so did our fortunes.

I do know that General Manager Alan Ford was in a very unenviable position because he and John were close friends. My guess is that had it been up to Alan he might have given John a vote of confidence and weathered the storm. The team's management committee was feeling antsy, and the coach as is always the case was a handy target. It's an unfortunate truism that when a coach is hired the process leading to his eventual firing is put in motion.

Following his dismissal John was granted permission to address the team. His farewell words were very emotional and a number of guys in the room shed some tears. I admit I was one of them. After the meeting Mike Lazecki came over to ask if I was okay. And I was okay. But I was sorry to see a fine man for whom I had enjoyed playing leave our football club.

Don Matthews

There were immediate rumblings about who would be John's replacement. One of the names that kept popping up was Don Matthews. The possibility presented an interesting dilemma for me because I had already formed a pretty negative opinion about Matthews from playing against him. Still it's important to get off on a good foot with a new boss. I decided to adopt a wait-and-see attitude. It's a good thing I did.

I was just as wrong about Don as I had been about Jack Gotta some years before, except in reverse. Though I hadn't looked forward to playing under Don he turned out to be an excellent coach.

The first difference Don brought to the team was reflected in our practices. With the team having just gone through a shakeup we all felt somewhat tense in practice. This by the way is usually the case after a midseason coaching change. Some players were worried that a Gotta-style housecleaning would be repeated.

Management, the media and some fans shared the opinion that a comfort zone had been extended to some veterans on the ball club. Don made it clear that one of his first priorities was to shake those players out of whatever comfort zone existed. I'm not sure many, if any, players felt they had the right to go half-speed in practice or play with anything less than total intensity in games. Certainly I personally did not then, nor do I now, believe in complacency—but I can say this: Don Matthews almost immediately raised the emotional level of our play.

What was more important though was that our team was still without Kent Austin and we continued to be mediocre. Nevertheless, in our first game with Don at the helm, we went into Edmonton and won a 44–41 barn-burner. As often happens in the first game after the arrival of a new coach, the team managed to put together one of our best efforts in some time.

Don was, and still is, very much his own man. He likes to gamble during games and he encourages his players to do the same. He made it clear that nobody on his football team would be cut for trying to do the little extras or for trying to make the big play. There is no doubt that Don's football philosophy provides fans with a very entertaining product.

One of his innovations on the practice field frustrated some of the team's long-time observers. Don's feeling was that if players were not directly involved in the drill being worked on, they should by all means relax. This meant they could sit or lie down on the field until it was time to be active again. The corollary of the methodology was that they were expected to perform at the highest level of effort and intensity when it came time. This was quite a reversal from how we had practiced in the past when fines were assessed any player caught sitting on his helmet. Most of the players enjoyed this element in the Matthews' practice regime, some more than others. Ray Elgaard was probably the first and best at sprawling out on the turf whenever the opportunity presented itself.

Don felt most comfortable in a small-town atmosphere, which should have been to his advantage in Saskatchewan. But he also was something of an introvert and liked as much as possible to stay out of the limelight associated with the game. He was probably as interested in promoting the team as John Gregory but preferred to put the players in the forefront. He encouraged us to become involved as much as we could with the various charities and organizations that approached us. His particular favorite was the Chili for Children program in Regina that provides hot meals to underprivileged children. Don went so far as to donate all of his speaking fees to the organization. It's unfortunate that almost from the start Don was misunderstood while he was in Saskatchewan.

His one vice, if it can be described as such, was his Harley-Davidson motorcycle. Don was requested by the *Leader-Post* to pose for a publicity shot while riding his Harley down the highway. The photographer asked him to appear without a helmet so his face would be visible. The publicity generated by the photo was largely negative as the province's safety advocates voiced their criticism of Don and the example they felt he was setting. The criticism was one of the few times I ever saw a group of Saskatchewan people, however small, behave in a narrow-minded fashion. The picture was not Don's idea. I never saw him without a helmet *except* in that one photo. Nevertheless, the whole affair may have soured some fans on Don and unwittingly contributed, however unfairly, to the negative opinion some had of him.

Don took pride in having a personal rapport with his players and was genuinely concerned when there was tension in the relationship. He spoke more than once about the strained relationship he'd had with kicker Lance Chomyc. Once, when Lance was having a bad season, Don invited him into his office to ask if there was anything he could do to make Lance more comfortable on the field and improve his success. Lance's reply was that Don should stop giving him the evil eye as he was heading onto the field for field goal attempts. Don would shake his head in the telling of the story and say, "As if I'd put the evil eye on my own kicker in the hope he's going to miss field goals."

Don had a couple of sayings he liked to use in the course of a season. On one occasion he brought all of us together to blast us about the way we had been playing and offered this comment: "Remember this, men, there is a pecking order on this team and I'm the head pecker." Another Matthews-ism was: "Shit rolls downhill and I'm at the top of the pile." We took that to mean that if heads were going to roll, his wouldn't be one of them.

As a keen observer of the game Don noticed things that may have escaped other coaches. For example, he approached me one day and told me he had noticed that my leg appeared to weaken as the season wore on. He suggested I reduce the amount of kicking I was doing during practice. He even went so far as to recommend I take a couple of days off from time to time to preserve the strength in my leg. The results surprised me. I noticed I had better pop in my kicking leg after those occasional days off, and I was still kicking strongly at the end of the season.

During the 1993 season I was fortunate to establish a CFL record for most consecutive field goals. I hit 28 in a row. It was a record I had always hoped to break but one I frankly didn't think I had much of a shot at because I had played my entire career in the prairie wind and weather. In fact Regina is noted for being pro football's windy city. At one point during the streak—I was at about 21 or 22 in a row at the time—Don Matthews opted to punt the ball rather than have me attempt a field goal that had little chance of success. Immediately there were accusations from a number of fans that the coach was trying to preserve my streak. Don and I reacted the same way to the charge. We pointed out that no coach (and certainly not Don Matthews) would put a player's individual achievement ahead of the team's.

As a matter of fact we kicked several long field goals during the streak. Often a coach will ask a place-kicker if he thinks he can make a particular field goal, and the best thing a player can do is be honest about the prospects. A kicker does his team no favor by telling the coach he can kick them from anywhere at anytime. This is especially important because of the CFL rule that brings a missed field goal back to the line of scrimmage for the opposition's possession. Those missed 55- and 60-yarders can give away some awfully good field position.

For the most part Don was fair with me. He had what I would call a Canadian attitude toward kickers, meaning that he understood the importance of kicking in the league and treated me the same way he treated other team members. I enjoyed the Matthews' years and was glad to see his subsequent success with Baltimore.

Ray Jauch

I first met our current coach during my one-practice tryout with the Winnipeg Blue Bombers in 1981. My first impression of Ray Jauch, formed during that brief exposure, was that he was a hard-ass tyrant. Not because he released me—in fact Ray was very considerate during that conversation—but because of the way he ran things on the practice field.

Ray first came to the Roughriders as an assistant to John Gregory, and I think it's fair to say I panicked when I heard he'd been hired. But once again my pre-judging of Rider coaches proved wrong. When John introduced us I refused to take Ray's extended hand, saying, "To hell with that. This guy cut me in '81, and for all I know he might be thinking about doing the same thing again." We had a good laugh. Then we shook hands.

A few seasons later Ray was appointed interim head coach when Don Matthews was ill. After the special teams warm-up preceding a game in Calgary, Ray called Glen and me over and in front of several people told me, "You're cut. Get dressed, you're out of here."

For about a two count I blinked and my mouth fell open. I didn't know what the hell was going on. Then Ray laughed and added, "Okay, you're re-hired. I just wanted to be the only coach in CFL history to cut Dave Ridgway twice." I'm hoping he doesn't decide to go for the hat trick.

In 1994 Ray became the head coach again, this time on a full-time basis, replacing the departed Don Matthews. At this stage, with Ray just entering his second season as *the man*, I can't offer the same perspective on him that I can with the other coaches, simply because he hasn't been at the post that long. (Not to mention that I'd like to remain employed for a while yet.)

I will say this: Ray has mellowed from the time I first saw him coach in Winnipeg. He isn't as quick to chew guys out, and he seems to have developed into a very capable teacher and leader as opposed to someone who just raises hell with players for a poor performance.

During the 1993 season, when Ray was still an assistant, I came out of a meeting and said to Ray Elgaard, "Hey, you know who Ray reminds me of? He reminds me of Luther" (from the TV series *Coach*). Elgaard looked at me and said, "Where have you been? I've been calling him Luther for two years."

Ray is noted for some of his one-liners. In our third or fourth game of 1994 we were leading a team that should have had a clear edge on us, given the number of key players we had lost prior to the start of the season. At half-time Ray went to the center of the room for the traditional pep talk, looked around at us for a while and finally threw his hands in the air. "Hell, I don't know what to say. I thought we'd be down by 14."

One of Ray's recurring practical jokes is a gem. It involves his getting a couple of guys to fake an altercation during a practice. Football players are able to stage make-believe fisticuffs that look very realistic. At about the time a full-scale donnybrook has erupted and everyone else has gathered around to watch the action, Ray pretends to lose it and tries to break up the fight himself. When the two are separated one of the guys mouths off, at which point Ray pulls a gun (a starter's pistol) and plugs him at close range. The effect is predictable. There is stunned silence and disbelief. Finally, when everyone realizes the whole thing is a setup, the place comes apart. It is hands down the most dramatic prank I've ever seen.

Ray Jauch is a very competent coach, but he hasn't forgotten that the game is supposed to be fun. I'd love nothing better than for him to be the third coach in franchise history to bring a Grey Cup to Saskatchewan . . . and for me to be a part of that team.

Millie *(Milson Jones)*

When the discussion turns to underrated players, Milson Jones comes to mind. The Jamaican-English-Canadian running back toiled in Saskatchewan from 1988 to 1992, having previously played with Winnipeg and Edmonton. Milson's name may not show up many times in the CFL record book, but he was enjoyed by fans and appreciated by teammates.

ROBOKICKER

My first recollection of Millie dates from when he was with the Eskimos in the early eighties. We went into Commonwealth Stadium where a very trim Milson Jones took a hand-off and raced 65 yards for the major. What stood out about him, in addition to his obvious talent, was that at a time when everybody with the exception of kickers had followed Billie Johnson's lead and was wearing white shoes, Millie did his scampering in a pair of black soccer shoes.

By the time he got to the Riders Milson had filled out to become the more rotund figure fans recall. But the talent was still there and by 1988 it was coupled with another vital commodity—experience. I have heard more than one Rider fan compare Milson's running style and his ability to run over people to that of the legendary George Reed. I never played with George, but I can testify it often took three or four tacklers to bring down Milson. So perhaps the comparison is valid.

Milson was what is known in football as a gamer. Nobody on the ball club was more mentally and physically prepared for the game. But practice and all other forms of preparing to play were another matter. Millie was habitually late for practice, for films, for meetings, for team meals, for taping. Whatever it was possible to be late for he was late for. But come game day Milson Jones was on time and he was ready.

Millie's intensity was evident during a game in Winnipeg when he was having a running feud with Bombers' defensive back Rod Hill. The conflict went on for about three quarters and Milson finally decided it was time to end it. Not long afterward the two of them met and had it out with some wrestling and a few punches. At one point Millie ended up on his knees and the next thing we saw was Rod Hill writhing around on the ground. Turned out he'd received a punch in the extreme lower abdomen. I'll tell you one thing, Rod Hill became a whole lot more civil out there . . . once he recovered.

Milson and I became good friends while he was with the Riders. Millie, mutual friend Troy Christian and I share a love of R & B music, particularly of the sixties and seventies vintage—people like the Ojays, Earth, Wind and Fire, the Stylistics, the Intruders and Barry White. Milson was pleasantly surprised that a couple of white boys enjoyed his kind of music, and we spent many hours reminiscing about growing up listening to all of those great tunes.

Milson didn't talk much in the dressing room, but when he did everybody listened up. He was one of the quiet leaders on the ball club. Because he had been to a couple of Grey Cups with the Eskimos (and had been Most Valuable Canadian in one) he was tremendously beneficial during 1989 when we made our own run to glory. We were a team of fledglings for the most part when it came to playing in the big one, and Millie's playoff experience and leadership, I believe, played a crucial role in our bringing the Grey Cup back to Saskatchewan.

Big Lew (Gary Lewis)

I will miss Big Lew, a longtime stalwart of the Roughrider defense. He joined the club in 1985 after coming out of Oklahoma State, and every year he came into training camp and won a job. He was a consistent performer, and those of us who played with him game after game believed Big Lew should have been voted to a whole lot more all-star teams.

While Gary was quiet in most respects, his presence was certainly felt around the ball club through his pranks and frequent appearances as the Phantom. He was also the main perpetrator of some infamous bathroom capers in the dressing room that featured a bucket of water spilling onto the unsuspecting occupant of a cubicle. Gary was not in any way discriminatory. He attacked pretty well anybody with the same enthusiasm, whether he was doing his annual switching of defensive backs' helmets, chin straps and underwear or tormenting the hoggies. Big Lew's retirement will bring to an end a colorful period of Rider history, but I personally hope he has passed the mantle of the Phantom to an equally colorful prankster.

Raz *(Dan Rashovich)*

In 1987 the Roughriders had the kind of recruiting year every team would like to have every year. That year we acquired several players who were to figure prominently in our Grey Cup success. Among the new Riders were our quarterbacking tandem of Kent Austin and Tom Burgess, popular defensive back Albert Brown, punter Terry Baker, receiver Don Narcisse and the man we call Raz.

There is, I think, a case to be made for stereotyping in the world of professional football. Take, for example, linebackers. They seem to come from a mold of off-the-wall, live-on-the-edge guys who play with reckless abandon and who put their bodies on the line every time they go onto the field. Players like David Albright, who put in six seasons with the team, Ray Bernard, an outstanding young player who regrettably is now an Ottawa Rough Rider, and Ron Goetz—all share a kind of Psycho Bill mentality on and sometimes off the field. Dan Rashovich is from that mold.

I met Raz when we were both at the Montreal Alouettes' training camp in 1987. I remember being in the kickoff huddle and never feeling so secure as when I saw the look in Dan's eyes. I knew if the opposition was going to make any kind of return it would have to be through at least one player who would die to keep it from happening.

My favorite story about Raz took place during one of the many Save-the-Riders telethons staged over the years. One featured Dan Kepley, a former Edmonton Eskimo and all-time CFL great, who had been brought in by the CBC. After the show a number of us got to talking, and Kep related the story of a recent illness that had all but claimed his life. As his condition worsened and he lapsed into a coma, a priest was brought in to administer last rites. Dan's recovery was miraculous and we were riveted by the telling of it.

The room was utterly silent as we listened to the man who had made such an amazing comeback from a brush with death. As Kep was relating how long he had been in a coma, Dan Rashovich finally broke the silence. "Gee, Kep," Raz said, "You'd think while you were in that coma they could've fixed your fingers."

You have to understand that Kep's hands are right out of Ripley's *Believe it or Not*. I mean these paws took a serious beating during his career as a linebacker. Several fingers do not go in the directions one expects fingers to go. Dan wrote a book with Jim Taylor a few years ago detailing his career. On the cover is a picture of one of Kep's hands sporting the five Grey Cup rings he won with the Eskimos. It's an effective cover—not pretty but effective. Those fingers tell a story in themselves.

After Raz's comment Dan Kepley laughed hardest of all. In fact maybe the only guy who wasn't laughing was Raz, who seemed to figure it was a legitimate question. That's linebackers.

ROBOKICKER

Narco *(Don Narcisse)*

Another player I would put in the vastly underrated category is Don Narcisse, who also joined us in 1987. Though he is sometimes criticized for a perceived lack of toughness Narco drops very few balls thrown his way. As for his toughness I would say Narco has taken as many vicious hits as any receiver I've ever seen, and afterward he has bounced up and gone back into the next play.

After our 1989 Grey Cup win the Riders had a video produced to commemorate the victory. In the video the Tina Turner song "Simply the Best" is featured from time to time. One of my favorite moments is a sequence showing Narco catching one over the middle for a 25-yard gain while the refrain "simply the best" plays in the background. The sequence is in slow motion, and every time I see it I am convinced there is an elegance to this brutal game we all too often overlook. Narco catching a pass is one of the best examples of it.

I have no doubt it is the poetry and the ballet of Don Narcisse's play that is in large part the reason my dad enjoys watching him so much. Narco has long been one of Dad's favorite players, so much so that he once asked him for an autographed picture—something Narco has never let me forget. Narco sent not only the picture but also several autographed football cards *and* a highlight film of a number of his catches that he put together especially for my dad. Since the incident Dad always reminds me to say hello to Don Narcisse. Narco's response to this is that one day my dad will adopt him and I'll have a little brother.

But Narco's most legendary characteristic has nothing to do with sports. It has to do with his bringing to football what Jack Benny brought to television. Put another way, Narco is frugal—

pure and simple—maybe the most parsimonious player ever to strap on shoulder pads. And he takes great pride in it.

The players receive a per diem from the ball club when we are on the road. When we return from road trips we often bet on how much of his per diem money Narco will have left. If, for example, each of us receives one hundred and fifteen dollars for a road trip, anyone guessing Narco has anything less than one hundred and eight bucks remaining in his pocket is going to lose the bet. Gary Lewis, who roomed with Narco on road trips, told endless stories about Narco's frugality. Narco's favorite dining experience is a buffet where he can load up enough food for three meals but only has to pay for one.

I'm certain that when Donald Narcisse decides to retire he will leave the CFL with nearly every dollar he made playing football. He also will carry out with his loot a bunch of team pass-catching records and probably some CFL records as well. No small feat when you consider he has played much of his career in the company of receivers like Ray Elgaard and Jeff Fairholm.

Kent Austin

The unfortunate circumstances surrounding the departure of Kent Austin from the Roughriders has sadly overshadowed his contributions to the team. Kent and his wife, Shelley, had concluded that leaving Regina was the best way to advance Kent's career. This decision led to Kent's request to be traded. Perhaps because of the way Kent handled the situation, refusing to discuss it with the media, the fans turned on him in a way I had never before seen. I can understand their irritation; they felt it was another case of an athlete taking and taking and then wanting out.

I haven't taken sides on the issue and don't want to now, but I will say two things: first, our sports media appeared to do their absolute best to make the issue more volatile than it was, almost to the point of a vendetta; second, Kent Austin is a great quarterback, probably the best I've ever played with, and I've had the good fortune to have played with some very good ones.

Kent may have irritated people with his penchant for running downfield to yell at officials or teammates, but this resulted from his burning desire to win. Kent was just as hard on himself as he was on a teammate who wasn't giving his all. I can't fault anyone who has that much desire to do the job at absolutely the highest possible level. I guess I was a little disappointed at the reception some of our fans gave him when he returned to Taylor Field with the B.C. Lions in 1994. I realize his leaving the province is still being taken personally; however, I hope one day we can put this aside and appreciate what he did on the field for the Saskatchewan Roughriders. Kent Austin is one of only two quarterbacks in the history of this team to lead us to a Grey Cup. And he did that brilliantly and with class.

Bobby Jurasin

Bobby Jurasin leads the Saskatchewan Roughriders in career sacks with 101 going into the 1995 season. He also holds the team record for most sacks in a single season with 22 in 1987.

Bobby, like Raz and some of the others, has the wild-man linebacker mentality, exemplified in Bobby's case by the bandanna he has made standard football equipment. I don't think I've ever known him to coast for even one play; he loads it up and brings it on every down. He commands respect for the way he plays the game and for his dedication to his family. He spends a great deal of time with his children, something I admire a great deal.

Before a game Bobby revs himself up. He paces around the locker room, screaming and swearing, Walkman in place, the heavy metal so loud it can be heard across the room.

Whenever I'm having a hot streak kicking field goals Bobby will stand beside me on the sidelines, and before he goes back on the field he'll say, "Hey Ridge, gimme some." We'll touch hands, not a handshake really, but just his way of having what's working for me rub off on him.

Bobby Jurasin is a winner. Like Poley and Aldag he is one of the most intense, dedicated athletes I've ever met. And he has poured every ounce of this dedication into the Saskatchewan Roughriders.

Pint *(Richie Hall)*

During my years with the Riders I don't know that I've seen a player endear himself more quickly to our fans than Richie Hall.

Known affectionately as Pint because of his diminutive stature (5' 6" and 160 pounds according to his last media guide) Richie played in 153 games in the CFL, not bad in a game usually reserved for men with a great deal more height and weight. The saying "It's not the size of the dog in the fight, but the size of the fight in the dog" is especially apropos in the case of Richie Hall. He came to us in 1988 and stayed until his release following training camp in 1992, a move that probably didn't increase Don Matthews' popularity with Saskatchewan football fans.

I think if you were to ask him, Richie would say he is ecstatic to have played so many games of professional football, about 150 more than he expected to play, considering his size.

I suspect his non-threatening stature combined with his cherubic, contagious smile was a big part of the reason Pint was so popular as a player and remains so as an assistant coach with the Riders.

Pooch (Scott Hendrickson)

As one of the hoggies Pooch has quickly filled the stereotypical shoes of the big men. He drives a pickup, wears cowboy boots, listens to country music, dips ('tween cheek and gum) and spits.

Bob Poley and Roger Aldag have retired, leaving only Mike Anderson of the old guard. Scott Hendrickson—along with Dan Payne, Chris Burns, Michel Lamy and Paul Vajda—are the Riders' new generation hoggies. They have already shown the ability to be as good as our great O-lines of the past. The only one who doesn't fit the stereotypical mold of the offensive lineman is Vajda. Fajita, as he is known to his teammates, is not as wild and reckless as the other young hoggies. Even more astonishing he has shown a penchant for dressing with real style on road trips, and he even maintains a stylish haircut. His battle to maintain his uniqueness will be uphill, I fear, given the likes of Pooch and company.

A couple of seasons ago Pooch noticed Glen Suitor and I bashing helmets after a successful field goal (admittedly a primitive celebration) and thought it would be a good idea if he got in on the act. On those occasions when I forgot to turn to him after Suits and I bashed, Pooch bellowed "Hey!" loud enough to be heard at the top of the stands.

A Few Good Men – The Recent Years

Scott Hendrickson is the Phantom! I'm pretty sure he placed the drawn and quartered roadkill gopher (not our ever-popular Gainer) in my locker a couple of seasons back. Before being considered a true team prankster a player usually has to spend several years in the league, and it speaks to the leadership Pooch brings to the team that he quickly became a major contributor to many inventive locker room pranks. Pooch leads by example on and off the field. He is a very physical, extremely rugged football player who is rapidly gaining a reputation around the CFL as one tough SOB to play against.

I've always tried to be on good terms with the hoggies like Pooch; it's a smart thing for a kicker to do. A quarterback needs to go further, even to the point of considering the hoggies part of his family. A few years back, after a particularly good season, I took the hoggies out for dinner. We went to the Keg and I stood the tab for the evening. We had a great time and I learned firsthand just how much food and beverage these guys can consume. I've been paying down my credit card balance ever since, going on twenty-six months.

A.B. *(Albert Brown)*

A.B. came to the Saskatchewan Roughriders in 1987 and like Richie Hall quickly became a fan favorite. He has great flair on the field and has developed into one of the premiere defensive backs in the league.

Albert is also a delight off the field, a kind of prairie answer to Yogi Berra and Casey Stengel. Though he's a bright guy Albert fractures the English language and has broken up the dressing room more times than I can remember. In fact his one-liners, most of the them inadvertent, have become so legendary that after Milson Jones was traded to Winnipeg he used to phone back to Regina every week to catch up on the latest Albert-isms.

On one occasion Albert came into the dressing room clearly upset about something and sat down next to Glen Suitor. Glen, sensing that something was wrong, asked, "What's up, A.B.?" Albert, who prefaces every statement with "Aw Dawg," replied, "Aw Dawg, I just heard one of the front office staff is making ninety thousand a year."

Suitor, without a hint of a smile, said, "Yeah, so what? I make twice that much."

To which Albert replied, "Aw Dawg, you make one-forty?"

Defensive backs need to communicate constantly on the field, and A.B.'s use of the language has resulted in some interesting exchanges. On one play the ball was thrown in the direction of Albert's man, and A.B. yelled, "Deddigo, deddigo, deddigo." A couple of plays later, Albert's call was "Yo, yo, yo."

When they got to the sidelines, Suitor went to Albert. "What the hell are you talking about out there?" he asked.

"Aw Dawg," said Albert, "'Deddigo, deddigo, deddigo' is 'there he goes, there he goes, there he goes' and 'yo, yo, yo' is 'yours, yours, yours.'"

During the 1994 season Albert had occasion to talk to Brent Matich, who has been our punter for two years and wears sweater number 13. A.B., apparently unable to put a name to Brent, started the conversation with, "Hey . . . uh . . . punter Dawg . . . uh . . . one-three Dawg . . ."

Albert is proud to be a Saskatchewan Roughrider. To prove it he arrived at training camp in 1993 with the name of his team emblazoned on his brand new Jimmy. It was a nice idea except the printing on the side of the vehicle announced to the world that the driver wore number 4 and played for the *Saskaghewan* Roughriders. A *Leader-Post* photographer happened

A Few Good Men – The Recent Years

to be on hand to capture it on film. Teammates tend to be merciless in those situations, and I think Albert was a little embarrassed by the whole thing. What had happened was the painter in Omaha, Nebraska, who customized the vehicle had never heard of Saskatchewan. When asked how it was spelled, Albert replied, "Aw Dawg, you know, just like it sounds."

The game of football wouldn't be nearly as much fun if it weren't for the characters encountered along the way. Albert Brown is certainly one of these personalities, with an ever-increasing mythology about him that will live on long after he is no longer playing football.

I meant it when I said it's the people who make this game special. It's not at all farfetched to suggest that each person I've played for, with and against has had at least some small impact on my life. Some have changed it profoundly. I wish I could mention them all, but that's clearly impossible. But I will remember them long after my career has ended and this book has found its way to the trunk in the attic. For me it is the people who are the game of football.

CHAPTER 9

I Got By With a Little Help From My Friend

Man, I did love this game. I'd have played for food money. It was a game. The sounds, the smells ...
—FIELD OF DREAMS, 1989

Glen Suitor was the Saskatchewan Roughriders' second-round draft pick in the 1984 amateur draft and the tenth player selected overall that year. He came out of Simon Fraser University with a reputation for being an aggressive hitter with a nose for the ball.

Glen began holding for place-kicks late in the 1985 season after Stew Fraser was traded to Ottawa and the ill-fated experiment with Joe Paopao had failed. Not many players wanted the holder's job because it added responsibility and pressure. Few can do the job of holding for place-kicks and do it well. In fact, when Glen suffered a badly sprained ankle late in the 1988 season, our attempts to find a replacement proved so futile it was finally decided that Glen would dress for the game just to hold for place-kicks.

So for 159 games, up to the end of 1994, Glen Suitor was my holder. During that time I attempted 517 field goals and made 421 for a success rate of 81.4 percent. And I'd be the first to admit my success has been in no small part because of Glen's great work.

While a good holder makes the process look easy, it's an important part of the game that is often overlooked. Many people don't understand the precise timing of a place-kick. Once I have begun my forward motion to the ball there is no turning back. Any errorwill result in a missed field goal. Glen's role was part technical and part psychological. His job, in the 1.2 to 1.4 seconds from the time the ball left the center's hands to the time my foot connected with it, was to catch the ball cleanly, get it onto the tee with the correct lean and lastly and most importantly spin the laces so they were away from me and facing the target. All this had to be accomplished while opposition players were charging up the middle and around the ends in an effort to block the kick or do whatever they could to disrupt the process. Glen did his job as well as anybody in professional football.

On one occasion when the snap was off target, Glen had to make a great move just to get his hands on the ball. Then, realizing he didn't have time to pin it, he set it down, spun it and jerked both hands out of the way. When I made contact with the ball Glen was not holding it, but it was still in position for that fraction of a second before toppling over. Because of Glen's ability to improvise in a split second, we made the field goal. There were others like it.

Without to my knowledge ever being assigned the role, Glen also took on the task of keeping me relaxed in the moments before big kicks. He had an uncanny knack for knowing when I was tensing up and an even greater ability to say just what was needed to help me relax. Suits knew me like no other player because we became over the years close friends on and off the field with the accompanying respect for each other's playing abilities that friends should have.

When Glen first took over the responsibilities of holding—amidst constant reminders from teammates, coaches and me of the great job the previous holder had done—Glen resolved to surpass Stewie Fraser in every technical and psychological aspect of the job. As a result he took as much pleasure as I have in establishing some of our CFL kicking records. He is proud that he held the ball for the 60-yarder in 1987, for the streak of 28 in 1993 and, of course, for the winning Grey Cup kick.

I can appreciate Glen's feelings because I went through a similar situation when I came to the Riders. For the first couple of years I heard endless good-hearted references to Doc Watson, the kicker from 1981. Many reminders came from our trainer, Ivan Gutfriend, who loved to refer to the strength of Watson's leg, his 59-yard kick and just about every other kick Doc made . . . over and over and over. Pretty much the same thing I did with Glen, come to think of it. My favorite dig at Suitor was to remind him that Stewie had been the holder for the *record-setting* (I liked to emphasize this part) eight-field-goal game in 1984. When we were able to kick eight for a second time in 1988, a big monkey was off Glen's back.

Glen strives to be the best at just about everything he does. Not only did he want to be the best free safety in the CFL (and many think he was) but he also wants to be better than his opponent at golf, Nintendo, Scrabble and I Spy with my Little Eye.

Glen is probably the most competitive person I know. I would rate myself a close second. We try to beat each other at everything we do, and if there is no competition associated with an activity we will invent one. We carried Game Boy and Pocket Scrabble on all flights and would even challenge each other when watching *Jeopardy*. Glen's motto when playing any-

I Got By With a Little Help From My Friend

thing was "If you're not cheatin' you're not tryin'." In Scrabble this led him to some very inventive word creations and some heated discussions about spelling and vocabulary.

Another of Glen's spins on competition is that he is a firm believer that the one who wins the last competition of the season is the reigning champion. Thus if I beat him eighteen times in a row but he wins the nineteenth and final game, he's the champ. This creative rule finally came back to haunt him in 1994. Throughout the year Glen had been able to beat me at golf almost every time out. Though the games were close, Glen, with the help of his two best clubs, the foot wedge and the scorecard pencil, dominated the season. For our last round of the year we headed out to Emerald Park in White City just outside of Regina. Glen won the first 18-hole round that day, but because the course was only days from closing for the year and we were about the only people out, we went around again. Much to Glen's chagrin I won the round, and before we could get out again, the first snow fell.

Glen and I are both Trekkies, but even there we cannot seem to avoid fierce competition. Glen is a huge fan of the old *Star Trek* series and believes that the universe revolves around Captain James T. Kirk. He knows, for example, that the *T* stands for Tiberius. In fact he even wanted to name his first son James Tiberius, but thankfully his wife, Elizabeth, prevailed and the firstborn male Suitor was christened Jared.

I like both the original show and *Star Trek: The Next Generation*, but because Glen is a purist, I will at the drop of a hat engage him in arguments on the subject of which is the better show. He is repulsed that *Generation* has a Klingon and a young boy on the bridge of the Enterprise and that in the early shows the security officer was a woman. I argue that the new Enterprise is superior to the original spaceship and that

Spock, McCoy and Kirk are relics in the same way leather football helmets and five-point touchdowns are relics. But the last word as far as Suitor is concerned is that Picard is not in the same league as James T. Kirk because—and this gives some idea of the intellectual level of his argument—Picard is bald. I contend by the way that Picard is secure in his masculinity and not caught up in the vanity associated with a full head of hair.

Glen's competitive nature drove him to duplicate one of Stew Fraser's bizarre shows of confidence in my ability: during a practice Stew held the ball with his nose while I kicked it. I would not personally want my face anywhere near the foot that propels a football at eighty miles per hour. But that didn't stop me from reminding Suitor of the kind of confidence his predecessor had showed in my right foot. Sure enough, one day during practice, Glen said, "Awright, damn it, let's get it over with."

Right then and there he got down, nose to ball, and I kicked it. Now *that* is a competitor. Actually there are probably those who would describe Glen's gesture in another way, including the coaches who howled as they watched the whole episode.

Our confidence in each other was put to the test during the 1988 season when Coach John Gregory decided to institute a fake field goal. The play was designed for Glen to take the ball and roll to the wide side of the field and throw to one of three outlet men downfield. The call was first made in a game against the Eskimos at Taylor Field. We were at about the Edmonton 20, facing third down, and as I trotted onto the field John yelled, "Fake . . . fake."

When I got to the huddle I told Glen we were going to run the fake. He became instantly excited because—like most defensive backs—he was a repressed offensive back. As we lined up for the kick I looked down at Glen, who was in the kneeling

I Got By With a Little Help From My Friend

position, and said, "Don't worry, I've got your back side." Meaning that when Glen rolled left I would block anyone charging in from the right, his blind side. Glen looked at me and nodded. Nothing more was said, but Glen knew beyond a shadow of a doubt our bond of friendship meant I would look after him.

The ball was snapped, Glen rolled behind me and headed left. I approached as if to kick, faked through the ball, then stopped and looked to the right to see if anybody was coming. Somebody was. The problem was there were two rushers coming. One I recognized as Larry Wruck, a damn tough linebacker. The other I didn't have time to identify except to note that he was very large and traveling very fast. I got myself down into a good blocking stance, determined to save my friend's life.

At this point things got a little hazy. I may have closed my eyes or I may have blacked out altogether. I do know this: both players blew by me untouched. I turned to look at Glen who was out there playing quarterback, completely unaware of the two Eskimos in hot pursuit, both with their hearts set on rearranging his body parts. As loud as I could I yelled, "Glen, look out! Look out!"

He apparently did not hear me, and as he opened his shoulders to the field—as a right-handed thrower running to his left must—the inevitable tackle took place. One hit him high, the other hit him low. The pass was a lame duck that fell harmlessly to the ground not far from where Glen lay buried in the turf. I ran over to see how he was and his right eye looked up at me through the earhole of his helmet.

He was slow getting up and I offered him a hand. He straightened out his helmet, looked at me groggily and said, "What happened? What happened?"

ROBOKICKER

"Glen," I said, "they made great moves."

Because we are friends Glen accepted my explanation without question. He nodded and limped off the field. The next morning he was in the trainer's room early for treatment—a lot of treatment—and after having ice packs applied liberally to his body he wandered into the film room to take a look at the fake kick to see what had gone wrong.

My phantom block must have been captured on videotape because not long after I received a phone call at home. It was Glen just out of the film room. "Just how deep a hole did you dig out there?" he asked. Others must have viewed those films as well because we didn't try many more fake field goals that year.

I hoped our friendship was strong enough for Glen to put the unfortunate incident behind him. But in the game Glen played in Calgary with a sprained ankle, the opportunity for revenge presented itself and it was too good for him to pass up. We were lined up for a point after. Bob Poley was doing the long-snapping and sent back one of his infrequent errant snaps. The ball bounced three times and then skipped over Glen's hands and by me. As it skittered back in the direction of the onrushing Stampeders Glen was able to get out of his crouch and grab the ball. He was hit immediately and the ball popped loose once again. This time one of the Stampeders scooped it up and was off and running for our goal line. (In the CFL, if the defending team returns a convert attempt to the kicking team's end zone, two points are awarded.)

I set out in pursuit of the ball carrier, trying to take an angle on him, and for a while things were going pretty well. Suddenly I was grabbed from behind by Stampeder Ken Ford, a very good and very big football player. He grabbed me so hard he turned me completely around so I was facing him as

I Got By With a Little Help From My Friend

he continued to run at full throttle in the direction of our end zone. Suddenly I found myself traveling through the air, still at a great rate of speed. And also traveling through the air, in a trajectory that would land him on top of me, was Ken Ford.

The human mind is a wonderful instrument that works quickly in stressful situations. I recall very well, while airborne, the two thoughts going through my mind. The first was that I would never walk again. I was coming off a bad back, and I was convinced it would never mend after this. My second thought was that Darth Vader was about to do me in. The reason for this thought was Ken Ford's smoked glass visor, which looked a lot like a costume piece from *Star Wars*. It's hard to see someone's eyes through those things, but I could see his mouth and he was smiling a very wide smile.

I landed and Ken landed on top of me just the way my mind had pictured it. My head hit the turf and rebounded up just in time to meet Ken's helmet on its way down. The collision took place near the Stampeders' bench and afterward I remember hearing a number of merciful Calgary players yelling, "Ridge, stay down. Stay down."

But I wasn't about to give them the satisfaction of thinking I was hurt. So I got up. I tried to take a step, but I couldn't get my legs to make contact with the ground. After pawing the air uselessly for several seconds I finally went down on one knee and waited for help. Glen Suitor and Ivan Gutfriend arrived at about the same time; Ivan, our faithful trainer, was unable to control the spasms of laughter that always seem to afflict him when I get banged around.

Glen had hobbled downfield to where the action had taken place. Despite the ankle injury he had made the effort to see how I was. I was impressed. But before I could express my gratitude Glen spoke. Glen Suitor, my teammate and good buddy, looked down at my crumpled body and said, "Ridge, I would have got a piece of that guy for you, but he made great moves."

While Suits and I are similar in many ways when it comes to athletic competition there are a couple of noteworthy differences when it comes to personal habits. For eight seasons we roomed together on the road and our contrasting lifestyles drove us crazy. I am a neatness freak to the point of being compulsive. Suitor, on the other hand, brings new meaning to the word *slob*. If you take the Felix Unger–Oscar Madison relationship from *The Odd Couple* and magnify it you have Suitor and Ridgway.

When we were on the road and checked into our room it was as if an imaginary chalk line had been drawn down the middle. My side was tidy; his was trashed. If he was reading a newspaper he didn't scatter it about in sections; that would be normal slob behavior and Suits was no run-of-the-mill slob. His newspaper was distributed page by page all over the room. Candy wrappers were not discarded in one pile; they were dropped wherever Glen happened to be when the candy was unwrapped. The room's furniture served as hangers for the Suitor wardrobe—the TV for socks, the lampshade for underwear and so on.

Some years ago I thought we were making progress when Glen discovered the closet and agreed to hang his clothes there. I was wrong. It was merely another creation of the devious Suitorian mind designed to irritate me. He used every hanger in the closet to hang up a total of one outfit. One hanger, one sock—one hanger, one tie—one hanger, one pair of undershorts—and on it went until the entire closet and every hanger in it was occupied.

There is a serious side to the friendship Glen and I enjoy,

I Got By With a Little Help From My Friend

and an incident during the 1989 Grey Cup season solidified the kinship that developed between us. We were coming off a loss to the Winnipeg Blue Bombers, our third in a row. The B.C. Lions came into Taylor Field the following week sporting a 4 and 8 record compared to our 6 and 6. It was a critical game for us as we tried to put a little more breathing room between our third-place standing and the fourth-place Lions.

With five seconds left in the game we were up by four points. On third down with the ball at our 53, B.C. quarterback Matt Dunigan sent three receivers to the same side of the field and threw up a jump ball. As Bombers' receiver David Williams went up for it, Glen flattened him, and with no time on the clock he was called for pass interference. Because a game cannot end on a defensive penalty, the Lions got another chance and went on to win the game.

There is no denying that Glen erred in taking a penalty on what should have been the last play of the game. He'd be the first to admit it. After the game he was quoted as saying, "I knew that time was running down but I didn't realize it had run out. I just tried to time my jump." The *Leader-Post* wrote that Glen looked "a lot like a condemned man awaiting escort to the gallows. His face buried in his hands, he sat hunched over on his stool facing into his cubicle."

The media and fans were quick to point out that all Glen had to do was let Williams catch the ball and then make the tackle to give us the win in a crucial game. But almost everyone who blamed Glen for the loss overlooked the very next play which saw Dunigan throw into the end zone, again in the direction of David Williams. This time Albert Brown was nailed for pass interference. That put the ball on our one-yard line, and on the next play Dunigan snuck in for the winning points.

In a way I credit the adversity associated with that play in 1989 with making Glen the player he became. I think he was a better ballplayer and a stronger person for it. I'm convinced this play did more than any other that year to pull us together as a team and prepare us for the run to the Grey Cup. Everybody felt bad for Glen and after the game we were a different group of athletes. We began to pull for one another and to develop the strong team chemistry that carried us to the Cup.

Unfortunately too many fans' reaction to that interference call was typical of the way they viewed Glen Suitor over the years. Many don't understand the responsibilities of the defensive secondary and in particular the safety position. Paradoxically some of the criticism of Glen's play arose from one of his most admirable qualities: he would never give up on a play. Often there were long pass plays where the receiver had beaten a defensive halfback or corner, but it was Glen, who after doing his job on the play, joined the chase and was seen as the player either making the desperation tackle or chasing the receiver into the end zone. So many times I have heard not particularly knowledgeable football observers say, "Well, there it is—Suitor got beat again."

One thing I do know is that no matter how much those comments hurt—and there are very few professional athletes who aren't stung by unfair criticism—Glen Suitor did not change. He continued the chase even when it seemed hopeless, and every once in a while he caught the runner and saved a touchdown.

Though perhaps not fully appreciated in Saskatchewan, Glen was one of the most respected safeties in the league. During Sacramento's first season in the CFL, quarterback David Archer, who played seven years in the NFL and a year in the WLAF, paid Glen the ultimate compliment. During the coin toss before the game, David looked over at Suits and told him he was the best safety in this league and one of the best he'd ever seen.

Glen Suitor is my best friend and I suppose it's natural I defend him. But I would ask nothing more than that critics take another look at the record of a player who holds the all-time Rider marker for interceptions and was four times a Western All-Star and three times a CFL All-Star. They might see what all of us who played with him saw—one of the best all-around athletes and fiercest competitors in the recent history of the Roughriders.

None of this in any way alters the fact that Glen Suitor could be a pain in the butt. His practical jokes were legendary, and he seemed to have an uncanny knack for pulling a prank and then dodging the blame. One of his favorite venues for driving teammates crazy was the airplanes where we spend so much time. If he saw somebody reading a book (Mike Anderson, who likes to read expensive hard cover first editions was often a target) Glen would wait until the book was left unattended. He'd then steal it, read the last few pages and return it unnoticed. When the reader took up the book again, Glen would approach to say, "Hey, are you reading *The Truth About Mrs. Jones?* Man, I can't believe she killed Bobby Ray Smith in the barn in the last chapter just because she wasn't pregnant after all." At this point there was always a lot of scrambling over seats and up the aisle as the victim tried to get his hands on Suitor's neck.

Glen was also the perpetrator of a prank that should go into the practical joke hall of fame. On a flight from Toronto to Regina, Suits and I were sitting immediately across the aisle from Bob Poley and Roger Aldag, who were getting set to play one of their endless games of crib. Before the game began, unknown to either Bob or Roger, Glen got hold of the deck and removed all the fives, a card critical to a successful cribbage game. The aircraft departed Toronto and for nearly three hours we listened to Polecat and Rodge complain bitterly about the bad hands they were getting. First one would say, "Dammit, I can't buy a hand." Then the other would mutter, "Hell, can't you deal me some cards just once?"

Suits and I were in spasms across the aisle. Finally, hours later, when the pilot announced we were beginning our approach into Regina, Glen pulled the four fives out of his shirt pocket, fanned them out in his hand and leaned toward the two cribbage players. "Hey Polecat," he said in his most innocent voice, "is this a good hand?" I think the only reason Glen survived the incident is that Poley and Aldag got into an argument about whose fault it was that they hadn't noticed the fives were absent from the deck.

Hoggies like Polecat and Rodge were a major target for the Suitor sense of humor. At the end of practice the O-line guys often get together, form a circle and put their arms in the middle. Then they raise their arms high and yell, "Yeah, Hogs!" Several times Glen managed to sneak an arm into the group and from the back, in a voice louder than any other, holler, "Yeah, fat guys!" He'd then run like hell to escape sure and sudden death. On one occasion, however, they caught him and made a hoggy pile—about a ton and a half worth—on top of him.

This was not the only time Suitor paid the price for his repeated pranks played on teammates. Prior to the 1992 playoff trip to Edmonton I was approached by several guys on the team, mostly offensive linemen, who told me they were going to use this trip to repay Suitor. They said I could either cooperate or be another victim. After about a millisecond of thought

I Got By With a Little Help From My Friend

I agreed to help. The plan was to tie up Glen, drop his drawers, put him on a hotel elevator and send him down to the main floor.

We were only in our room on the eleventh floor of the Westin Hotel for a few minutes when there was a knock at the door. I opened it and seven or eight guys burst into the room and swarmed over Glen. First they tied a pillowcase over his head—that had been part of our deal since they wanted me to videotape the prank, and I didn't want Glen to know I had even an unwilling part. Then they bound him hand and foot and carried him to the elevator, me in hot pursuit with camera rolling. They secured an elevator and threw in the defrocked Glen. Someone pressed the buttons for the fifth and third floors as well as the lobby. This was to allow us to get in another elevator and be waiting in the lobby when Glen arrived.

That week Edmonton was also hosting the Canadian Finals Rodeo, and the Westin was the center for the entire rodeo community that had descended on Edmonton in boots, jeans and Stetsons. We got to the packed lobby ahead of Glen as planned and cleared a semicircle around the elevator descending with our naked free safety aboard. We were surrounded by cowpokes and cowpokettes who didn't want to miss what they figured was some kind of action. At last the door opened . . . but Glen wasn't on the elevator.

The event was instantly transformed from comedy to crisis. Nobody had any idea where Glen was, but we all knew there would be hell to pay if one of our key starters for the playoff game got hurt during some tomfoolery. I headed for the room to see if Glen had somehow made it back there, and the rest of the guys deployed themselves around the hotel. I got to the room and looked out at the street below to see an ambulance pulling up in front. At this point I became really concerned, as did Mike Anderson, who arrived at the room just in time to see the scene unfolding on the street below. Fortunately at this moment Glen poked his head around the corner and came into the room. To say he was irate is to put it very mildly indeed, and he went uncharacteristically silent for the rest of the trip.

Later I learned what had happened. One of the floors we had arranged for the elevator to stop at happened to be the pool floor. When the door opened and Glen smelled the chlorine from the pool he rolled off the elevator, got himself to his feet and worked his way to the pool. He heard someone inside and used his head, still in the pillowcase, to bang on the door. The janitor working inside was an older Chinese gentleman who didn't speak a lot of English. When he saw Glen he initially didn't want to have anything to do with what could have been, for all he knew, a Mafia hit. Finally he agreed to cut Glen loose. As soon as he was free Glen found something to cover himself with and got back to the room.

The next day Suits was still mad as hell and went to every one of the guys and vowed to get even with them one by one. I think he eventually exacted his revenge on most everybody, and I don't think there was much complaining from anyone when his turn rolled around.

On May 15, eighteen days before our 1995 training camp, Glen called to tell me he was retiring from football. Three days earlier he had been offered a job with TSN as a color analyst on their CFL telecasts. He had a choice of maybe playing one more year or moving into a career that could last ten or fifteen years. I think he made the right choice and will do an excellent job as a sports broadcaster. He is extremely knowledgeable about the game and is a big a believer in the CFL.

I Got By With a Little Help From My Friend

I knew he would hang 'em up before I did. Nevertheless, his leaving is tough for me, not only because I lose an excellent teammate, but also because I lose a best friend. I owe Glen Suitor a great deal of credit for the success I've had. I'm the first to admit that the records I've achieved, the all-star recognition I've received and the success rate I'm pretty proud of wouldn't have happened had Glen not been the player holding the football for me. His skill as a holder, his willingness to put in the time after practice to work with me on our timing, his ability to calm me in tough situations and most of all his being there for me during the toughest periods of my professional career and personal life are things I will carry with me for a very long time.

One last thing. I won our last game of golf together. That should give me bragging rights forever.

CHAPTER 10

Thrown for a Loss

I believe we have two lives . . . the life we learn with and the life we live with after that. —THE NATURAL, 1984

MINE HASN'T BEEN a fairy tale career; I doubt such exists. There have been some memorable moments, experiences I will always cherish. And there have been a few I'd just as soon forget. I have experienced both extremes of the emotional spectrum, from the frustration and feelings of futility of my early years in the league to the euphoria of playing on a Grey Cup winner.

When I was cut by the Montreal Alouettes in 1981, it marked the first time I had been told I was not good enough. While I was growing up, when teams were being picked out in the school yard, I was either doing the picking or one of the first picked. The sudden realization that my athletic ability was no longer automatically recognized and respected was psychologically devastating.

What followed my first Montreal experience, as I made my way back to the University of Toledo to finish my education, was a period of intense dejection and disillusionment. When I arrived in Toledo the first thing I did was pack away my kicking shoes, tees and footballs. I had resigned myself to the fact that my dream of playing professional football was over. Although I knew there were guys who went through six or seven tryouts before finding a place on a team's roster, I felt other teams would simply do what Montreal had done, which was to assure me they wanted me to do only the place-kicking duties, then release me because I wasn't an all-purpose kicker. My bitterness reached the point that I did not attend any of my school's games that entire season.

On the positive side I applied myself academically as I had never done and the results were astounding. My grades weren't Dean's Honor Role, but they were easily the best I had achieved throughout my academic life and I was proud of them. Apparently there really was some kind of correlation between studying and academic success. Of course, professors had been telling me that, but I had scrupulously avoided heeding their advice.

Being released by the Alouettes and subsequently by the Blue Bombers in what didn't amount to a tryout was certainly not the last adversity I would face during my career. Though my first professional season had plenty of highs and very few lows, what followed for the next few years was much more akin to a nightmare than the fulfillment of the dream to play professionally. When Joe Faragalli was fired in 1983, it was like losing a close friend, and I had a lot of trouble handling the situation on an emotional level. To make matters worse there was the ongoing feud between General Manager John Herrera and my good friend and confidant, punter Ken Clark. As is usually the case in management–player disputes, management won and Clarkie was dealt to Ottawa. The trade, following closely on the heels of the Faragalli firing, was doubly hard to take. I admit a big part of the problem was me. I came to the CFL with a kind of emotional naiveté, and the things I saw happening to people in the hard world of professional sports shocked me.

I wasn't alone. Earlier, when the Riders dumped Lyall Woznesensky, Ken Clark's best friend, the Woz came around to say good-bye to the guys. When he'd gone, Kenny, whose locker was next to mine, turned to me and said, "That's what sucks about this game. The best thing you can do is not get close to anybody."

Equally troubling throughout the 1983–85 period was the Riders' bad play on the field. We won five, six and five games respectively over a three-year period, and whoever said it's more fun to win than to lose was right on the money. And it's not like we were losing a whole bunch of squeakers. Some of the scores were flat out embarrassing: in 1985 alone we lost 33–12 to Montreal, 49–3 to Winnipeg, 33–9 to B.C. and 51–14 to Hamilton.

My personal statistics were atrocious. My percentages of field goals made during the same three-year period were 62.9, 66.7 and 60.5. Our offense just didn't get the ball close often enough, and I was attempting kicks at the very edge of my range. While it doesn't excuse what was admittedly poor kicking, the average length of missed kicks over those three years was 43.3 yards in 1983, 47.5 yards in 1984 and 45.1 yards in 1985. In 1985 I hit six uprights or crossbars, five from outside 50 yards, which is outrageous bad luck. Thankfully nothing like that has happened since.

My confidence certainly suffered during that time. While it didn't excuse my performance I found it very difficult to do the job well when management had little idea what it was doing and my own coach didn't respect me or have faith in me.

Thrown for a Loss

Surely it's not coincidence that when I returned to the Riders under John Gregory in 1987, my percentage shot up to 83 percent and has stayed there ever since. That's when stability came to the team under the leadership of Bill Baker and subsequently Alan Ford, and the results on the field, not only for me but for the whole ball club, improved dramatically.

I have for years been a practitioner of the power of positive thinking. I was introduced to the works of Norman Vincent Peale by University of Toledo Assistant Coach Dan Simrell. Peale's theme is simple but effective: how good you will be at an endeavor depends entirely on the amount of practice and dedication you put into it; but once you have arrived at your goal your continued success depends on the amount of belief you have in your ability. "Self-confidence equals positive production" is how Peale phrases it and I think he's right. Conversely self-doubt leads to mediocrity. Athletes, like people in all walks of life, are insecure. I am no different. Insecurity about my ability has dogged my career.

The worst thing the athlete who finds himself in a slump can do is press. If he presses for improvement and fails, the tendency is to get down on himself. The combination of high pressure and temporarily poor performance can cause irreparable damage to his self-confidence, which is the key to long-term success, and can lead to questioning his ability. From there it's a short journey to the end of a career.

The key to longevity in professional sports is consistent productivity. When this falls off, management, media and fans rightly demand an immediate return to the former level of performance. Loyalty doesn't enter into it. Professional sports is the definitive what-have-you-done-for-me-lately business.

My mediocre play in the mideighties was disappointing, but it paled in comparison to one brief, horrible moment in

1992. It took place on the grass field of Edmonton's Commonwealth Stadium during the Semi-Final playoff game with the Eskimos. With 22 seconds showing on the clock, Sean Fleming kicked a 44-yard field goal to give Edmonton a 22–20 lead.

What followed was another last-gasp drive downfield authored by Kent Austin and an attempt at a game-winning field goal from the Edmonton 40 with time expired. The kick was not a gimme but it was certainly makeable. Then, in the words of the *Leader-Post*'s Darrell Davis, "Ridgway slipped. The snap from Bob Poley was pinned by Suitor, and Ridgway, the league's all-time accuracy leader, stepped toward the football, and planted his left foot on the thawed grass of the only grass field in the CFL." The article then quoted me as saying, "No long story. I slipped. I was wearing the same cleats I always wear here . . . if I miss left or right, at least I gave it a try, but I slipped. I'm going to think about this for a long time."

And, believe me, I have. The slip was the biggest single disappointment I have experienced as an athlete. I did everything exactly as I normally do in such a situation. Exactly as I had done in the Grey Cup game three years before. Except this time, when I planted my left foot on the field for the kick, a piece of turf tore away and I fell.

My right foot actually did meet the ball as I was on my way down. When I hit the ground I heard the double-thump sound no kicker wants to hear as first my foot hit the ball and then the ball hit the back of one of our linemen. When I got to my feet I saw the dejection of my teammates contrasted with the ecstasy of the Eskimo players who were jumping around in the victory dance that seconds before I had been confident we would be doing.

In my frustration I slammed my helmet to the ground so hard that it was never usable again. The walk to the dressing room, as teammate after teammate patted me on the back to console me, was the longest of my career.

I had missed important field goals before but never one where failure meant the end of our season. The post-game locker room was, as can be imagined, stone quiet but for the crush of reporters who gathered around my locker and fired questions. I explained that I was certain I had worn the right footwear. The field, when we started the game, was frozen and by the end it had begun to thaw. When I put the tee down and looked at the grass where I would plant my foot for the kick, it seemed fine.

Most reporters were gracious in their questions and their comments. All but one. Near the end of the scrum a female reporter approached my locker. To this day I do not know who she was, but she asked, "How does it feel to have let down your teammates and cost them the game?" I looked up and said, "Is that what they're saying?" To which she replied, "Oh yeah." I was too stunned to say more. I regret that the next year I refused to do an interview with Edmonton reporter Joanne Ireland because I mistakenly thought she was the woman from the year before.

We had a couple of hours before our departing flight and stopped to get something to eat. I felt estranged from the other guys on the team, not because they were blaming me for the loss, but because for them it was a little like a funeral when people struggle to come up with the right words to comfort the bereaved. I wound up sitting with Bob Poley, Roger Aldag and Norm Fong in a Chinese restaurant. We talked about everything *but* what had happened on the field at Commonwealth Stadium. Bob Poley would soon retire from the Riders, and I would have given a lot to have his final play as a Roughrider turn out differently.

Bob, like virtually all my teammates, was both generous and gracious about the slip. As a matter of fact so were the Eskimos. Larry Wruck was quoted as saying that if the game had been played at Taylor Field or on artificial turf, "Ridgway makes that field goal and Saskatchewan wins." Gizmo Williams, who by the way happens to be the best kick-returner on the planet, said, "I know if he hadn't slipped, he'd have made it."

The headline the next day in Regina read, "Ridgway Slips, Riders Fall." Terry Jones' story in the *Edmonton Sun* read, "Just Dumb Luck." And one of my favorites was a cartoon by Dave Elston in the *Calgary Sun*, although admittedly when I first saw it I didn't think it was too damn funny. The cartoon shows Glen Suitor holding the ball while I am no where to be seen, but my dialogue balloon says, "I've fallen and I can't get up."

I couldn't believe how wonderful most of the fans were. I received mail from all over Canada, not only from Rider supporters but from people who had seen the game and just wanted to send a few words of encouragement. A letter even arrived from a prisoner in Stony Mountain Penitentiary, who had written to wish me well. I have kept pretty well all of that mail, a huge stack, as a reminder of how forgiving football fans can be.

As is to be expected there were some people whose comments hurt. "Careful you don't slip, Dave," was a favorite. But those people were a small minority.

Some media reports were decidedly less generous than most teammates, the western media and fans. The *Globe and Mail* quoted that most reliable source, "the unidentified Saskatchewan player," as saying, "He refused to change his cleats when we all did at half-time. He nearly slipped on a convert earlier but he still wouldn't change... he was stubborn and unprofessional and a lot of us are unhappy about it." To set the record straight on this point, only two players changed their footwear at half-time. Those two were Glen Suitor and Kent Austin, who changed *to* the shoes I had on. And I know neither was the anonymous spokesperson.

Even Calgary place-kicker Mark McLoughlin got into the act. "He should've known by the end of the game what the footing would be like," he said. "He should have had proper footwear on by then. A guy the caliber of Ridgway shouldn't have made that mistake." The remark just didn't sound like what I expected Mark would say. We should know there are enough people around waiting to dump on kickers; we sure don't need to do it to each other.

A couple of days after the infamous slip, as I was leaving Taylor Field, I ran into Don Matthews in the parking lot. He stopped me and said, "There's something I'd like to tell you, and it's something I once heard Hugh Campbell say to Dave Cutler. I don't want you to ever become so arrogant as to believe that your kicks win or lose games for us. There were probably fifty things that happened in the course of that game that, had they been done differently, wouldn't have allowed the game to come down to a field goal."

Don Matthews' advice was the beginning of my attempt to put the incident in perspective. Since then my deliberations usually go something like this: *Millions of people in the world go to bed hungry every night. They have never heard of Dave Ridgway and don't give a damn about a missed field goal. Their struggle is more important than the fortunes of a guy who kicks footballs for a living in Regina, Saskatchewan.* Having done that bit of philosophizing, however, I always come back to the simple and obvious truth: if the slip was the proverbial character builder, selfishly speaking I would gladly sacrifice a little character for another shot at that kick.

During the 1992 and 1993 seasons I went through one of the most difficult periods of my personal life, a separation from my wife and children and a subsequent divorce in 1994. This was one time that being easily recognized in the community was a drawback. It seemed everyone in the province was familiar with my marital situation and more than willing to comment on it. I realize being a public figure leaves me open to every kind of conjecture from people who think they *know*, but overhearing some of their comments certainly didn't make things easier. Public scrutiny of private matters is something I, like every professional athlete, had to learn to deal with. Most often the recognition was enjoyable. Only during that extremely difficult personal period was being a public figure in Saskatchewan a liability.

The agony of the separation and even the divorce itself was nothing compared to the pain of having my children taken several thousand miles away from me. Nancy and I were married in 1982 in Cleveland, and in 1992 she returned to Ohio to pursue a Master's degree. After we decided to separate in December of that year, I returned to Regina to find I had been served with a restraining order to keep me away from my sons. What followed was the toughest, cruelest situation I have ever faced as our divorce was fought out in distant American courts under a legal system marked by its lack of sympathy for the rights of fathers. Nancy's counsel was determined to prolong my agony as long as possible, and the divorce dragged on for twenty months.

I was naive at the outset, believing Nancy and I would divide our assets equally, I would pay child support and in return receive fair access to my boys. This was not to be the case. As a result the one thing I had pledged would never happen in my life—a repeat of the painful separation of family I had experienced during my childhood—became a reality. In retrospect I know I could have been a better husband, but I also know this: I am a great father.

Nancy and I have two beautiful boys: Christopher Dallas and Drew Bradley. The times together with my sons are the most important in my life. Christopher is a super kid. Like a typical proud father I see him as intelligent, perceptive and remarkably athletic. He has reached the age at which he is starting to question why Dad doesn't live with him, his brother and his mom. I have a difficult time explaining it to him because I become extremely emotional when he questions me about it.

Drew is still in a world of his own, as he should be at four years old. He's a wonderful little tough guy and quite big for his age. He has no idea what has happened, and his biggest worry right now is how many dinosaurs he can line up on the kitchen table. He is great fun to talk to on the phone. I get choked up when he says he's going to come and see me later. He doesn't yet understand how far he is away from his dad.

Following the 1989 Grey Cup the players received what I believe is one of the nicest championship rings ever designed. Christopher has had his eye on my ring since he was twenty-four months old, and now whenever he sees it he comments that it will be his. This is exactly what I intend. If my football career can bring one more achievement I want it to be another championship with the Riders so both my sons can have a Grey Cup ring. I would happily trade every record and personal accomplishment for that second ring.

I want to do everything I can to maintain as good a relationship as possible with my boys. They mean everything in the world to me. I don't think Nancy has any idea just how much I love them. If she wanted to find a way to hurt me through the divorce she certainly succeeded by moving our boys two thousand miles away.

I would love to have a civil relationship with my ex-wife and her family; after all, they're the ones taking an important role in bringing up my sons. I'm thankful Nancy is a good mother and her parents are fine people. They have taken their daughter's side and I can't expect them to do otherwise. Divorce is devastating for the entire family as I learned as a teenager, and I'm glad Nancy has a support system to lean on. Nancy's father, Nick, took almost as much interest in my football career as my own dad. In fact Nick has been crazy about football all of his life, growing up in the shadow of Cleveland Stadium, home of Lou "the Toe" Groza, Jimmy Brown and the other members of those storied Cleveland Browns football teams.

Nancy was a big part of the success I experienced in my football career, and she supported my aspirations in good times and bad. We were together for fourteen years, four years of dating and ten of marriage. I can't believe that after so much time together there can be hatred. I hope at some point we can both recognize how important it is to the growth and security of our sons for us to be friends. For now, there is a good deal of animosity, fostered, I believe, by her legal counsel. I've recognized my mistakes and have accepted my rightful share of responsibility for the breakup of our marriage. And I know I have to learn to make the best of a lousy situation.

As has likely happened to everyone who has gone through a marriage breakup, some mutual friends melted away, feeling they had to choose sides. Others didn't. Without the help of several people, notably my good friends Troy Christian and Randy Pollock, I'm not sure what might have happened to me during that difficult period. Troy knew how much the separation from Yin and Yang (Chris and Drew) depressed me and saw to it I was seldom alone for the first several months.

I didn't let many teammates know what I was going through. Glen Suitor was about the only one, and he did exactly what you'd expect a best friend to do: he kept me company by busting my chops at one of my simulated football strategy games. The people I really leaned on a tremendous amount and who did everything possible to help me through the separation were the Roughrider front office staff. Alan Ford and Jill McDougall were wonderful; they supported me as if I were family. This meant a lot to someone whose nearest family member was a few thousand miles away. They showed they cared about me, not as a ballplayer but as a person. At other times when I just needed to talk, Liz Measner, Vickie Poitras or Barry Taman took turns trying to cheer me up.

The last and most recent adversity I have faced is my first major injury. Injury in a violent sport like football has to be accepted as part of the game. Though I'd had back problems since my sixth season in the league and the occasional pulled muscle, it wasn't until 1994 that I was sidelined (in game thirteen of season thirteen for those with a superstitious bent). I suffered a severe tear of the quad muscle in my thigh. The best efforts of trainer Ivan Gutfriend and our medical staff couldn't get me back before the end of the season. Teammate Dan Farthing, who is knowledgeable in the field of physiology, suggested that the injury might have simply been an accident waiting to happen, the muscle gradually weakening and finally letting go. I think he's probably right.

Though some may suggest a kicker shouldn't get hurt because he doesn't get involved in the physical part of the game there are occasions when a kicker is thrust into the play in the role of blocker or tackler, and while it doesn't happen often, it *does* happen. In addition, the very act of kicking a football 40, 50 or 60 yards puts the same kind of strain on the leg and lower body as a pitcher's arm experiences when it hurls a baseball at ninety miles per hour. There have been kickers (Lui Passaglia comes to mind) who have been plagued by injuries during their careers.

In my own case I give a great deal of the credit for my relatively injury-free career to Ivan and our medical staff, Dr. Jack Alexander (who also delivered both my sons) and Drs. Ron Ailsby and Donovan Brown. Ivan is tremendously skilled at what is a difficult and underrated job. His value to the organization is in his ability to reduce the number of injuries and to speed up the return to the field of players who are hurt.

The toughest part of being injured, and I'm sure most professional athletes would say the same thing, is not being a part of what's happening on the field. I hated having to stand on the sidelines and watch somebody else doing my job even though Paul McCallum, who was obtained on loan from the B.C. Lions, did a great job for us. What was troubling was that it wasn't *me* out there doing what I'd practiced a lifetime to do.

Being hurt reinforced how much I love this game and how much I want to continue to play it for some time yet. It forced me to recognize that I am getting older and that I have to put more effort into physical conditioning to ensure my body will get me through a complete season.

This was reinforced by Suits, who took me aside at the end of the 1994 season, and as only a friend can, told me it was time I got on a better program for strengthening during the off-season and a consistent maintenance conditioning program during the season. He was absolutely right. I hope if anything the injury that kept me out of the last six games of the 1994 season will actually end up prolonging my career. One thing I do know, I never again want to experience the frustration of having to stand on the sidelines and not be able to contribute to what's happening out on the field.

After a tough loss a few years ago, I watched the film *The Natural*. A line from Glenn Close stuck with me: "I believe we have two lives . . . the life we learn with and the life we live with after that." If adversity is part of the life we learn with, I hope I've come to the life I live after that.

CHAPTER 11

The Twilight Zone

Pendleton: You wanna know something? At my age in any other business... I'd be young.
Corkle: Well, look at it this way. Pretty soon you'll get into another business and have a real life, you know?
Pendleton: I don't know what that means. This is the only business I know that's real. —HEAVEN CAN WAIT, 1978

NEXT TO THE BIRTH of my two sons, playing football in Canada and in particular in Saskatchewan has been the greatest thing to happen to me. I've been coached for the most part by some of the finest people in the game and have played against and alongside some remarkable athletes, many of whom I'm proud to call friends. I've done all that and been paid for doing it.

As a matter of fact I've been paid pretty well for doing something I now love more as each year goes by. As a Canadian Football League player I don't earn the kind of salary that has become the norm in other leagues and in other sports. The CFL has made an effort, somewhat to the chagrin of its players, to implement a system of financial responsibility for member teams. In reality the league had no choice. With a struggling economy and increased competition for consumers' entertainment dollars, fiscal restraints were needed to ensure the league's long-term survival. It's pretty simple math. Teams can't continue to spend more on players' salaries and operational budgets than they take in at the gate.

But while the math may be simple the implications of the decisions made are anything but. As the 1995 season approached and the province of Saskatchewan prepared to host its first Grey Cup game, the fans made one thing clear. They quite rightly felt that the Riders couldn't afford a repeat of the exodus that followed the 1993 season when we lost Jeff Fairholm, Jearld Baylis, Charles Anthony, Kent Austin, Craig Hendrickson and Barry Wilburn, all of whom went elsewhere in search of what they felt was fair market value for their services. Though we fielded a competitive and highly entertaining team in 1994, there was real concern about the effect of another mass departure. I shared this concern and at the same time I sympathized with General Manager Alan Ford, who has to balance fielding a winning team with the need to keep costs under control.

It's a conundrum, no doubt about it. Overspend and the 2.1 million dollar deficit we currently carry grows bigger and soon all the telethons in the world won't keep us afloat. Underspend and the product on the field suffers, the fans stay home and we're sunk anyway. It's a difficult and delicate juggling act small market general managers must perform, and often it seems they're damned if they do and damned if they don't.

The vast majority of CFL players do not earn enough money to retire once their playing days are over. In fact many earn less than minor league hockey and baseball players. While we have a few highly paid stars under the league's marquee player distinction, even those players—Flutie, Austin, Dunigan, Archer, et al.—would be making several times their present salaries if they played in other leagues. I don't begrudge any of them a penny of what they earn. They're good for their teams, the league and the fans. Only Rocket Ismail stands out as a clear exception.

The rest of us fall into another category. As a result many CFL athletes are preparing themselves for life after football by seeking employment while their football careers are still in progress. By acquiring the skills and experience necessary to earn a living after our playing days are over, we hope to make the transition to a life away from football less painful.

Throughout my tenure as a Rider I have been fortunate to gain valuable work experience. For a period of time I was employed by NewGrade Energy and Federated Co-ops of Saskatchewan working on the Heavy Oil Upgrader project in Regina. It was a field in which I previously had little or no expertise; however, with the help of several capable and patient senior process personnel I soon developed an excellent working knowledge of the systems employed in heavy oil upgrading. From there I moved on to Giles Communications of Regina and learned some of the ins and outs of the public relations and advertising business.

I made a brief foray into the food and beverage industry when Jeff Fairholm and I opened Mutt and Jeff's sports bar and restaurant with Jack Nicolle. It was one of the greatest learning experiences of my life and something both Jeff and I really enjoyed. Jack is now the sole proprietor and I honestly don't know how he does it; I had no idea how much time and energy goes into the running of a quality restaurant.

A number of players have regarded self-promotion as another way of bringing their earnings more in line with what athletes in other sports take home. Unfortunately, in the CFL, both the league and member teams often hindered the player who wished to promote himself. In recent years the attitude of the league has changed, and a number of us have appreciated

The Twilight Zone

the opportunity to establish co-promotions with businesses in our respective CFL cities. A couple of years ago I followed the lead of Kent Austin and Ray Elgaard in establishing a promotional package with an automobile dealership. The deal—with Auto Gallery Suzuki in Regina—calls for me to be available for on-sight promotions and to represent the company at various functions in return for the privilege of driving one of its vehicles. I think the arrangement has been beneficial for both of us and I've certainly enjoyed working with the Auto Gallery people. I have also entered into an agreement with Thompson's Marine Connection of Regina. While it may seem to be something of a contradiction—a marine outfit on the prairies—Saskatchewan is blessed with some of the finest fresh water lakes in the country, and the business is doing well. In addition I have a personal and business relationship with Amtrak Communications—a long established radio and cellular telephone company in the province.

On occasion some fans have taken exception to players' involvement in these kinds of promotions. When Jeff Fairholm was with the Riders he appeared on a television talk show wearing clothing displaying the logo of a firm he was doing some work with. During the program a caller claimed it was a disgrace Jeff was not wearing Roughriders' apparel while appearing on television. Jeff, never shy about speaking his mind, told the fan it was none of his business. And to be honest I agree. When I'm appearing on behalf of the team and often when I'm not, I will wear something that denotes my association with the ball club. But if I have a chance to provide some exposure for another organization I'm working with, then I don't consider that I'm breaching my allegiance to the Saskatchewan Roughriders. In fact most players go out of their way to promote their teams and the league. I include myself among this number.

Many players also are heavily involved with the various charitable organizations that request our assistance. I count it a privilege to have been able to support the Terry Fox Run, the Regina Humane Society, the Cancer Society, the Diabetes Association, the Multiple Sclerosis Society, the Tamarac Foundation, the Learning Disabilities Association of Saskatchewan and the United Way. I have always been particularly interested in working with groups involved with children. One of the things that has pleased me most about my association with Auto Gallery owner Tom Glenn is an annual fund-raiser he hosts that helps to ensure that every child in Regina hospitals at Christmas receives a gift. A couple of years ago David Pitcher, Jeff Fairholm and I joined Santa Claus in delivering the gifts. Last year Ray Bernard joined in. It is one of the most meaningful Christmas experiences I have had.

I've also enjoyed being active on the Saskatchewan and western Canadian banquet circuit. I've probably visited with more people in the four corners of the province of Saskatchewan than most politicians. Which, in a roundabout way, brings me to a topic I'm often asked about—what I would like to do when my playing days are over. I've given the issue considerable thought and have decided that politics, either at the provincial or federal level, may be the career that will follow football. Through the highs and even the lows of my career, this province has been very good to me, and I'd like to give something back to its people, who are the envy of every franchise in our league. While I concede politics may be new ground for me, I've succeeded as a rookie before, and I have some realistic ideas about where to begin and what I want to accomplish.

I don't know exactly when I will begin to try to pry open those political doors. But I can't think of a better place to build a career after football. If there are drawbacks to living in

Saskatchewan, they are few, and they are far outweighed by the province's most valuable resource—its people.

I have found after many years playing here that on the whole the football fans are loyal not only to the Roughrider organization but to its players. Ron Lancaster and George Reed are still revered and still the subject of conversation years after their retirement. Roger Aldag is already held in similar esteem. Not a bad fate when you think about it. The truth is I've become pretty passionate about this province. During the early 1980s, when the Roughriders weren't a very good football team, whenever we heard of disgruntled players on other teams asking to be traded, the cry almost always was accompanied with the footnote "anywhere but Saskatchewan." Yet players were often surprised by what they found. Punter Gerry McGrath went so far as to pronounce the place as "great—not at all what I expected."

I couldn't agree more.

CHAPTER 12

We're Taking on Water but the Ship Isn't Sinking

... spirit of achievement, teamwork. You might say the game embodies what has made our country great. It's a great game. ... —THE LONGEST YARD, 1974

THE SPECTACLE OF THE POSSE galloping back and forth between Las Vegas and Jackson and finally riding into the sunset in the spring of 1995 serves as a metaphor for what has gone wrong with the Canadian Football League. Only a few weeks from training camp, eager new franchises and struggling established teams awaited some sign of leadership that might affirm the league's credibility in the minds of skeptical fans. What they got instead was Commissioner Larry Smith writhing his way through another crisis. Teams and fans had no schedule, no divisional alignment and no playoff structure. A league that can ill-afford the errors and pratfalls that have plagued it stubbed its toe once again.

During the thirteen seasons I have played in the CFL I have seen the league in good times and bad and have watched enormous changes take place. Over the last decade Canadian football, like other professional sports, has faced problems typical of the entertainment business: rising costs, a volatile econ-

We're Taking on Water but the Ship Isn't Sinking

omy and increased competition for the public's discretionary income. Nevertheless, with dedicated leadership at the league level and for the most part competent and committed owners, the CFL historically has been able to meet these challenges successfully. More recently, however, and particularly during the last four or five years, we seem to have taken two steps back for every step forward.

When an organization faces the difficult challenges the CFL now confronts, management blunders, real or apparent, receive special attention from a zealous media, which reinforces the negative opinions of our league's all-too-eager detractors. As a result the public perception is that the continued existence of the CFL is tenuous at best. Prior to the 1995 North–South divisional alignment, the only healthy Canadian franchise in the East was the Winnipeg Blue Bombers, a team geographically located in the West but placed in the Eastern Conference to give the division a workable number of teams. Two of the remaining three Eastern Canadian teams, Hamilton and Ottawa, are in continuing desperate straits and the other, Toronto, is invariably mentioned whenever discussions about NFL expansion take place. In the West both Calgary and Edmonton required massive season ticket drives in order to remain viable going into the 1995 season, something familiar to residents of Saskatchewan.

My belief in Canadian football has remained constant through the confusing and troubling recent history of the league. I have had several opportunities to head south but the bottom line has not necessarily been financial. The truth is I enjoy the football played in this league. It is the most exciting and entertaining football played anywhere, and I'm convinced it is played by outstanding athletes. I'm not suggesting the football played in the NFL is not good football.

It's simply a very different game played by a very different type of athlete.

My opinions on the game of football have not been formed solely on the basis of the attention I pay to the CFL. I watch bantam and high school football in Regina; I follow and enjoy the Canadian Intercollegiate Athletic Union (CIAU) and to a lesser extent I watch American college ball and the National Football League. During the seventies I watched the old World Football League, then the United States Football League and more recently the World League of American Football.

For the most part the NFL bores me. I have enjoyed, like any other football fan, the greatness of people like Joe Montana, particularly in his glory years with the 49ers, and more recently Steve Young, as both men teamed up time after time with Jerry Rice. I have admired the poetry of Dan Marino throwing to his great receivers. And let's not forget Warren Moon, who has proven to be as dominant a passer in the NFL as he was in the CFL. But all too often the spectacular play of these and other gifted players is overshadowed by the three-yards-and-a-cloud-of-dust football typical of the game south of the border. It has been said and bears repeating: great *players* don't necessarily make great games. Exciting *plays* makes great games and in that regard Canadian football is unrivaled.

We have all watched disgustedly as players from opposing teams appeared to go through the motions and finally walk off the field in the closing minutes of an NFL game because it was for all intents and purposes over. In the CFL, with the twenty-second play clock and three downs, it is possible to score two or three times in the space of a couple of minutes, and very few games with the exception of the occasional blowout are decided much before the final gun. The spectacular playoff run of the B.C. Lions in 1994 exemplifies what I think is the greatness of the CFL. The Lions won both their playoff contests and a thrilling Grey Cup game all with time running out on the clock. I'm not sure how you can make football more exciting than this.

The emphasis on offense in the Canadian Football League is characterized by the array of great throwing quarterbacks who have electrified crowds over the years. Lancaster, Etcheverry, Liske and Jackson—the list would easily fill a page. In keeping with the tradition of great passers the CFL currently employs its most spectacular group of throwing quarterbacks ever. Tracy Ham, Matt Dunigan, Kent Austin, David Archer—these guys love to throw the football. Atop the list is Calgary's Doug Flutie, who has won the Most Valuable Player Award four years in a row. He is without doubt one of the most entertaining athletes playing the game on either side of the Forty-ninth Parallel. Having these quarterbacks in the CFL means the ball spends a lot of the time in the air, which generally leads to more scoring. That's exciting, that's what fans want to see and that's what they see in the CFL. The following comparison of average points scored per game in the NFL versus the CFL appeared in *Canadian Football Illustrated:*

	NFL	CFL
1983	43.7	51.6
1984	42.4	50.7
1985	43.1	45.4
1986	41.0	47.9

The difference becomes even greater as we compare recent years:

	NFL	CFL
1989	41.2	54.7
1990	40.2	61.9
1991	38.0	64.2
1992	37.5	57.4

I realize football purists will say defensive football is interesting, even entertaining, and I agree. But, at a time when a number of major sports are looking at ways to increase the amount of scoring in their games, my contention is that the CFL, because of its rules, the dimensions of its field and the type of athlete it attracts, already has the desired ingredients in place.

Which isn't to say defense is absent in the CFL, not at all. The reason for the difference in points scored between the CFL and NFL (and a coinciding difference in total yards gained per game) is that to be successful in three-down football the ball *has* to be in the air. Tony Gabriel, in his book *Double Trouble*, makes the excellent point that the passing game results in another of football's most thrilling plays—the interception—also being front and center in Canadian football. Yet, despite the excitement that is clearly the most outstanding feature of our league, we continue to hear about sagging attendance in some venues, declining or nonexistent profits in several others and the threat of the collapse of the entire league. These were the dangers the CFL faced at the end of the 1992 season when expansion began.

While declining attendance in CFL cities is a concern it must be understood in relation to market area population or we run the risk of interpreting attendance levels as an overall decline in interest in our game. The following comparison of CFL and NFL attendance as a percentage of population puts the issue into perspective. CFL teams may have experienced problems with attendance, but they still fare very well in comparison with their American counterparts. Regina has by far the highest attendance levels relative to population but we note that most Canadian cities have higher relative attendance than U.S. cities.

We're Taking on Water but the Ship Isn't Sinking

ATTENDANCE PER CAPITA IN THE NFL

CITY	1986 CENSUS METRO POP.	AVERAGE ATTENDANCE	PER CAPITA PERCENTAGE
†Green Bay/ Brown County	524,000	56,621	28.45
Buffalo	1,175,600	78,348	6.66
New Orleans	1,307,000	67,663	5.18
Kansas City	1,575,400	75,778	4.81
Indianapolis	1,237,000	50,991	4.12
Denver	1,858,000	73,851	3.97
Cleveland	2,769,000	71,059	2.57
Cincinnati	1,729,000	44,159	2.55
Phoenix	2,030,000	51,025	2.51
San Diego	2,370,400	59,354	2.51
Pittsburg	2,284,100	55,116	2.41
Minnesota	2,387,500	57,303	2.40
Tampa Bay	1,995,100	47,189	2.37
Seattle	2,421,000	54,835	2.26
Miami	3,001,000	67,240	2.24
Atlanta	2,737,000	57,067	2.09
Dallas	3,766,000	63,759	1.69
Houston	3,642,000	56,565	1.55
Detroit	4,620,200	66,746	1.44
Washington	3,734,200	50,221	1.34
New England	4,110,000	45,371	1.10
San Francisco	6,042,000	62,685	1.04
Philadelphia	5,963,300	61,097	1.02
††NY Giants	9,060,000	73,021	0.81
††NY Jets	9,060,000	66,463	0.73
††LA Raiders	6,885,000	48,955	0.71
Chicago	8,181,000	58,229	0.71
††LA Rams	6,885,000	45,401	0.66
NFL Totals	97,149,800	1,666,110	1.72
NFL Average	3,469,600	59,504	1.72

†Green Bay plays three home dates in Milwaukee (pop. 1,571,700). Combined pop. 1,770,700 makes per capita percentage 3.20%—6th best in the NFL
††New York, Los Angeles populations split in half for two teams.

ATTENDANCE PER CAPITA IN THE CFL

CITY	1986 CENSUS METRO POP.	AVERAGE ATTENDANCE	PER CAPITA PERCENTAGE
Regina	192,000	23,833	12.41
Winnipeg	652,000	25,110	3.85
Calgary	754,000	28,167	3.74
Edmonton	840,000	30,511	3.63
Hamilton	600,000	17,533	2.92
Ottawa	921,000	22,022	2.39
Vancouver	1,603,000	28,444	1.77
Sacramento	1,385,200	16,973	1.23
Toronto	3,893,000	25,433	0.65
CFL Totals	10,840,200	218,026	2.01
CFL Average	1,204,666	24,225	2.01

And this brings us to expansion, or to put it more accurately, expansion into the United States since the Canadian Football League brain trust has apparently concluded that expansion in this country is not feasible. On this point I'm not sure sufficient investigation has taken place to warrant such a blanket assessment. The problem, of course, is the lack of stadiums in cities other than Montreal. To date there simply hasn't been anyone stepping forward who is ready to make the financial commitment required to build a thirty- to forty-thousand seat facility. Nevertheless, experimentation in uncertain Canadian markets could hardly have had more disastrous results than some of the league's forays into supposedly solid American locations.

I stress that like most CFL players I am not opposed to expansion into the U.S. But I have three concerns: that expansion seems to have taken place on a haphazard basis without sufficient homework done in advance of franchise approvals; that expansion into the United States is seen as the *only* way of ensuring the survival of the CFL; and that the integrity of the

We're Taking on Water but the Ship Isn't Sinking

Canadian game is not being adequately protected and preserved.

There is no doubt that our commissioner's frenzied rushing here and there, desperately doling out franchises, was embarrassing for the league. The impression throughout 1992–93 was that if *any* American were to indicate even passing interest in owning a CFL team there would be a news conference forty-eight hours later to announce the newest franchise approval. That was followed inevitably by the sheepish announcement some weeks later that the interested party lacked money, a stadium and fan interest and that the CFL would regrettably be looking elsewhere.

Despite head office false starts and fumbles the inevitable expansion took place with the Sacramento Gold Miners joining the league in time for the 1993 season. They were followed by the Las Vegas Posse, the Shreveport Pirates and the Baltimore whatevers. Then came the demise of Nick Miletti's Vegas franchise, the relocation of Sacramento to San Antonio and the addition of Birmingham and Memphis. Although the expansion to the United States can hardly be given rave reviews to this point, the league continues its fast-track move south. Recently Larry Smith told a Calgary talk show it would be preferable for the league to expand in an orderly fashion—step A, then step B, then C and so on, but it couldn't afford this luxury; instead steps A, B and C all had to happen at once.

I disagree. I believe such haste has led to the problems we have seen. Also troubling is something of a Catch-22 at work here. If expansion into the U.S. fails, the survival of our league is in grave danger. If, on the other hand, the American experiment succeeds, the commissioner and league governors may face another problem—the threat of a league dominated by its

American partners, particularly if we ever arrive at a point where U.S.-based teams are the majority.

While Americans are for the most part good neighbors there is an inevitable tendency for the bigger to roll over the smaller. I think it was Woody Allen who said when the lion and the lamb lie down together things aren't going to be so good for the lamb. I am concerned that American dominance will lead to an attempt to force rule changes. This will surely lead to an erosion of the very things that make our game distinct and exciting—three downs, a bigger field, twelve players—and maybe even a name change to something like (God forbid) the Continental Fast Football League. I don't think it's inconceivable that a group of even moderately successful American teams may eventually decide to split off and set up a league of their own. This would put the Canadian teams right back where they were at the end of the 1992 season.

I'm concerned that one of the biggest stumbling blocks to the success of expansion south may be the attitude of the American football fan. The unfortunate truth is that most Americans see the CFL as an inferior, minor league product. Some may be willing to give the Canadian game a look but very few will concede, no matter how great the evidence, that there is a brand of football more exciting than their own. The average American has the attitude that if something is not invented in the United States, it can't possibly be good. This is in startling contrast to our own unfortunate belief that if something is Canadian it *must* be inferior.

An incident during our 1994 visit to Louisiana brought home the reality of the image problem we face in the United States. The day before our game several of us made our way to a Shreveport shopping mall. In an athletic wear store, the clerk, a young male, asked about our Roughriders' logo. We

We're Taking on Water but the Ship Isn't Sinking

explained that we were there to play against the Pirates. The clerk then asked, "Have you guys ever thought of playing pro?" It is an attitude we encounter over and over when we travel to the United States, and it is one of the biggest challenges facing our commissioner and the owners of American-based teams. If the negative public perception can be overcome I believe even the Gleibermans may be successful in places like Shreveport. People in the South love their football and if we can show them how great a product we have, franchises like Birmingham, Memphis and Shreveport may turn a profit. Of course, they will be helped by the large number of CFL free agents heading south to play in their home country for better money under better tax laws.

Birmingham has a special problem. It will have to survive in a market fiercely loyal to its two powerhouse college teams, the University of Alabama and Auburn University. We shouldn't kid ourselves for a minute that the CFL is going to threaten the survival of either the Crimson Tide or the Tigers. Add to this the fact that the Birmingham football fan has seen the coming and going of two World Football League teams, the Americans in 1974 and the Vulcans in 1975, the United States Football League Stallions from 1983–85 and the World League of American Football Fire from 1991–92. One can forgive Alabama football fans for being a little jaded about professional football. Even a big-money owner like Art Williams could have his hands full there. An article by Kevin Scarbinsky in the *Birmingham News* echoes the perception problem Canadian football has in Alabama: "Other men with deep pockets and bottomless egos have tried to sell minor league football before. What will he [Williams] say when the Birmingham fan discovers there is no Emmitt Smith or Steve Young in the CFL? And there isn't. What will he do when he discovers that the choice between a Southeastern Conference game involving Alabama, and a CFL game, is no choice at all for the Alabama fan? And it won't be even when the Alabama game is only available on TV."

When I read comments like this I hope Mr. Williams is able to shove it down Scarbinsky's throat. Unfortunately history and a whole lot of attitudes exactly like Scarbinsky's are against the Birmingham franchise. I hope this is one time history does not repeat itself.

It's important to note that not everyone is against us down there. Former Auburn coach Pat Dye said about our brand of football: "It's fun; it's an offensive game. It's a fast-paced game and it's wide open. If the people of Alabama will accept it and learn it, they will thoroughly enjoy it. It's just exciting football; there is nothing in the world boring about Canadian football. Alabama fans who want to see wide open offense will see it."

I am also worried about San Antonio, a franchise facing many of the same problems as Birmingham. Murray McCormick, in early 1993 in the *Leader-Post*, quoted the sports editor from the *San Antonio Union Express*, Barry Robinson, who wondered why the CFL wanted to include San Antonio in its expansion plans: "Why San Antonio? And I hate to say that about my own town. We were among the worst in attendance in the USFL, the World Football League and had the worst attendance in the World League of American Football. We have a bad history of attendance."

Given this kind of feedback from an individual much closer to the sports scene in San Antonio than anyone in the CFL, one wonders at Larry Smith's dogged desire to sow a franchise on such barren soil. Not surprisingly the original San Antonio franchise never made it to the starting gate and the result was another black eye for our league. Yet only two years later the

CFL approved the move of the Sacramento Gold Miners to the Texas city where 150 years ago a band of gallant men died trying to defend a tiny fort against an attack from the Mexican army. Owner Fred Anderson may be facing the same odds as Crockett, Travis, Bowie and the rest of the defenders of the Alamo.

One other note here. If expansion is as successful as the CFL movers and shakers envisage, what will be the reaction of the NFL decision makers? Will they be content to stand idly by while we make a dent in their stronghold and their wallets? I doubt it. What has up to now been fairly idle chitchat about NFL expansion into Canada and a return to Baltimore may become much more than mere talk.

Another major concern with expansion has to do with the apparent assumption that moving into the U.S. is seen not as a part of the solution to the league's problems, but as the *only* solution. I am disturbed that the marketing of the CFL and the consolidation of existing Canadian franchises seems to be less a priority at the league level than helter-skelter expansion south. League officers, so eager to divvy out questionable American expansion franchises, adopt a particularly hard-line toward flagship Canadian teams with threats to relocate them if certain financial conditions are not met quickly. Apparently the best marketing ploy the CFL can offer is to threaten fans: buy so many season tickets or lose your team. This may be the reality of the situation, but surely we can sell our game on a more positive note than that. Lean and mean may be necessary, but it needs to be applied on both sides of the border. Had this been the case from the outset we may have avoided some of the humiliating distractions the league really didn't need.

Finally and perhaps most importantly I am disturbed by what I see as an erosion of the Canadian-ness of our game, a trend I fear may increase as more Americans purchase CFL franchises. The commissioner has vowed that the Canadian Football League will retain its uniqueness no matter where the games are played. He has been quoted as saying, "The CFL brand of football, wide-open, three-down football with an emphasis on offense and speed is what we will export. The league has unique qualities that have allowed it to survive this long and we will not let that uniqueness be lost just for financial gain."

These are worthy sentiments, but I'm not convinced of Larry Smith's sincerity. In 1994 we found ourselves playing in Shreveport on a field that, in addition to being one of the worst I have ever played on in my life, had shorter end zones than CFL regulations call for. In Las Vegas we played in the UNLV stadium, again with shorter end zones and with a narrower-than-regulation field that necessitated the hash marks being moved. And, of course, we find ourselves playing against teams with completely American rosters.

In addition to being one of the few professional sports with different sets of rules for different teams (even baseball with its designated hitter in one league and not the other has to deal with the problem only during the World Series) it seems to me that Commissioner Smith's pronouncements notwithstanding we are in danger of losing many of the elements—and the people—that have made this game *our* game. Unquestionably a move is afoot to slash Canadian content on existing Canadian rosters. Canadian players are understandably upset.

The CFL's drive to reduce the number of Canadian players on rosters may do massive and irreparable harm to the football currently being played in the Canadian Intercollegiate Athletic Union. With the reduction or removal of quotas for Canadians on the rosters of CFL teams and the resulting reluctance of teams to take the time to develop Canadian newcomers to the league, it follows that Canadian kids coming out of high school who are serious about pursuing careers in professional football will more and more be forced to turn to American colleges with their extensive and expensive programs to get the grounding they need. That would be unfortunate. It would be a shame were the CFL to eliminate players like Dave Sapunjis, Ray Elgaard, Jeff Fairholm, Chris Walby, Blake Marshall and so many others simply because it was no longer viable to sign the Canadian kid who might need a little time to develop his talent in favor of the American who may initially be a little further along.

Some critics hold that nationality should not be a factor in roster selection. I remind them that we live next to a giant neighbor with a huge population, enormous wealth, a monstrous communication machine and an unrivaled national self-esteem. This attitude was exemplified by the prediction of former CFL player and now television commentator James Curry, who stated that the Sacramento Gold Miners, with their American roster, would go 18 and 0 in their first season in the league. His punditry was proved absurdly wrong when the Gold Miners failed to even make the playoffs, but the real wonder is that someone who supposedly knows the game could say something so inane.

Regulated Canadian content on team rosters is not a nationality or a skills issue though I admit management has a point when it says there aren't enough Canadians to give teams depth at certain positions. It's a money issue, plain and simple. If rosters are opened up to an unlimited number of Americans there will be so much competition for jobs that the league will be able to institute a WLAF-style position-by-position salary cap and salaries will drop. The result will be a weakening of the CFL's talent base as our star players opt to try their luck in the NFL. Even borderline CFL players may head south, feeling that NFL practice rosters will pay more than a CFL job that falls under the constraints of a salary cap.

The elimination of Canadians has another implication for the league. When we lose our Canadian content we also lose a valuable link with the community. For the most part it is the Canadian players who stay in the community in the off-season doing charity work and promoting their teams. Maybe we could learn a lesson or two from the citizens of Quebec. I have admiration for the energetic effort of Francophone Canadians to preserve their culture and language though I can't agree when it expresses itself in a sense of nationalism that would break up Canada. But perhaps some of this nationalistic fervor and dedication is needed as our CFL decision makers grapple with the complex problems associated with expansion into the United States.

If there was any doubt about how Canadians feel about American encroachment on one of their national institutions they sent a strong message during the run-up to the 1994 Grey Cup between Baltimore and the B.C. Lions. There was a lot more to that game than a friendly rivalry between teams from opposite sides of the border. It was the first time an American team was in the running to win our Canadian Football League trophy. It also was one of the few times Canadian patriotic pride and nationalism rose up and made itself heard as it had during the legendary Canada–Russia hockey battles. It manifested itself in a tremendous coming together of support for the Lions. The game presented an opportunity for us to beat a team that is based outside Canada and doesn't even play by our rules.

When I came into the league in 1982, I made a promise to

myself that I would not attend a Grey Cup game unless I was one of the participating players. I broke this promise for the first time in 1994 as I realized that getting to one championship game in thirteen seasons just wasn't enough. I went to Vancouver to cheer on the Lions.

The league in cooperation with CP Rail had invited a few current players and several CFL alumni to join the surviving members of the 1944 Grey Cup champs from Montreal, the Navy Combines (St. Hyacinthe-Donacona) on a train ride from Calgary to Vancouver through the Rockies to commemorate the fiftieth anniversary of their championship. It was a wonderful experience. I can rest easy in the knowledge that football players don't change from one generation to the next. The players on that 1944 squad—people like Dick Swarbrick, John Crncich, Moe Segal and Sam Abbott—talked about doing exactly the same things back then that my teammates and I do now.

The game, I have to say, was almost as exciting as the 1989 match the Roughriders played in. It was the perfect situation: the team of the host city versus the invaders from south of the border. The game lived up to its advance billing, and while it wasn't the best-played Grey Cup ever staged it was among the most entertaining and was a fabulous showpiece for our game, complete with the last-play heroics that are a trademark of Canadian football.

The post-game tirades by several members of the Baltimore team were the only downside. Among those heard from after the game, only Coach Don Matthews and quarterback Tracy Ham displayed real class. This doesn't surprise me as both men are great competitors and have the best interests of the league at heart. However, the comments of several other Baltimore players were utterly tasteless. Was there controversy? Of course, there almost always is. Did Ray Alexander catch the critical pass that set up Lui Passaglia's twin shots at the game-winning field goal? I don't know. Did this call or any other cost Baltimore the game? Not likely.

Calgary sportswriter Murray Rauw's game story included a good sampling of the Baltimore whining: Charles Anthony, a former teammate of mine, said, "They took the game; they didn't want an American team to win the Grey Cup. We played against thirteen men all year anytime we played a team from Canada. This league will never grow this way. They need some ethics." Karl Anthony, Most Valuable Player of the game and former Calgary Stampeder, complained, "If I was B.C. I wouldn't even want to take that win. . . . We knew it would be like this. It was no secret." Mike Pringle, runner-up for the CFL's Most Outstanding Player Award for 1994, sniveled, "If the league isn't going to be fair, they should put more teams in damn Canada instead of the States, put a team in Montreal or something. I know it wasn't a big stink like this after the World Series. I know we didn't cry about that, but that's a pro league." Irvin Smith, Baltimore cornerback, whined, "The referees gave them two opportunities to win the damn game in the last minute and thirty seconds. . . . Karl Anthony told me two days ago if it was a close game, the referees would keep that cup in Canada." Chris Armstrong, former Edmonton Eskimo, summed up: "That's been going on all year. Every time we're in a close game we lose because of the officials."

Many people by the way thought Baltimore wouldn't have appeared in the Grey Cup at all but for an errant call by an official in the Eastern Final against Winnipeg that led to Baltimore's only touchdown. The major was scored by none other than Karl Anthony, one of the main complainers. Nothing like a little selective recall to soothe the soul.

We're Taking on Water but the Ship Isn't Sinking

Then there was another former teammate, Jearld Baylis, telling a reporter for the *Vancouver Province* he wouldn't talk to any "#@*#% Canadian reporters." I was especially disappointed at Charles and Jearld, who for four and eight years respectively earned good livings in "damn" Canada.

A few points the complaining Baltimore players might want to note: it was a completely Canadian offensive line that blocked for 213 rushing yards against an totally American defensive line; it was a Canadian fullback, Sean Millington, who rushed 13 times for 85 yards; and it was a defensive line featuring three Canadians that held Mike Pringle, the all-time single-season CFL rushing record holder, to 71 yards on 18 carries. Finally it was another "damn" Canadian who made the kick on the last play of the game after Baltimore failed to move the ball.

I hope the Baltimore players' comments came out of the frustration and the emotion we all feel in the immediate aftermath of a tough loss. The CFL now needs both Americans and Canadians for this league to work, and it needs us working together for the betterment of the league. As long as games are officiated by human beings, there will be bad calls. But no thinking person can honestly believe officials base calls on geography. Cross-border rivalry can be good for the CFL. A cross-border war of words can only do it harm.

Expansion into the United States may be necessary and even desirable as a means of saving the CFL from going the way of dinosaurs and fizzies. I applaud the commissioner and the league governors for making a bold and innovative move. I only question the speed of the move and the efforts to protect our game for Canadian players and fans. If we can eliminate some of the blunders (euphemistically referred to as "growing pains" by B.C. Lions owner Bill Comrie) in executing expansion and renew our commitment to preserve the Canadian identity of the CFL, I believe the future of the Canadian Football League can be a bright and exciting one Canadians *and* Americans will support.

CHAPTER 13

That Championship Season

Maybe is powerful stuff, son. The road to heaven is paved with maybes. You got a dream, you hold onto it. Everybody needs a dream. —TALENT FOR THE GAME, 1991

THE 1989 SEASON BEGAN much like others in the eighties. Though we had come off a decent year in 1988 with our first playoff appearance in what seemed like a millennium, there was no particular reason to think 1989 would be the year when the dreams of a lot of people would at last come true.

Training camp was once again to be staged at the University of Saskatchewan and sixty-nine hopefuls headed for the city of bridges. Among the highly touted rookies were Dan Payne, a 6' 7", 275-pound lineman, quarterback Bobby McAllister of Michigan State, who had pretty good college credentials but who didn't make the team, and defensive tackle Chuck Klingbeil from the University of Northern Michigan, the same school that brought us Bobby Jurasin. Chuck suffered a rib injury during camp and wound up going home and rejoining us later when he was sufficiently healed up. During the camp I signed a new contract for three years plus an option year.

ROBOKICKER

We played three preseason games that year as General Manager Alan Ford worked out a deal with Winnipeg's Cal Murphy to squeeze in an extra game. We met the Bombers at the Gordie Howe Bowl in Saskatoon and won 37–7. We followed with a 28–24 win over the Eskimos in Regina and suddenly a feeling of heady optimism was in the air. We had, after all, beaten two pretty good football clubs. We managed to bring everybody back to earth with a thud as we were bombed 30–13 in our last preseason game by the Lions in B.C. Place.

The day before our regular season-opener against Calgary, Nick Miliokas wrote an article in the *Leader-Post* entitled "What Do You Do After You've Done It all?" The piece was extremely complimentary toward me and referred to the 1987 and 1988 seasons, which had admittedly been good ones. "Ridgway's accuracy, his consistency, his dependability have brought him the respect and the recognition he was talking about that day in Vancouver, but they have also created a situation which is certain to produce pressure, as high expectations usually do. Pressure, of course, is something that every athlete experiences and place-kickers are no exception. Ridgway has learned to live with pressure, he has shown he can handle it, he has known good times and bad times in Saskatchewan.... He survived a general manager named John Herrera and a head coach named Jack Gotta. He has responded to every challenge that has come his way and at the age of thirty, he's in the prime of his career, he's on a roll, he is ... Robokicker."

Nick was right on the money with his insights regarding pressure. I suppose it's true I've created an identity I have to live up to. Fans expect me to make every field goal I attempt. So do I. Had I been a little more erratic throughout my career, expectations might not be quite as high. On the other hand, had I been an erratic kicker, there might not have been a career at all. One thing I can say, no one puts more pressure on me to produce than I do.

Our season-opener that year was not only one of the most exciting in the history of our ball club but also was among the most heart-stopping games ever played in Taylor Field . . . period. We were trailing the Lary Kuharich Stampeders 26–6 after three quarters. Tom Burgess replaced Kent Austin midway through the third quarter and led us to 17 points in the final two minutes of the game. We scored a touchdown with 1:51 remaining, then recovered the ensuing onside kick. Four plays later Tom hit Don Narcisse in the end zone from the 42-yard line.

On the next Stampeder possession quarterback Danny Barrett attempted a pass to Larry Willis, who had the ball deflect off his hands and right to defensive back Jeff Treftlin. Jeff fell out-of-bounds and we had the ball back with a little time still remaining on the clock. We ran five consecutive running plays and then kicked a 42-yard field goal to win the game as time expired. I remember this kick. It was a beautiful night in Regina as we lined up on the left hash. Although I hit the ball well it didn't go down the middle and in fact barely slipped inside the left upright. It was the kind of kick a kicker tries to help with a little body English as it's in flight. Though my kicks sometimes have a tendency to fade this one decided to stay straight. It was a good thing. The game and the way it ended was a kind of omen, but at the time none of us knew it. We were just happy to win one that seemed pretty well out of reach.

We went to 2 and 0 with a 42–37 shoot-out victory over the B.C. Lions the following week. One of the highlights of the game was a Bobby Jurasin touchdown pass reception of 39 yards on a short yardage play. Later Bobby said he was all right about catching the pass but was scared to death about running with the ball. He ran well, as it turned out, and ended up carrying three defenders into the end zone. After he'd scored Bobby spiked the ball and then ran under the goalposts to signal the score with arms down at his sides as they do in Aussie football.

In game three of the season we were beaten 34–17 by the Tiger-Cats at Taylor Field in one of those classic summer thunderstorm games. Vicious, black clouds rolled in and we played half the game in a monsoon. For a while the rain was so thick it was impossible to see the other sideline. I kicked a couple of field goals in the game—one a 37-yarder into the wind and driving rain that was as difficult as any I have ever attempted. Because of the volume of rain there wasn't a dry ball in the park. I think the reason I made the kick was that the ball was soaked, which made it heavy enough to cut a path through the wind.

In game four we beat the Bombers 29–27 in Winnipeg. The next day one of the headlines in the *Winnipeg Sun* read, "Lightning Can't Stop Ridgway." I had kicked five field goals in the game. For the second week in a row we played in a torrential downpour. I was quoted in the story as saying that the storm had followed us from Saskatchewan to Winnipeg. At one point, after lightning cracked directly overhead, the referees ordered everyone off the field. I was standing on the sidelines when that bolt of lightning and the ensuing clap of thunder tore through the Manitoba sky. Gary Lewis, one of the tallest players, not wanting to be a human lightning rod, threw himself onto the turf.

We pounded Ottawa 58–22 in our fifth game of the year and had a 4 and 1 start to the season. During the game Ray Elgaard became the Riders' all-time leader in pass receptions, besting the 328 catches made by former record holder Chris DeFrance. (Hugh Campbell had 321 and George Reed 300 in their careers.) Clearly Ray was already among a very elite group of athletes and would soar to still greater heights in the years that followed.

Game six was in Hamilton and we were beaten 46–40 by the Tiger-Cats, which meant we had lost both games of our home-and-home series with the Tabbies, a point that became significant later. The loss marked the beginning of a slump. We were beaten by B.C. 37–25, then shellacked by Edmonton 45–19 at Commonwealth Stadium. Suddenly we were only a .500 football team. The Eskimos, on the other hand, had suffered only one loss to this point in the season.

We then lost the Labor Day Classic 28–20 to the Blue Bombers for our fourth straight defeat. Much of the optimism of the fans and media disappeared like the air in a punctured balloon. Our next game was pivotal. We went into the new SkyDome and knocked off the Argos 29–24. We won in dramatic fashion, scoring 16 points in the last three minutes. I would certainly put the Toronto game among the key moments that year. Mike Anderson was quoted afterward as saying prophetically, "This is a great psychological lift for us. In November we can look back at this, point to it, and say it's the turning point of our season."

The following week, in a typical Taylor Field wind, we handed the Eskimos their second loss of the season, 48–35. Of the 83 points scored that day, 70 were scored with the wind at the back of the scoring team. On those days it's critical to have the wind advantage in the fourth quarter. We trailed 35–27 going into the final quarter and with the wind behind us chalked up 21 points to win going away.

Never ones to enjoy prosperity for too long, we managed

to lose 36–27 the following week to an Ottawa team that had won only one previous game that season. Dean Dorsey kicked seven field goals and I was asked after the game by an Ottawa writer about Dean's performance. I was in a terrible mood over the loss to a team we should have beaten, and I said, "No big deal." When I saw the quote the next day in an Ottawa paper, I felt so bad I phoned Dean at home to congratulate him for having a great day and to apologize for my remark.

Game thirteen was at Taylor Field against the B.C. Lions and was *the* turning point of the season, which may sound odd because we lost to the Lions 32–30. This is the game that saw Glen Suitor called for interference on the final play. But the resulting loss brought the Saskatchewan Roughriders together, and more than any other moment of the season it set the stage for our run to the Grey Cup.

We dropped to 6 and 7 and B.C. closed to within two points of us at 5 and 8. We went into Calgary and, in what had become a crucial game for us, handled the Stampeders 39–26 to even our record at 7 and 7. The game had particular significance for our Rob Bresciani, a graduate of the Regina Rams' program. Because we had several injuries to starting receivers, Rob got the nod. When it was over he had made six catches for 194 yards and one touchdown. Twice he literally stole the ball out of the hands of Stampeder defenders and on another, with Tim McCray juggling the ball and about to drop it, Rob swept it up before it touched the ground for another outstanding reception. If ever a guy came off the bench to have an impact day, it was Rob Bresciani that day in Calgary.

Kent Austin also had a big game, setting an all-time Riders' single-game passing record at 492 yards as he went 29 of 37 with three touchdowns and no interceptions.

In game fifteen we knocked off the Argonauts 24–18 at Taylor Field. Going into the game, Argo Coach Bob O'Billovich was 6–0–1 in Regina and it was nice to finally beat him. The following week the Stampeders came into Saskatchewan and beat us 23–17 and once again our record was even.

Just before game seventeen defensive tackle James Curry left the team. He had been through arthroscopic surgery on his knee twice that year and had been forced to miss our two previous games. Prior to this time he had been having a huge year with 16 quarterback sacks in our first 14 games. James had wanted to play in our previous game, but Coach John Gregory felt he wasn't physically ready to go and told him he wouldn't be dressing. According to the *Leader-Post*, James felt missing the game would cost him a chance to earn some of the incentive bonuses in his contract so he left the club, returning to his home in Reno, Nevada.

It was a tough loss for the ball club and an unfortunate situation for James, but it was a story with a surprising ending. Rookie Chuck Klingbeil, having recovered from his training camp injury, was inserted into the lineup in James' spot and went on to play a major role in the playoffs and Grey Cup game.

In our last two games of the season we beat Calgary 34–19 and suffered a lopsided 49-17 loss to the Eskimos. The Edmonton game was a massacre, plain and simple. We had been decimated by injuries and were no match for the Eskimo team that finished the year at 16 and 2 (9 and 0 at Commonwealth Stadium).

We finished with a 9 and 9 record and weren't exactly riding a wave going into the playoffs. Nevertheless, we felt good about the Western Semi-Final in Calgary, having beaten the Stamps in three of our four meetings that year.

After a sluggish start we put together some impressive drives and were nursing a 23–9 lead going into the third quarter. Midway through that quarter, Kennard Martin ran it in three yards for the Stampeders, and Mark McLoughlin added a field goal a few minutes later to pull Calgary to within four. Then in the fourth quarter, after Calgary quarterback Danny Barrett injured his ankle, Terrence Jones came into the game and tossed a 36-yard touchdown pass to Mark Zeno, who outjumped Richie Hall to give the Stampeders the lead with 2:24 left in the game.

We got the ball back and Kent Austin moved us to the Calgary 50. On second down John Gregory sent in Brian Walling with a draw play. Brian had come to us only three weeks before from the Edmonton Eskimos' practice roster, and suddenly here he was front and center in one of the key plays of our entire season. Brian took the draw and rambled almost untouched fifty yards into the end zone to restore our lead. We added a field goal in the final minute and the game ended 33–26—our first playoff victory since 1976.

This was the good news. The bad news was that we would now face 16 and 2 Edmonton. We weren't given much of a chance against the mighty Eskimos, and to tell the truth I can't blame those who cast us in the role of the biggest underdogs since Custer. Some Edmonton scribes had picked the Esks to win by as much as 30 points, a reflection partly of the year they'd had and partly of the attitude of the city everybody loves to hate. Eskimo cornerback Andre Francis stated the Edmonton thinking going into the game: "There's no sense trying to put a false, humble act on when that's just not us." Defensive lineman John Mandarich went further: "We're going to write them off. We're going to totally dominate them. It's going to be a write-off; we want a write-off; there's no doubt we'll shellac them." Dave Elston capped it off with a cartoon in the *Edmon-*

ton Sun sports page depicting a sheep wearing a Saskatchewan Roughriders' football helmet. The cartoon was captioned "Sacrificial Lamb."

The big plus for us, in addition to the overconfidence of the Eskimos, was that the lineup we would field for the Western Final bore little resemblance to the injury-wracked group they had pounded a few weeks earlier in our season finale. And there was something else. We knew we could expect a repeat of the tremendous fan support we had received the week before in Calgary. We were right. Fans descended on Edmonton, having traveled not only from Saskatchewan but from all over Western Canada to show their Rider Pride. There is no doubt they were a factor in the final outcome of the game.

In front of over thirty-five thousand fans we beat the Eskimos 32–21. The early part of the game actually followed the pregame predictions. Edmonton scored on their first two possessions to lead 10–0. Ray Elgaard said afterward that having the game start this way was the best thing that could have happened to us. He was right. The Eskimos, who had been touting themselves for the entire week, had to figure the game was in the bag.

I hit a 44-yarder to get us on the board. Then early in the second quarter came a play that was to be as big for us as the Walling run the previous week. Linebacker Eddie Lowe knifed in and blind-sided Eskimo quarterback Tracy Ham, who coughed up the ball. David Albright scooped it up and galloped 62 yards for a major. Suddenly the score was tied in a game a whole lot of people thought we had no right to show up for.

On the following Edmonton possession Eddie Lowe came up big a second time and intercepted a Tracy Ham pass, which he returned to the Edmonton 42. Five plays later, Kent hit Ray

Elgaard with a six-yard strike in the end zone, and guess what? Custer had risen from the dead.

The Eskimos weren't out of it yet. By early in the third quarter they had regained the lead, 20–17. Tom Burgess, who came in when Kent was injured, pulled us back in front when he teamed up with Jeff Fairholm for a 46-yard touchdown. On the ensuing kickoff linebacker Tuineau Alipate hit Eskimo returner Keith Wright and jarred the ball loose. It was recovered by Don Narcisse, and four plays later Tom tossed a 14-yard touchdown pass to Elgaard to give us an 11-point spread.

From this point our defense played textbook football, and perhaps the greatest upset in CFL history went into the books. It was a game we probably shouldn't have won. But that's the great thing about sport. If the best team always won there would be no point in playing the games. We refused to be intimidated by either the Eskimos or the pregame talk and played sixty minutes of damn good football to win. It was a tremendously satisfying feeling to beat them, and as Bobby Jurasin said after the game, "The best part is that we're sixty minutes away from getting that Grey Cup ring." Dave Elston's sacrificial lamb had turned wolf, the subject of his next cartoon.

So many times over the years we had left Commonwealth Stadium with our tails tucked between our legs for a long, miserable trip home. The departure from Edmonton after that Western Final victory was the sweetest in my memory. And then it was on to Toronto.

The Saskatchewan Roughriders had last gone to the Grey Cup in 1976. Only one player on the 1989 team, Roger Aldag, had been on the 1976 squad, and due to an injury he had not played in the Grey Cup game itself. Thirteen seasons later, most of them without even making the playoffs, Aldag and a completely new cast of characters would finally return to the game that decides the professional football championship of Canada.

The *Leader-Post*, in its November 20 edition, carried the three-inch-high headline in the sports section: "GREY CUP BOUND." That was typical of the reaction all over the province to our win in Edmonton. When we arrived back at the Regina airport an estimated twenty-five hundred fans turned out to greet us. Saskatchewan's football faithful had waited a long time to celebrate, and they were intent on making up for lost time. The emotional uplift was something I had never experienced in my athletic career and was that much more meaningful coming after all of those years of frustration and failure. So many times we had made those trips back to Regina after yet another butt kicking in Somewheresville, Canada, and often as the plane was making its descent into Regina, Roger Aldag would turn and say to those close enough to hear, "Well, I wonder if the brass band is waiting for us this time." On most of those occasions the welcoming party was a few wives and friends who had showed up to provide sympathy and rides home.

Without wishing to overstate the importance of the 1989 season to the Saskatchewan population at large, I have often felt the Roughriders' long drought was something of a metaphor for the economic and agricultural hardships our province endured through much of the 1980s. Our playoff success provided a rallying point for its hardy and beleaguered citizens. John Gregory made this point during our team rundown back in Regina when he said the game in Edmonton had been a great win for us as players and staff, from front office personnel to souvenir sellers, but it also had been a tremendous victory for the people of Saskatchewan. John, as

I've mentioned, spent the off-seasons traveling to all corners of the province speaking at banquets and functions. So when he spoke of our victory over the Eskimos in terms of what it meant to the people of Saskatchewan, he knew what he was talking about.

We didn't have much time to savor what we had accomplished in Edmonton. We flew home Sunday night, practiced the next morning and were immediately into the process of preparing to leave for Toronto. Obviously the normal procedure of going into the visiting city twenty-four hours before the game was abandoned in the case of a national championship. We'd be in Toronto a full five days in advance of Grey Cup Sunday in order to allow us to participate in the media mayhem leading up to the game and to become acclimatized to the stadium in which we'd play.

Before we left, there was a noon civic pep rally and Roger's brass band finally made its appearance. As we were preparing to leave the rally, a good friend of mine, Thomas Siarkos, co-owner of an excellent Regina eatery called Memories, approached me, wished me luck and gave me a book of matches printed up for the restaurant. On the front were the name and logo of the restaurant and on the back were the words: "Sask. Riders, 1989 Grey Cup Champions." That moment encapsulated both what was expected of us and how important winning the Grey Cup was to our fans. I still have that matchbook. I kept it as a reminder of what the Grey Cup means to a lot of people in this country.

Our upset of the Eskimos wasn't a hit with everybody. Among those who were evidently shocked by the outcome of the Western Final were the brass at Air Canada. We were told the airline had contingency arrangements in place to get Edmonton fans to Toronto, but no such plans existed for extra flights out of Regina. This led to an interesting predicament: how to accommodate the myriad fans now frantically trying to get to Toronto in time for the game. Among them were the players' wives, some of whom directed considerable anger at the football team for allowing the situation to happen. Carolyn Stevenson, wife of offensive lineman Vic Stevenson, was quite vocal and went so far as to make the media aware of the problem. The crisis was eventually overcome and the wives got to Toronto, but it provided an interesting sidenote to the lead-up to the game.

The team flew out of Regina on Tuesday evening and arrived in Toronto in the predawn hours. As we passed the SkyDome on the way to our hotel, I was suddenly reminded of something. When we had played that pivotal late-season game against the Argonauts, our season was in danger of going down the drain like so many before it. But we had come to the SkyDome and won a game after trailing 24–13 with less than three minutes remaining. Now I was reminded of what had taken place on the bus leaving that imposing structure after our first visit. In the post-game excitement after the earlier win, some of the veterans on the team—Poley, Aldag, Mike Anderson, a couple of others and I—agreed to make a commitment to come back for one more game in November. Looking back on it now, I realize making a pact like this is right up there with saying, "Let's make a commitment to win the lottery." Still, that quiet little agreement came back to me as we once again passed the SkyDome in the early hours of a cold Ontario morning.

On our first day of practice we immediately became aware of the almost constant demands placed on players and coaches by the media. For most of us who were experiencing our first Grey Cup, the coverage in the days leading up to the game was mindboggling. That is not a complaint. I'm very much aware that the attention paid to the game and the festivities surrounding it are reasons why the Grey Cup has become a national institution.

We had arrived in Toronto during a cold snap, which shouldn't have posed a problem since the game was being played indoors. That's apparently what our rotund equipment guru, Norm Fong, thought because he had neglected to pack our sweats for the trip. The temperature in the Dome for our first practice was near freezing, and we were out there in our shorts. A loud chorus of bitching was directed at Normie, and he was forced, much to his chagrin, to contact Danny Webb, the Argonauts' equipment manager, to borrow their sweats for our subsequent practices. To ensure that his error would never become public, Norm insisted we wear the sweats inside out so the Argos' emblem couldn't be seen by anyone watching us practice.

I was surprised how loose a group we were in those first practices. We were businesslike about getting the work done, but the tension level didn't appear much higher than normal and certainly nowhere near what might be expected for a collection of mostly first-time Grey Cuppers. I took a lot of practice kicks during the course of the week, more than usual, mostly because I was concerned about the conditions indoors, which can sometimes be rather deceptive and certainly differ from kicking in the outdoors.

The SkyDome is cavernous and the scoreboard, known as the Jumbotron, takes considerable getting used to because once it lights up it requires concentration to divert one's attention away from it. Of particular interest to me was kicking field goals in the direction of the SkyDome Hotel with its huge expanse of windows behind which the guests in their rooms were clearly visible. So visible in fact that one amorous couple had attracted the attention of thousands as they made their passion public some months before during a Blue Jays' game. Several times during practice Glen and I mulled over the odds of a similar performance during the Grey Cup game. There hadn't been that kind of excitement since the 1975 game when a crazed streaker warmed up the opening ceremonies in Calgary on an afternoon when the thermometer read minus twenty-five Fahrenheit.

On Thursday, during a team brunch, Suits and I discussed the fact that our long-suffering locker room assistant, Shorty Mitchell, was not with us in Toronto. The team had not brought him to Toronto because Shorty was not officially a team member, but we were all keenly aware of the contributions he makes. He personifies Rider Pride. His collection of Roughrider memorabilia is without doubt one of the most extensive anywhere and includes at least one of every Roughrider football trading card in history.

Before the brunch wrapped up I asked Coach John Gregory if I could say a word to the team. He agreed so I stood up and said, "Listen guys, Shorty isn't here. He's a person who has done a lot for all of us and has stood by us through thick and thin, and I think he should be here with the team." I asked for a show of hands to see how many guys would chip in to pay for Shorty's flight and accommodations. Everyone in the room raised his hand.

Management made the arrangements to get Shorty to Toronto, and the next day he was at practice decked out in his familiar Roughriders' jacket, cap and locker room slacks . . . the ones with the twenty-four inch inseams. At the end of practice John called us together and told us Shorty had something to say. Shorty stood in the middle of the group and told us how much what we had done meant to him. The *Leader-Post* ran a picture of Shorty addressing the team and I know everyone felt his money was well spent. It was worth it to me see a tear in that grizzled old eye.

One of the unfortunate asides to Grey Cup week was the general apathy of the people of Toronto. As the week wore on I got the feeling more and more that the average person in Toronto didn't give a damn. We'd take a cab ride somewhere and when the cabby found out who we were and why we were there, the reaction was usually a yawn. This typified the attitude we encountered over and over throughout the city. The vast majority of people in Toronto had apparently decided to ignore the nation's football championship about to be played in their hometown. Milson Jones, who had been to two previous Grey Cups with the Eskimos, summed up Toronto's civic spirit well. "When we were in Vancouver, you could feel the pulse of the city. Toronto needs a resuscitation." As it turned out it was their loss because they missed the game of the century, a point the Toronto media grudgingly conceded in the stories that followed the game.

The atmosphere in Toronto finally became festive when the Saskatchewan fans arrived en masse. When the festival organizers saw fit to cancel the Grey Cup parade the Rider fans held their own. Actually they held several. Had it not been for all of those Saskatchewan people who drove, flew or took the forty-eight hour bus charters to Toronto, it would have been almost impossible to detect any difference between that weekend in Toronto and any other in the year. We were told that back home the whole province was in a frenzy. This came as no surprise.

It also came as no surprise that every Roughrider was focused intensely on the game. Every team has its party animals and the 1989 Riders were no different. But even these players kept their carousing and staying out late to a minimum. Suitor and I confined most of our off-field activity to going out to eat, seeing a few friends or doing a little shopping. On one occasion, as we were walking south on Yonge Street toward the lake, we heard a band playing. We kept walking and suddenly from around a corner came a hundred or more Roughrider fans all decked out in green and white and following "The College Nine," a group of talented but lunatic University of Saskatchewan musicians who are a Saskatoon tradition.

Suits and I realized that if we were recognized by the mob there was a better than average chance we might not actually make the game. So we jaywalked to the other side of Yonge and doubled back to the Eaton's Centre to hide out. I'll be damned if we no sooner got into the mall than in they came singing the Roughriders' fight song and having the kind of good time the whole city of Toronto should have been having.

Grey Cup week provided an opportunity for me to renew acquaintances with former CFL great Garney Henley. I had met him in 1976 when he had evaluated my kicking and written a letter of recommendation I used in applying to schools in the United States in pursuit of an athletic scholarship.

I knew Garney was a member of the Hamilton staff, and I was excited about seeing him after all that time and having the opportunity to thank him in person. There is no doubt in my mind that what Garney Henley did for me played a large part in my eventually becoming a professional football player.

On Thursday after our practice, I changed and went back out onto the field for the Tiger-Cats' practice. I saw Garney on the sidelines and went to him, offered my hand and introduced myself. I reminded him of what he had done thirteen years before and told him I wanted to thank him. He asked me about my college experience, and we chatted about that for a while and then he said, "And what are you doing with yourself now?"

When I was able to recover, I said, "Well, I'm playing for the Saskatchewan Roughriders. I've been place-kicking for them for seven years, and I'll be playing against you on Sunday." I hadn't expected Garney Henley to remember me from thirteen years earlier, but I was surprised he had never heard of me and didn't know I would be kicking against his team in the Grey Cup game. Still it felt good to thank in person the man who had helped me start my career.

One former Tiger-Cat, however, did remember me. In one of the post-Grey Cup articles in the *Leader-Post*, sportswriter Darrell Davis quoted former Hamilton kicker Ian Sunter as claiming me as a protégé. Sunter, who kicked a last-second field goal to beat the Roughriders in the 1972 Grey Cup, said he had taught me how to kick. My response was: "Not true. My dad, Len, taught me how to kick." My only contact with Sunter had been at a job fair in high school at which he was representing professional football. I told him I was working on becoming a kicker. I don't recall his answer, but I'm damn sure it didn't have the slightest impact on my career.

As the week progressed the general mood of the team changed. As the pressure began to mount, guys became more and more irritable. I was probably the moodiest of all, as I tend to be in such situations. At times like these Glen Suitor called me the dickhead. The week seemed to drag and the endless interviews began to get on our nerves. The question I was asked over and over was how I'd feel if the game came down to a last-second field goal. My stock reply became that I didn't think it would happen, but if it did I'd think about it then. I really didn't think it would happen. My feeling was that with two offenses as potent as these, one was likely to blow the other out.

By Saturday's practice my frame of mind came pretty close to fitting Suitor's description. There was no escaping the emotion and constant reminders of why we were there. I just wanted get on with the game. I think most players on both teams felt the same way. Milson Jones, who couldn't wait to get on the field, said during practice, "That's enough foreplay, let's get to the real thing."

As usual the practice before game day was pretty much restricted to some light work on special teams. In fact the whole week was very much like a normal week of the season insofar as practices were concerned. Coach John Gregory didn't vary our routine much and avoided the tendency to do a bunch of rah-rah stuff, which was unnecessary anyway. He hadn't done that for either of our playoff games, and he knew it wasn't needed for this game either. In professional sports the athletes are quite capable of preparing themselves for the big game and seldom require the win-one-for-the-Gipper pep talk.

I awoke game day morning and distinctly recall having the jitters, something that doesn't usually set in until later in the day. Our pregame meal was one of the quietest in memory. There was little conversation. Following the meal John Gregory asked some veterans—Roger Aldag, Ray Elgaard, Gary Lewis, Milson Jones and me—to join the coaches at their table. He informed us that he wanted the five of us to accept the trophy after the game. It was a wise move on his part. He conveyed a calm certainty about the outcome and his confidence in us. There was no doubt in his mind we were going to win.

Different players have different rituals they go through on

game days beginning with when they arrive at the ballpark. On our club that year it was about an even split between the players who traveled to the stadium on the team bus, which usually arrived about two hours before kickoff, and those who preferred to get there earlier. By earlier I mean four or five hours and in extreme cases—for guys like Aldag, Poley and Jurasin—even more before game time.

I had taken the team bus to the stadium almost all the time. But for the Grey Cup game I arrived three hours before kickoff. As had been the case with the pregame meal, the locker room was extremely quiet. The kibitzing and joking normally part of the atmosphere was completely absent. Arriving early was the only thing I did differently that Sunday. I tried to follow the rest of my preparation ritual as closely as possible. This meant that when I got to the locker room I first changed into my equipment, including pants, socks and shoes, leaving only my shoulder pads, game jersey and helmet for later. Then I tried to relax.

Over the years Glen Suitor and I developed a ritual of going onto the field early to play a little game. Most often the game involved the two of us standing about fifteen yards away from the goalposts and throwing footballs at one of the uprights. The one who first hit the upright five times won. Intent on not deviating from our routine, Glen and I went onto the playing surface of the SkyDome and played a game of hit the upright. Then we spent some time, again according to our normal pattern, working our way down the field and back with me throwing the ball and Glen breaking to it to get loosened up and accustomed to the stadium lighting. At this point we went back into the locker room to wait for the call for special teams—kickers, long-snappers, holders and kick-returners—to go out for their warm-up.

During the interlude between Glen and I coming off the field and the call for the special team warm-up, the stadium staff had opened the gates and fans had begun streaming into the SkyDome. It was about an hour before kickoff, and we were unaware what had taken place. So when we went onto the field a second time, we were taken completely by surprise: the stands were already about one-third full and the stadium lights had been turned on. The effect was dazzling. As the fans saw some of the players making their way onto the field, they began to cheer—no, they roared. My guess was that ninety percent of them were Saskatchewan fans. The air was electric.

After the special team warm-up the rest of the players came onto the field for the stretch period and a few offensive and defensive drills. Then it was back to the locker room to await the player introductions. As I was passing our bench en route to the locker room, I heard a voice from the front row of the stands yell, "Hey, Ridgway!" I looked in the direction of the voice and saw Stew Fraser. He was dressed in his old number 11 and his face was painted half green, half white. We gave each other a giant hug, which left a generous amount of his green paint on one side of my face. Seeing my old teammate and friend, who had driven in from Moncton, New Brunswick, gave me a huge lift.

This good feeling was almost offset by a Tiger-Cat fan seated nearby who called out, "Ridgway, you're gonna choke." The prediction was accompanied with the familiar hands-around-the-throat gesture. Minutes away from the kickoff of the biggest game of my life, this was not something I particularly needed.

And finally, after all the waiting and all the rhetoric and all the endless distractions, it was time to play. The Grey Cup introduction of the players is a much bigger production than at any time during the season, forming part of the pomp and ceremony that precedes the kickoff. It was as we were waiting to be introduced that the guys finally began to release their emotions in a chorus of chatter, trash-talking and pounding on one another. The starting defensive team was introduced and as soon as these twelve guys were on the field the rest of the 1989 Saskatchewan Roughriders ran out with Roger Aldag leading the way. Roger was so pumped up I thought he might throw the game's first block during the coin toss.

The captains of the two teams met at midfield, and though I was one of the five guys representing our team, I have no idea who won the toss. We kicked off so I suppose Hamilton must have won, but that's only a guess. We lined up for the kickoff and the official blew his whistle. I was as fired up as anybody and I practically sprinted at the ball. I hit it pretty well although it stayed fairly low and kind of helicoptered downfield instead of traveling in the usual end-over-end fashion. There was no turning back. The game of our lives, in the words of Sherlock Holmes, "was afoot."

Our first couple of offensive possessions were pretty tentative and didn't generate much production. The game's first points came via the right foot of Hamilton place-kicker Paul Osbaldiston. Paul had been good on 6 of 6 in the 1986 Grey Cup and over the years had established himself as an excellent kicker of pressure field goals.

On our next possession the offense shook off their early jitters and began to move the ball. However, the drive ended when an old friend and former Rider, Frank Robinson, batted a Kent Austin pass up in the air and then made the interception. It was poetic justice for a guy who had been an superb team player for the Riders. Our defense held and it felt to me that we were now into the game in every way.

That Championship Season

A couple of possessions after the Osbaldiston field goal, the Tiger-Cats marched down to within touchdown range, but quarterback Mike Kerrigan missed with a couple of passes. Osbaldiston made good on another three-pointer and we were down 6–0 early in the game. We got on the board just after this when Terry Baker unloaded a huge punt from the Hamilton 48 for a single at the 10:41 mark of the first quarter. It was a precursor of the career day Terry was to have, something largely overlooked in the media coverage of the game. He wound up with a 46.5-yard average for 6 punts, his longest being 62 yards with another going out-of-bounds at the Hamilton two-yard line. On the other side of the ball, Paul Osbaldiston, who also handled the punting duties for Hamilton, kicked five times for an average of 46.6 yards, equally outstanding.

On Hamilton's subsequent possession, Tony Champion caught a 13-yard touchdown pass from Mike Kerrigan and with the convert Hamilton led 13–1 at the 14:45 mark of the first quarter. The unenviable task of covering Hamilton defensive back Tony Champion, coming off a spectacular year, had fallen to Harry Skipper. Harry admitted before the game there was no way he was going to shut down the likes of Champion; the best he could hope for was to minimize the damage Champion would do.

Things didn't look all that good at this moment, and the thought went through my mind that we had waited a long time to get to the Grey Cup game and we had better get started soon if we wanted to stay in the game. I was struck by the realization that this might be the only opportunity I'd ever have to play in a game of this magnitude, and I made a conscious decision to take in everything about the game. I walked over to the sidelines, got down on one knee and, during the television time-out following the Hamilton touchdown, looked around at the SkyDome and the crowd. In the upper reaches of the stadium a haze hung in the air. I vividly recall the glass of the SkyDome Hotel, the reflections of lights around the stadium and the predominance of green and brass of the SkyDome architecture. I guess what I wanted to do was not just play in a Grey Cup game but remember and appreciate it.

On our second possession of the second quarter we moved the ball from our 48 to the Hamilton 5, and on first down Kent threw a touchdown pass to Ray Elgaard. That touchdown marked, I think, an important point in the game. We realized then that we could do the things we had done successfully for much of the season and it was time to put aside all the hype and get down to playing some ball.

Nevertheless, the Tiger-Cats took the ball after the kickoff and marched from their 53 to our 30. Kerrigan then hit Derek McAdoo with a touchdown strike and, bang, we were in the hole again 20–8. On the first play after the kickoff Austin loaded up for our first big play of the game, a 75-yard pass and run to Jeff Fairholm for the touchdown. Suddenly, at the 8:28 mark of the second quarter, it was clear we were in the middle of a shoot-out. It was also clear that anybody who had made the decision to turn the game off when we were down 13–1 had committed a sports fan's worst mistake. This game was going to be a wild one.

The half ended with Hamilton leading 27–22. Other than for converts and kickoffs I did not get on the field until the last play of the half for a 50-yard field goal attempt. I was short and wide with the kick and Wally Zatylny ran it out to the Hamilton 12 to end the half. I went to the locker room at half-time with mixed emotions about how the game had gone to this point. On the one hand, I was delighted we had come back and were right in it going into the final thirty minutes. On the other hand, I wasn't thrilled with my own contribution, having missed on my only opportunity.

The locker room was very upbeat in sharp contrast to the atmosphere prior to the game. Everyone felt we were moving the ball well and had taken control of the game in the second quarter even though we were trailing by five points. Most players would have liked to dispense with half-time and get back out on the field right away. John Gregory obviously felt the same way because he said very little other than that the game was within our reach and to go out and take it in the second half.

The first-half statistics reflected the shoot-out the game had been to that point. Mike Kerrigan had completed 15 of 22 passes for 207 yards and two touchdowns. Kent Austin had thrown 21 times and completed 12 for 220 yards and three touchdowns. Hamilton had 17 first downs to our 12. McAdoo had rushed 13 times for 64 yards for Hamilton. Our own rushing game was pretty much non-existent with Kent carrying the ball twice for eight yards and Tim McCray having only two carries for five yards.

Tim was another player I would put in the unsung hero category of the game. Despite not being used extensively as a kick-returner during the regular season, he had returned three kicks for 99 yards in the first half alone, the longest being 49 yards. It was a credit to Tim that when he realized we weren't going to be running the ball a lot, he simply went out and made his contribution by blocking in the backfield, catching passes and playing superbly on special teams.

The most important statistic from the first half was the time of possession: Hamilton had the ball for 19:41, almost double our 10:19. It was clear our defense, despite giving up 27 points, had played well. We would have to control the ball a hell of a lot more in the second half if we were to have serious designs on winning.

The second half of the Grey Cup game went by in a blur. On our first possession we moved from our 46 to the Hamilton 27 and I kicked a field goal. If ever there was a good omen for our club and for me in particular it was this kick. I kicked from the right hash at the 34 yard line and the ball banked in off the right upright. I had seldom if ever bounced one in off a post (though I'd had more than my share rejected by uprights and crossbars) and I took it as a positive sign.

We had taken the lead 34–30 by the end of the third quarter and the stage was set for a wild finish. We opened the scoring in the fourth quarter at the 1:12 mark with a field goal, capping a march that had included a 53-yard pass to Mark Guy. On Hamilton's first possession of the final quarter Glen Suitor intercepted a Kerrigan pass on our 40 and returned it 18 yards. This was our only interception of the day. But on the very next play we gave it back to them. We tried a trick play with Elgaard going in motion behind our quarterback, taking a pitch and throwing a pass. Unfortunately it was picked off at the Hamilton 22.

Then our defense came up with a big play of its own. On second down Chuck Klingbeil sacked Kerrigan for a 20-yard loss that was very close to being a safety. Chuck, who had replaced the departed James Curry, had a tremendous game and was eventually voted Defensive Player of the game.

At the 8:39 point in the quarter Paul Osbaldiston kicked his fourth field goal and was now, dating back to 1986, 10 of 10 in Grey Cup play. With less than half a quarter to go it began to look like my prediction to the media might be incorrect. This game could end up being decided by a late field goal.

That Championship Season

We added an important 20-yard field goal at 13:02 to make the score Saskatchewan 40, Hamilton 33. This gave us what turned out to be a crucial seven-point spread. Hamilton elected to take the ball at their own 35 rather than receive a kickoff. What followed was a great do-or-die Hamilton drive downfield that was tinged with more than a little controversy. Kerrigan completed an 18-yard pass to Lee Knight and followed with a nine-yard completion to Rocky DiPietro. On second and one McAdoo carried for six yards to our 42. On the next play Kerrigan threw for Tony Champion, and it appeared Harry Skipper had made contact with the Hamilton receiver as he went for the ball. There was no call and Tiger-Cat Coach Al Bruno went nuts on the sidelines. On the following play Kerrigan threw to the other side of the field to Earl Winfield, and this time the flag was thrown on our rookie defensive back Steve Wiggins. I can't even say it was a makeup call for Bruno's tirade as Steve had pretty well mugged Winfield. This put Hamilton on our 11 and our bench went very quiet. Kerrigan handed off to McAdoo, who was stopped after a two-yard gain. On second down Kerrigan tried a quick pass to DiPietro. Once again there was little doubt we caught a break as an obvious interference wasn't called. Rocky was furious.

Of course, all the missed call did was heighten the drama and set the stage for the impending heroics of Tony Champion and then of Kent Austin and our offense.

And while all of this was going on a nervous place-kicker was wishing his team was ahead by three or four touchdowns.

CHAPTER 14

The Kick – Part Two

Don't worry about this one . . . you miss it—we lose. –CADDYSHACK, 1980

IN EVERY TEAM SPORT there are players who, when the money is on the line, want the ball. They want to take the last-second shot from three-point range, they want the call to the mound with the bases loaded in the ninth and they want to try the last-second field goal in a championship game. When I first entered professional football I was not one of those players.

To be honest the games I still enjoy most are the ones in which we are up by at least twenty points with less than a minute to go. Everybody is kibitzing on the bench, there's no pressure and the only issue left in doubt is who's going to pour the Gatorade on the coach. I add, however, that particularly in the second half of my career I have not been reluctant to kick in the situation in which we found ourselves in the 1989 Grey Cup game. I have confidence in myself under pressure; I can do what is required, mentally and physically, to come through for my team.

This was the final thought I allowed myself in the seconds preceding the snap of the ball for the most important kick of my life. I was relaxed, thanks in part to the words Glen had just shared with me. I was ready. At that moment I turned my mind to the mechanics of place-kicking: the push off with the right foot, then two steps, left, right, plant with the left and bring the right leg through in an arc perfectly in line with the spot exactly in the middle of the uprights.

From this point everything happened subconsciously. Over the years I have trained my body to perform the necessary motions by habit. In a pressure situation that's exactly how I want it to be—nothing should happen any differently from the hundreds of kicks that preceded it.

For me the Grey Cup kick was like a slow-motion sequence in a movie. The snap was true, the hold perfect and the ball was away. Both Glen and I were trained, like golfers, to keep our heads down and concentrate on the place the ball was pinned for a solid one-count after the ball is airborne. On this kick we brought our heads up sooner than normal. I knew as soon as I looked up that the ball was dead center. The kick was good!

My first feeling was a mix of relief, pride and joy all at the same time. I remember yelling, "My God, we did it!" and as I did, Glen was coming out of his stance, arms raised to signal it was good. I too stabbed my arms in the air, and Glen and I embraced as our teammates ran to join the celebration. Glen was babbling, I have no idea what; maybe I was too. There is no way to describe the elation I felt in that split second after I realized the thing I had prepared and trained for all of my life had just happened.

The first guy back to us was Milson Jones and I'll never forget how calm he was about the whole thing. Millie, with no hollering, kind of sauntered back to us, shirt hanging out, and hugged both Glen and me. Seconds later the rest of the guys arrived and after that pandemonium reigned.

When the kick went through the uprights something happened that I will cherish all of my life. It didn't to my knowledge make any of the highlight films or media coverage. But it was special. It was also one of the most decent gestures I have ever experienced in a game where we are taught the opposition is the enemy. Hamilton kicker Paul Osbaldiston had been stationed in the end zone so he could kick the ball back out to avoid the single point and preserve the tie in the event the kick was wide. As I came off the field I felt a tap on my shoulder. I turned and Paul was standing there, right hand extended, with the ball in his left. He said, "Congratulations, I thought you might like to have this." He handed me the ball.

I took it from him and shook his hand, but for one of the few times in what has been a fairly talkative life, I was speechless. Had our situations been reversed I might have kicked the ball up into the stands in frustration. I hope not because I know in that moment Paul Osbaldiston showed what being a great competitor is all about. The ball still occupies a prominent place in my home and whenever I look at it, as I often do, I think not only of the kick but of the selfless gesture of the CFL's Wizard of "Os."

When we got to the sidelines the celebration continued for a few seconds as I was greeted by "Duke" Ellingson and Terry Baker. But before we could get down to some serious jubilation I heard the call, "Kickoff team . . . kickoff team." That's when I realized two seconds were left on the clock and we would have to kick off to Hamilton. Tiger-Cat Coach Al Bruno had decided not to take the ball on his 35 and elected instead to try some kind of trick play on the return.

We went onto the field and huddled up for the kickoff. I called the squib, but when we lined up I saw Hamilton had left a huge gap between their 45- and 20-yard lines. Instead of the

The Kick – Part Two

squib I kind of pooched it into the open space between Tiger-Cat players. It was almost as precise a kick as the field goal that preceded it. Hamilton's Steve Jackson fielded the ball and punted it downfield in the hope we might fumble and they could run it in for seven.

On the kickoff Suitor, John Hoffman and I stayed back as safeties. The only player I didn't want to touch the return kick from Jackson was me. Fortunately it took a nice bounce right to Glen and he ran it out-of-bounds. The 1989 Grey Cup game, the 77th in the history of the CFL, was over.

The on-field celebration was something I don't think anyone in the SkyDome that day—players, coaches or fans—will ever forget. John Gregory's carefully laid plans for the acceptance of the Cup were almost immediately derailed. When Bill Baker, commissioner of the CFL, announced, "Ladies and Gentlemen, the 1989 Grey Cup Champions, the Saskatchewan Roughriders," Ray Elgaard leaped onto the podium, grabbed the microphone and began yelling into it. I'm not sure what Ray was yelling, but it reflected the kind of emotion we were all feeling. This was the cue for everybody else to scramble onto the platform to try to get a hand on the Cup. I was near the back of the group, and as I tried to climb on the platform I got bumped off. I laughed and stepped back to watch the guys who actually made it up there. I had been given a ball cap with "Grey Cup Champions" on it and I doffed the hat to my teammates.

The Grey Cup was passed from hand to hand until everyone on the team had held it at least for a moment. One of the biggest roars from the fans went up when Roger Aldag finally got his hands on the Cup. Thirteen years after he had watched from the sidelines as an injured rookie, Roger was at last able to be a full participant in his own Grey Cup triumph. Every one of us felt something special when Roger hoisted the Grey Cup high over his head. For me, despite the glorious careers of Reed and Lancaster, the two Saskatchewan boys—Roger Aldag and Bob Poley—will always share the title "Mr. Roughrider."

It wasn't until the players started to make their way to the locker room, about twenty minutes after the game had ended, that the fans started to leave. I didn't get to the locker room for close to forty-five minutes after the final gun because of the number of interviews I was requested to do on the field.

I was fortunate to receive one of the game's Most Valuable Player awards. Kent Austin was selected as Most Valuable Player in the game; Chuck Klingbeil received the Defensive MVP award and I was chosen for the Dick Suderman Memorial Award as the game's top Canadian. It was a tremendous honor for me as there were several outstanding efforts turned in by Canadians on both sides of the ball. Jeff Fairholm, Ray Elgaard and Rocky DiPietro were among those equally deserving.

Scott Oake of the CBC was the first reporter to get to me as the game concluded; he caught me just as I was coming off the field after making the kick, but we had to postpone our interview until after the ensuing kickoff and the presentation of the Cup. When we did get together his first question was: "What were you thinking about as you made the kick?" My answer was that I wasn't thinking about anything, which was probably true at the actual moment of contact with the ball. Scott then asked if there was anybody to whom I'd like to dedicate the Grey Cup victory. I was glad he asked the question, which gave me a chance to salute the people of Saskatchewan, the most extraordinary football fans on the planet.

One of the subsequent TV interviews turned out to be a little controversial. In answer to the question, "What was I planning to do that night?" I responded, I thought tongue in cheek, that someone would have to pull me out of the gutter.

The Kick – Part Two

Later the Riders and the league office received a number of letters decrying the terrible example I had set for the youth of our nation. To be honest the remark was made thoughtlessly, in jest and in the spirit of the moment. Still I said it, and looking back on it, I wish I had answered differently.

Eventually I was able to make my way to the locker room, and as if to give the lie to my comment to the CBC, the champagne was gone. Next time I want to win by a bunch so I can be one of the first players to sip the bubbly. The atmosphere in the dressing room was chaos. Reporters were everywhere and I was interviewed a few more times. A couple of photographers wanted pictures of me kissing the Grey Cup, a request with which I was happy to comply. Glen and I were asked to pose for a number of photos together including one I liked a lot of Glen pinning the Cup as he would a football and me getting ready to kick it.

Gradually people began to leave and peace settled over the locker room. At last only five people remained: Ivan Gutfriend, Norm Fong, Bob Poley, Roger Aldag and me. A celebration was going on back at the hotel, but I was in no hurry to bring to an end that moment in time. The feeling was eerily reminiscent of the scene in the remake of *Heaven Can Wait* in which Warren Beatty and a couple of other players are sitting in the locker room after their Super Bowl victory, savoring the moment. Each of us was deep in his own thoughts. When the five of us finally decided to leave we were the only people who used the team bus to travel to the hotel. The others had made their own way or traveled in the company of family and friends.

The lobby of our hotel was packed and I was quickly separated from Roger and Bob. It was a bit of a job getting to the victory party. A couple of policemen guarding the staircase had to be persuaded I was a player and actually belonged at the party. My wife, my in-laws and my son, Christopher, were already there, but both Nancy and Christopher were suffering from a touch of flu. In addition the wives were flying out on a special early morning flight, and the combination of illness and the early flight had not surprisingly dampened Nancy's enthusiasm. She, her mom and dad, and Christopher left not long afterward for their hotel. I visited with some of my teammates and their families and after a few minutes left for my room. For a couple of hours, as the adrenaline stettled, I watched a news channel. Every twenty minutes or so the screen flashed "1995 Grey Cup . . . Saskatchewan 43 – Hamilton 40." It might have been the best evening of TV in my life.

The next morning Glen and I made our way to Pearson Airport where a large number of people from Saskatchewan were awaiting flights back to Regina. There were lots of smiles and pats on the back as we made our way through the departure area.

The flight to Regina was without a doubt the rowdiest I have ever been on, culminating in a pillow fight involving most of the players and even some fans. It got a little out of hand. When we arrived at Regina things still hadn't settled down, and the pilot circled the airport and told us he wasn't going to land until we returned to our seats, put on our seat belts and shut up. This brought the situation under control. A lot of us were speculating about how wild the reception would be as we came off the plane. But when we entered the terminal almost nobody was there except a TV camera crew. When we asked what was going on we were told people had been asked to stay away from the airport in favor of a celebration at Taylor Field.

When we got to the stadium it was very cold. Night was falling and the stadium lights had been turned on. We got off the bus near our locker room and went inside to wait for the moment when we would be introduced to the fans. We remained beneath the grandstand for about twenty minutes unaware that above us were some eighteen thousand people waiting to greet their team.

A platform and podium had been erected on the field and we waited for our names to be called. John Gregory and the other coaches were introduced first, and then John brought the players out one at a time. Nancy and Christopher were at the park, and when I was introduced I had Christopher in my arms. When a huge roar went up, as it did for all the players, Christopher's head snapped around, and he stared in awe at the stands. My own reaction was about the same as once again it was brought home to me just how much the Riders mean to these wonderful, crazy people. The last two players to be introduced were Roger Aldag and Bob Poley, who fittingly came out together carrying the Grey Cup.

Since that day in November of 1989 I have often had people say I won the Grey Cup with the kick. I disagree. Football is a game in which individual players often receive too much praise when things go well and too much criticism when they go badly. I was glad to contribute my share to the most important win of our lives—nothing more and nothing less than any Roughrider who took to the field that day in Toronto.

In all the media reports that followed, I don't think anyone said any better what we felt about the Grey Cup win than center Mike Anderson. Seconds after the final gun Mike looked into the television cameras and jubilantly yelled to all of Canada, "We're the 1989 Grey Cup Champions and that'll live forever, baby!"

Mike was right. We had climbed out of the rubble of the long, lean years and reached the pinnacle of Canadian professional football. We had believed and we had made others believe. That's what made winning the Grey Cup special. At a time when sport is fast becoming big business, finally it is the team and the game that count. The Grey Cup game was the culmination of a growing process that had taken place over many years for me personally and for the team. We had grown as athletes into a very good football team, and we had grown as people to have faith in one another and our ability to do what it takes to be a championship team.

If I didn't know this before I learned it that November night on a street of Toronto. Some hours after leaving the Grey Cup celebration I realized I hadn't had anything much to eat since the pregame meal. Room service at the hotel had closed at midnight so I decided to walk the short distance to Yonge Street to see if I could grab a bite. When I got there all the restaurants were also closed. It was a wintry night and I was dressed only in a light jacket so I started back to the hotel. I looked up at the stars visible through the city lights and chuckled as a newspaper headline came to mind: "Dave Ridgway Kicks Field Goal in Grey Cup—Then Dies of Starvation."

As I was walking head down, collar up, into the cold wind on a surprisingly deserted Yonge Street, I saw a group of young men coming my way. They were clearly Rider fans—some had their faces painted half green and half white—and they were celebrating. They were singing the Riders' fight song, "Here we go, Riders, here we go." They had come all the way from Saskatchewan to cheer their team on and this night was theirs.

As they got closer one of the group broke away and grabbed my arm. He looked me straight in the face and in his best Foster Brooks' voice said, "Hey, buddy, how about them Riders?"

He didn't recognize me. I laughed with them and for a moment shared in a salute to my team and the game of football. I said, "Yeah, how about those guys?" and continued my walk back to the hotel.

THE DAVE RIDGWAY RECORD

The old cliché that records are meant to be broken is absolutely true. Nevertheless, fans are often interested in the records and achievements that make up a player's career. I present my numbers here for those fans who love statistics. They were compiled by one such fan, my good friend Guy Scholz.

Dave Ridgway, CFL RECORDS

1. All time field goal accuracy leader   531/689 for 78.2%
2. Most field goals in a single season   59
3. Most field goals in a single game   8 (twice)
4. Longest field goal   60 yards
5. Most consecutive field goals   28
6. Most selections as a place-kicker to a divisional all-star team   7
7. Most selections as a place-kicker to the CFL all-star team   6
8. Tied for most field goals in one quarter   4
9. Tied for longest kick-off   95 yards
10. Best field goal accuracy for single season   90.6%

NOTE: *Ridgway is first or tied in 10 CFL kicking categories—more than any other place-kicker in the league. He is in the top five in 10 other categories and in the top 20 in 21 various league categories. In addition to his CFL records, Ridgway holds 20 Saskatchewan Roughriders' marks.*

ROBOKICKER

Dave Ridgway, SEASON *by* SEASON

REGULAR SEASON

		SCORING					FIELD GOALS		
YEAR	GP	C	FG	S	PTS	T	G	AVG	LK
1982	16	34	38	15	163	51	38	74.5	53
1983	16	31	22	14	111	35	22	62.9	47
1984	16	30	28	13	127	42	28	66.7	55
1985	16	25	23	15	109	38	23	60.5	52
1986	18	34	37	8	153	50	37	74.0	50
1987	17	23	49	4	174	57	49	†86.0	†60
1988	18	45	†55	5	†215	66	55	†83.3	53
1989	18	49	†54	5	216	68	54	†79.4	53
1990	18	47	†59	9	†233	72	59	†81.9	53
1991	18	56	†52	4	216	61	52	†85.2	52
1992	18	50	36	7	165	47	36	76.6	47
1993	18	51	†48	1	196	53	48	†90.6	50
1994	13	35	30	3	128	39	30	77.1	52
TOTAL	230	510	531	103	2,186	679	531	†78.2	†60

AVERAGE PER SEASON

	SCORING				FIELD GOALS		
GP	C	FG	S	PTS	T	G	AVG
17.7	39.2	40.8	7.9	168.2	52.2	40.8	78.2

PLAYOFFS

		SCORING					FIELD GOALS		
YEAR	GP	C	FG	S	PTS	T	G	AVG	LK
1988	1	2	1	1	6	2	1	50.0	13
1989	3	11	9	0	38	12	9	75.0	44
1990	1	3	2	0	9	3	2	66.7	32
1992	1	2	2	0	8	2	2	100.0	27
1993	1	1	2	0	7	2	2	100.0	33
TOTAL	7	19	16	1	68	21	16	76.2	44

†CFL Leader
GP = Games Played / C = Converts / FG = Field Goals / S = Singles / PTS = Points
T = Tried / G = Good / AVG = Average / L = Longest Kick

The Dave Ridgway Record

ALL-TIME CFL POINT LEADERS

		SEA	TDS	C	FG	S	PTS	AVG
1	Passaglia	19	1	792	637	256	2,966	156.1
2	Cutler	16	0	627	464	218	2,237	139.8
3	Ridgway	13	0	510	531	103	2,186	168.2
4	Kennard	12	0	509	394	149	1,840	153.3
5	Ruoff	14	0	401	384	219	1,772	126.6
6	Chomyc	9	0	412	337	75	1,498	166.4
7	Osbaldiston	9	0	330	338	147	1,491	165.7
8	Organ	12	2	391	318	105	1,462	121.8
9	Hay	11	0	363	308	124	1,411	128.3
10	Sweet	14	0	327	314	73	1,342	95.9
11	McLoughlin	7	0	379	291	86	1,338	191.1

ALL-TIME CFL ACCURACY LEADERS

		SEA	T	G	AVG
1	Ridgway	13	679	531	78.20
2	Westwood	4	198	150	75.76
3	Dorsey	8	290	219	75.52
4	Chomyc	9	457	337	73.71
5	Passaglia	19	888	637	71.73
6	Baker	8	210	149	70.95
7	McLoughlin	7	413	291	70.46
8	Fleming	3	160	112	70.00
9	Osbaldiston	9	485	338	69.69
10	Hay	11	445	308	69.21

OTHER NOTABLES

		SEA	T	G	AVG
1	Sweet	13	457	314	68.71
2	Kennard	12	592	394	66.55
3	Organ	12	502	318	63.35
4	Cutler	16	790	464	58.73
5	Abendschan	11	300	159	53.00
6	Robinson	14	353	171	48.44

SEA = Seasons Played / TDS = Touchdowns / C = Converts / FG = Field Goals
S = Singles / PTS = Points / AVG = Average per Season / T = Tried / G = Good

ABOUT *the* CO-AUTHOR

David A. Poulsen has been an actor, rock singer, high school football coach and college instructor. No stranger to the world of professional sport, he is a former rodeo competitor and clown and is now a respected commentator and television broadcaster for rodeo with credits that include CTV "Wide World of Sports," TSN Sports and guest appearances in *The Black Stallion* television series and the motion picture *Convict Cowboy* with Jon Voight. In 1987 his story "The Welcomin'" won the Alberta Culture Short Story Competition. He has written a trilogy of young adult novels, a collection of short stories and a novel, *Don't Fence Me In*. David A. Poulsen lives near High River, Alberta.